D1526737

Reforming Education

FOURTEENTH ANNUAL YEARBOOK
OF THE AMERICAN EDUCATION FINANCE ASSOCIATION
1993

Reforming Education

The Emerging Systemic Approach

Editors

Stephen L. Jacobson
Robert Berne

CORWIN PRESS, INC.
A Sage Publications Company
Thousand Oaks, California

For information address:

Corwin Press, Inc.
A Sage Publications Company
2455 Teller Road
Thousand Oaks, California 91320

SAGE Publications Ltd.
6 Bonhill Street
London EC2A 4PU
United Kingdom

SAGE Publications India Pvt. Ltd.
M-32 Market
Greater Kailash I
New Delhi 110 048 India

Printed in the United States of America

Library of Congress Cataloging-in-Publication Data

Reforming education : the emerging systemic approach / edited by
    Stephen L. Jacobson, Robert Berne.
        p. cm. — (Annual yearbook of the American Education Finance
    Association ; 14th)
        Includes bibliographical references and index.
        ISBN 0-8039-6098-0 — ISBN 0-8039-6099-9 (pbk.)
        1. School management and organization. 2. Educational change.
    3. Schools—Decentralization. 4. School, choice of. 5. Education—
    Finance. I. Jacobson, Stephen L. II. Berne, Robert.
    III. Series.
    LB2805.R43 1993
    371.2—dc20   93-6442
                                                                 CIP

93 94 95 96 97 98 10 9 8 7 6 5 4 3 2 1

Corwin Press Production Editor: Rebecca Holland

Contents

Preface

For the past decade, ever since the release in 1983 of the National Commission on Excellence in Education's report *A Nation at Risk*, the reform of education has been an issue of national importance in the United States. *A Nation at Risk* purported that America's economic preeminence in the global marketplace was being threatened by an erosion in the quality of its public schools. In response, the United States began to reorder its educational priorities and excellence soon replaced equity as the nation's primary educational objective. Numerous reform proposals moved quickly from rhetoric to implementation. States began mandating higher starting salaries and alternative approaches to teacher compensation, longer school days and school calendars, and higher academic standards through a return to "basics" and increased graduation requirements. Farrar (1990) reported that, by 1986, 44 states required more courses for high school graduation than they had in 1980. As Petrie (1990) observed, "The common wisdom is that the first wave of educational reform, initiated by *A Nation at Risk*, was characterized by the imposition of top-down reforms which essentially asked us to do more of the same, but do it better" (p. 14).

But simply asking schools to "do more of the same" failed to recognize the systemic nature of the educational enterprise (Petrie, 1990). Though schools and teachers could be asked to do more, there was little chance that they would "do it better" unless significant changes were made in how schools were organized and run. First wave reforms thus gave rise to a second wave of educational reforms, which were perhaps exemplified best by the Holmes Group (1986) report, *Tomorrow's Teachers*, and by the Carnegie Forum (1986) report, *A Nation Prepared*. These reports placed teachers at the center of reform and called for a restructuring of the teaching profession and the school workplace. Recommendations in these reports included improving teacher preparation, establishing national standards for licensure, and moving toward professionalization to alter traditional teacher responsibilities and role relationships.

Concurrently, evidence from the business community suggested that entrepreneurial "excellence" was more likely to be achieved by corporations "chunking" into smaller, more manageable, organizational structures because it allowed greater flexibility in response to changes in consumer preferences and the market (Peters & Waterman, 1982). The educational reform movement incorporated these lessons from the private sector, and, as a result, school decentralization through an increase in site-based management (SBM) and greater local autonomy became attractive policy alternatives for many school districts, especially those in the nation's major urban centers.

Other significant issues that have commanded the attention of educational reformers in the United States over the past decade include parental choice, privatization, the development of national curricula and standards, and a reconsideration of existing school funding mechanisms. Yet these issues, indeed the whole movement toward reform and restructuring, were not peculiar to the United States during the 1980s and 1990s, nor were they particular to education. Schools in other developed nations—the United Kingdom, Australia, and Canada, for example—also began experimenting with reforms such as decentralization and site-based management, greater parental choice, and the development of national curricula, in the belief that they could enhance their economic competitiveness. Other nations, such as Germany, the Eastern-bloc countries of the former Soviet Union, and the republics of the newly formed Commonwealth of Independent States, were having to reform their schools simply to keep abreast of the rapidly changing social, political, and economic realities that resulted from Gorbachev's policy of "perestroika."

There is a great thirst for mutual understanding and mutual communication in the world. It is felt among politicians, it is gaining momentum among the intelligentsia, representatives of

culture, and the public at large. And if the Russian word "perestroika" has easily entered the international lexicon, this is due
to more than just interest in what is going on in the Soviet Union.
Now the whole world needs restructuring, i.e., progressive development, a fundamental change. (Gorbachev, 1987, pp. 253-
254)

This book, the fourteenth yearbook of the American Education
Finance Association (AEFA), is devoted to a review and appraisal of
the "educational perestroika" that has occurred over the past decade,
both in the United States and abroad. Diverse educational reforms,
some first implemented in response to *A Nation at Risk*, have been in
place long enough that they have been examined empirically and
need no longer simply be the subject of speculative discussion. The
chapters in this book examine the present and future of educational
reform. This work is intended to serve as a logical follow-up to
discussions about school reform presented in earlier AEFA year-
books, particularly the 1985 yearbook, *The Fiscal, Legal, and Political
Aspects of State Reform of Elementary and Secondary Education* (Mueller
& McKeown, editors, 1986), and the 1987 yearbook, *Attracting and
Compensating America's Teachers* (Alexander & Monk, editors, 1988).

Overview of Contents

This book is divided into three parts. The first part examines school
reform initiatives in the United States, while the second part examines
reform initiatives abroad. Both parts begin with a chapter that examines the school reform movement within the broader social, political,
and economic contexts from which it emerged in the 1980s. These
introductory chapters are then followed by chapters devoted to specific reform initiatives that are intended to capture for the reader the
diversity and evolution of this worldwide reform movement. The last
part of the book considers the future of school reform in light of the
rapidly changing social, political, and economic realities of the "New
World Order" of the 1990s and twenty-first century.

Part I contains seven chapters that explore reform initiatives in the
United States. In Chapter 1, Fuhrman, Elmore, and Massell review
briefly the history and context of school reform in the United States
through the 1980s and find that, while the reform movement gener-

ated considerable activity, it had little influence over school processes related to learning. They characterize early reforms efforts as being "broad, but not deep," with "multiple interventions" having "low coherence." They then examine the more promising "systemic" approach to reform that has evolved during the first years of the 1990s—an approach that attempts to combine coordinated state policies with restructured governance.

In Chapter 2, Richards, Fishbein, and Melville look at cooperative performance incentives (CPI), paying particular attention to the experiences of districts in South Carolina. They contend that CPIs can work in schools and that the apparent success of CPIs in South Carolina was the result of their ability to overcome many of the obstacles engendered by such previously touted reform initiatives as individual, merit pay incentives.

In Chapter 3, Malen provides an overview of the professionalization of teaching using Rowan's (1990) "network structures" as an analytic framework. She concludes that the strategy of expanding teachers' roles in organizational decision making and professional development/peer assistance has produced mixed results. For some teachers, these added responsibilities have provided rewarding opportunities to pursue interests, acquire knowledge, and interact with others, while, for others, it has simply produced "confusion, skepticism, frustration, overburden, and exhaustion." Malen argues that a shortage of key resources, most notably time for teachers to carry out their new responsibilities, has limited the success of this strategy and has produced negative side effects within network structures.

In Chapter 4, Hess looks at decentralization, shared decision making, and school-based management as central themes in the reform movement of the 1980s. Specifically, he examines the decentralization of Chicago's public schools and their return to community control. He reports that community control in Chicago has reempowered local actors and opened the way for an advocacy of organizational and curricular diversity as an alternative to the rigid and stultified institution public schooling had become.

Through a preliminary assessment of negotiated reform, Koppich and Kerchner, in Chapter 5, explore the emerging nexus between school reform and changes under way in labor relations. They contend that union and management are becoming increasingly sophisticated in distinguishing between structural and political obstacles to change. Koppich and Kerchner conclude that, by an expansion of scope, and through the use of waivers and trust agreements, collective bargaining between districts and their teacher unions is evolving into a principal tool moving the parties toward the joint operation of schools.

Using the micro-political conception of "logics of action" as developed by Bacharach and Mundell (1993), Cooper, in Chapter 6, considers educational choice from the perspective of four key constituent groups: school consumers, voters, organizations, and professionals. Cooper's analysis reveals the complexity of choice, coming as it does "from so many quarters, with so many different meanings, policies, and purposes." He concludes that, in the future, schools, not districts, must be the center of choice-making. Cooper contends that this shift is essential in light of competing "logics of action" because it would enable voters more voice in how "their school" is run, would focus on consumer and producer interactions, and would allow teachers more opportunities to be decision makers.

In light of growing concern over the cost and efficiency of reform initiatives in the United States, Monk and King, in Chapter 7, consider the usefulness of cost analysis to the design, implementation, and study of school reform. Applying cost analyses to evaluations of reforms in the education of at-risk students and reforms in pupil assessment practices, Monk and King conclude that, while numerical estimates of costs are of interest, a good cost analysis provides insight into the origins and implications of costs, which may prove to be far more meaningful if a reform is to be successful. They argue that this conceptually oriented type of cost analysis should be pursued more seriously if the fiscal dimensions of reform are to be better understood.

The four chapters that constitute Part II focus on reform initiatives abroad. In Chapter 8, Fowler, Boyd, and Plank examine school reform and restructuring as an international phenomenon that must be studied in light of political changes that are truly historic in dimension. They contend that school reform in the English-speaking world has been driven by a conviction that the incorporation of market forces is the key to more effective and efficient education systems. Education reform in Western Europe, on the other hand, has been reluctant to "unleash market forces," seeking instead to use education to "regain, maintain, or increase the legitimacy of the political system" and to raise significantly the educational level of the general population to capture high-tech and flexible production industries.

In Chapter 9, Ribbins and Thomas focus primarily on school reforms in England and Wales between 1987 and 1992. Quality, diversity, increased parental choice, greater autonomy for schools, and greater accountability were the major reform themes during that period. Ribbins and Thomas contend that, taken as a whole, the reforms contained a fundamental contradiction; that is, they required the implementation of a national curriculum and national system of pupil assessment that centralizes schooling while at the same time the reforms sought to create an educational market that would decentralize decision-making power. Ribbins and Thomas contend that it will be "headteachers" who, in shaping the implementation of these reforms, will be crucial in resolving this conflict.

In Chapter 10, Brown considers an initiative called voluntarism, or benevolence, which addresses two key problems confronting Canadian public schools: (a) a general shortage of resources, which is a consequence of competing societal priorities, and (b) the rigidity associated with large districts that inhibits their meeting local needs. Brown views benevolence as a promising avenue for school improvement, because it enables schools to acquire needed resources and build connections with parents and the community. Brown concludes that, while the state can pay the bills, it cannot love a school and that benevolence can produce "schools with heart."

In Chapter 11, Mitter and Weiss describe current transformations in the educational systems of the former East German Länder, their effects on education in the West German Länder, and the radical challenges these reforms pose for a "united" Germany. Mitter and Weiss point out that school reform in Germany must, among other things, overcome two significant residuals of Marxist-Leninist ideology: (a) students who have an internalized shyness of making choices and decisions and (b) thousands of teachers who had formerly been loyal executors of official East German doctrines. The tendency to impose "Western" attitudes on "newcomers" opens educational reform to charges of "colonialism." Nevertheless, the authors point out that the challenge of reunification, and the social and economic crises it has spawned, make the transformation of education in Germany an undertaking of critical importance, particularly in light of alarming outbreaks of extremism among young adults in the East.

In the final part, Guthrie considers the future of school reform in light of an emerging "New World Order." Guthrie contends that Western nations increasingly view schooling as instrumental in enhancing their supply of human capital and thus promoting further economic development. These nations have much and hope to "acquire" more. Education in the Third World, on the other hand, is shaped by economic adversity, the result being that school systems in these nations have little but must "accomplish" more. In any case, Guthrie finds that national economies are being transformed by rapid communication, expanding information, and technological innovation, and future schools will increasingly be called upon to expand the pool of human talent beyond a narrow intellectual elite. As a result, Guthrie sees an overarching change in the extent to which education policy and practice will be politicized. This shift, he predicts, will make educational practitioners more accountable to laypersons; increase skepticism regarding evaluations undertaken by educational professionals; forge greater linkages between education agencies, government planning efforts, and the policymaking process; and encourage added dependence upon internationally oriented performance comparisons.

Guthrie also expresses concern about the absence of any significant governmental efforts to intensify educational research or development of technology to enhance school productivity. He concludes by reminding educators of the "New World Order"; in addition to national economic development, there are still many other masters worthy of being served including acculturating new citizens, ensuring social cohesion and civic order, facilitating social mobility, developing artistic and aesthetic tastes, and contributing to individual fulfillment.

The reform of education is a path just begun; only the future knows where it will lead:

We are all students, and our teacher is life and time. I believe that more and more people will come to realize that through *restructuring* in the broad sense of the word, the integrity of the world will be enhanced. Having earned good marks from our main teacher—life—we shall enter the twenty-first century well prepared and sure that there will be further progress. (Gorbachev, 1987, p. 254)

Acknowledgments

Orchestration of an edited volume such as this rests upon the collective efforts of numerous individuals. I consider myself incredibly fortunate to have had the opportunity to work with so many fine people through the course of this project. I want to begin by thanking Van Mueller, past president of the American Education Finance Association, for giving me the chance to undertake this work; Austin Swanson, chairman of the Department of Educational Organization, Administration, and Policy at the State University of New York at Buffalo, for providing the resources necessary to complete it; and Gracia Alkema of Corwin Press for her patience and good nature through a series of unintended delays.

I am especially indebted to the book's contributors, whose timeliness and professionalism made this work a relatively painless task. I would also like to thank my coeditor, Robert Berne, whose careful and insightful reading of the drafts helped shape the final product. Collectively, the expertise of these individuals, as reflected in the chapters that follow, turned this work into an important learning experience for me—one I hope that the reader will share.

I would also like to acknowledge the clerical support I have received from the Graduate School of Education at SUNY/Buffalo. Specifically, I want to thank secretaries Sally Claydon, Pat Glinski, Nancy Myers, Carol Norris, and Linda Pogorzelski for helping with so many odds and ends, and Barbara Shircliffe, a graduate assistant, who made sure that all the book's references and citations were in order.

I would like to single out David Monk for a special acknowledgment. Since my doctoral studies at Cornell, he has been both a mentor and a friend. David's scholarship inspires his students to high standards and his gentle humor reminds us that we can have fun in the process.

Finally, special thanks to my family, Anita, Josh, and Kim, and my parents, Anne and Leo, for their unflagging support. I especially want to thank my daughter Carrie for letting me use the computer in her room. I am very lucky to have you all in my life.

STEPHEN L. JACOBSON

References

Alexander, K., & Monk, D. (Eds.). (1988). *Attracting and compensating America's teachers.* Cambridge, MA: Ballinger.

Bacharach, S., & Mundell, B. (1993). *Organizational politics in schools: Micro, macro, and logics of action*. Unpublished paper.

Carnegie Forum on Education and the Economy. (1986). *A nation prepared: Teachers for the 21st century*. New York: Author.

Farrar, E. (1990). Reflections on the first wave of reform: Reordering America's educational priorities. In S. Jacobson & J. Conway (Eds.), *Educational leadership in an age of reform* (pp. 3-13). New York: Longman.

Gorbachev, M. (1987). *Perestroika: New thinking for our country and the world*. New York: Harper & Row.

Holmes Group. (1986). *Tomorrow's teachers*. East Lansing, MI: Author.

Mueller, V., & McKeown, M. (Eds.). (1986). *The fiscal, legal and political aspects of state reform of elementary and secondary education*. Cambridge, MA: Ballinger.

National Commission on Excellence in Education. (1983). *A nation at risk: Imperative for educational reform*. Washington, DC: Government Printing Office.

Peters, T., & Waterman, R. (1982). *In search of excellence*. New York: Harper & Row.

Petrie, H. (1990). Reflections on the second wave of reform: Restructuring the teaching profession. In S. Jacobson & J. Conway (Eds.), *Educational leadership in an age of reform* (pp. 14-29). New York: Longman.

Rowan, B. (1990). Commitment and control: Alternative strategies for the organizational design of schools. In C. Cazden (Ed.), *Review of research in education* (pp. 353-389). Washington, DC: American Educational Research Association.

About the Contributors

Robert Berne is Associate Dean and Professor of Public Administration at the Robert F. Wagner Graduate School of Public Service, New York University. His research and publications focus on educational policy and finance, and local government finance. He is the coauthor of *The Measurement of Equity in School Finance* (Johns Hopkins University Press, 1984) and *The Financial Analysis of Governments* (Prentice-Hall, 1986). He has recently published *The Relationships Between Financial Reporting and the Measurement of Financial Condition* (Governmental Accounting Standards, 1992). He has worked with and directed state commissions on education finance and governance and has testified in school finance court cases.

William L. Boyd is Professor of Education at Pennsylvania State University. His specialty in research and teaching is education policy and politics. He holds a Ph.D. from the University of Chicago. He is the author of seven books, including *Education Policy in Australia and America*, *Private Schools and Public Policy: International Perspectives*, and *Choice in Education, Potential and Problems.* He was a Visiting Fulbright Scholar in Australia in 1984 at Monash University and Deakin University, where his project was a policy analysis of the reorganization of the State Education Department of Victoria. With a grant from the Bicentennial Swedish-American Exchange Fund, he conducted research in 1990 on education reform efforts in Sweden. In 1990-1991 he was a Visiting Fulbright Scholar in Britain, in the Department of

Political Theory and Education at the University of Liverpool. He has served as president of the Politics of Education Association and is a member of the U.S.-Australia Education Policy Project.

Daniel J. Brown undertook his graduate studies at the University of Chicago and then served as professor at the State University of New York at Buffalo. Currently, he teaches in the educational administration program at the University of British Columbia. He has written two books, titled *Decentralization and School-Based Management* and *Decentralization: The Administrator's Guidebook to School District Change.* Along with the continued study of school-based management, his interests focus on the ways in which schools attract gifts of time and money (voluntarism) and how schools seek private resources (enterprise).

Bruce S. Cooper is Professor of Educational Administration and Policy Analysis, Graduate School of Education, Fordham University. A Ph.D. graduate of the University of Chicago, he has taught at the University of Pennsylvania and Dartmouth College. His most recent books are *Labor Relations in Education: International Perspectives* (Greenwood), *Graying Teacher: Pensions and Early Retirement* (ERIC and the University of Oregon) with Frank Auriemma and Stuart Smith, and *The School as a Work Environment: Implications for Reform* (Allyn & Bacon) edited with Sharon Conley. Recent research includes extensive studies of school resource allocations, with the goal of tracking funds from the source to the classroom.

Richard F. Elmore is Professor of Education and Chair of the Department of Administration, Planning and Social Policy at the Graduate School of Education, Harvard University. He is also a senior research fellow of the Consortium for Policy Research in Education. His research focuses on state-local relations in education policy, school organization, and educational choice. He teaches regularly in programs for public sector executives and holds several government advisory positions. He holds a doctorate in educational policy from the Graduate School of Education at Harvard University.

Daniel Fishbein received his Ed.D. in educational administration at Teachers College, Columbia University, in 1992. He currently teaches science at Riverdale Country School in New York.

Frances C. Fowler received a Ph.D. from the University of Tennessee, Knoxville. Her major was educational administration, with minors in political science and social foundations. For 15 years, she was a classroom teacher in the public schools of Tennessee, during which time she was a leader in a teachers' union at the local and state levels. Since August 1990, she has been Assistant Professor in the Department of Educational Leadership at Miami University. She teaches politics of education, policy analysis, American school governance, and school law in the Educational Administration program. Her research interests include interest representation in educational policymaking, the impact of governance structures on policymaking, and comparative educational policy. She has published articles in the *Journal of Educational Policy, International Education, Education Week, Phi Delta Kappan,* and other journals.

Susan H. Fuhrman is Professor of Education Policy at Rutgers, the State University of New Jersey, and Director of the Consortium for Policy Research in Education, which conducts research on state and local education policies and finance. She is the author of numerous articles, research reports, and monographs on education policy and finance. She is the coeditor of the 1990 Politics of Education Yearbook and serves on the editorial board of the *Phi Delta Kappan.* She has served on numerous task forces, including the Standards Task Force of the National Council on Educational Standards and Testing and the New Jersey Task Force on Educational Assessment and Monitoring. She was a consultant to the Ford Foundation's program on educational management and finance for 10 years. Between 1986 and 1992, she served on the school board in Westfield, New Jersey.

James W. Guthrie received his Ph.D in educational administration from Stanford University. He is currently Professor of Education in the Graduate School of Education at the University of California at Berkeley. He has served as the Irving R. Melbo Distinguished Professor at the University of Southern California in 1984 and was a Fellow at Oxford University, Department of Educational Studies, in 1989. In 1990 he was selected the American Education Research Association's first Senior Fellow. He directs, with Michael W. Kirst of Stanford University, Project PACE (Policy Analysis for California Education). He was the editor of the American Educational Research Association-sponsored quarterly, *Educational Evaluation and Policy Analysis* (1985-

1991). He has written extensively on matters of educational policy, evaluation, and the reform of educational systems and has written widely used textbooks in school finance, educational administration, and strategic planning, including *Education Finance and Policy: Enhancing Education Equality, Efficiency, and Liberty,* with Walter I. Garms and Lawrence C. Pierce, and *Ed School: A Brief for Professional Education,* with Geraldine Clifford.

G. Alfred Hess, Jr., was trained as an educational anthropologist, receiving a Ph.D. from Northwestern University. He is Executive Director of the Chicago Panel on Public School Policy and Finance, a multiracial, multiethnic coalition of 20 nonprofit agencies dedicated to improving public education in Chicago. He has been instrumental in providing public scrutiny of the finance and budgeting processes of the Chicago public schools and has been a key participant in school reform in Chicago. His numerous publications in the area of urban education reform include *School Restructuring, Chicago Style* (Corwin, 1991).

Stephen L. Jacobson is Associate Professor of Education and Coordinator of the Educational Administration Program in the Graduate School of Education at the State University of New York at Buffalo. He received his Ph.D. from Cornell University, and his dissertation was named cowinner of the American Education Finance Association's Jean Flanigan Award for Outstanding Research in the Field of Educational Finance in 1988. Prior to entering higher education, he was a special education teacher with the New York City Public Schools. His research interests focus primarily on the school workplace, rural education, and educational reform. His most recent works include *Educational Leadership in an Age of Reform* (Longman, 1990), with James A. Conway, and *Helping At-Risk Students: What Are the Educational and Financial Costs?* (Corwin, 1992), with Patricia Anthony.

Charles Taylor Kerchner is Professor at the Claremont Graduate School in Southern California, where he directs the program in educational leadership. He has studied teacher unionism for more than a decade and is coauthor of *The Changing Idea of a Teachers' Union* (Falmer, 1988) and numerous articles and book chapters. Before coming to Claremont in 1976, he was on the faculty at Northwestern

University, where he received his Ph.D., and was a member of the Illinois Board of Higher Education. He also served on the staff of the *St. Petersburg Times* (in Florida) in a number of editorial and managerial positions.

Jennifer A. King is a doctoral candidate studying educational policy and administration at Cornell University. She has taught writing at Marquette University's Upward Bound program and is currently a Research Assistant for the Consortium for Policy Research in Education (CPRE). Her primary research interests include urban education policy, issues of educational productivity, and multicultural education.

Julia E. Koppich is a lecturer in the Graduate School of Education and Deputy Director of Policy Analysis for California Education (PACE) at the University of California at Berkeley. She previously served in a staff position with the California legislature, worked as a classroom teacher, and was staff director for the American Federation of Teachers in San Francisco. She earned a Ph.D. in educational policy analysis at the University of California at Berkeley. Her research interests focus on the politics of education, public sector labor relations, and the politics of school reform. She is also a founding partner of Management Analysis and Planning Associates, an independent consultant firm specializing in organizational analysis and development.

Betty Malen is Associate Professor in the College of Education, University of Washington. She received her Ph.D. in education policy and administration at the University of Minnesota. Her research focuses on the politics of various education reform initiatives and includes studies of the enactment and implementation of career ladder and school-based management policies.

Diane Massell is Research Associate with the Consortium for Policy Research in Education. Her current research focuses on state approaches to setting the agenda for new instructional guidance policies and will appear in a forthcoming book published by the Association for Supervision and Curriculum Development. Similar work on national standard setting efforts and curriculum policies is also under way. In addition, she is preparing a study on state and local barriers to new science curriculum.

Paula Melville received her Ed.D. in educational administration at Teachers College, Columbia University, in 1993. She is a former high school administrator and teacher of emotionally disturbed children.

Wolfgang Mitter is Head of the Department of General and Comparative Education and Director of the Research Council at the German Institute for International Educational Research at Frankfurt/Main. In addition, he has teaching responsibilities at Frankfurt University. His main research interests are comparative education and educational policy. He is active in numerous international educational research bodies. Currently, he is President of the World Council of Comparative Education Societies and a member of the German Commission for UNESCO. He is also editor, since 1981, of the journal *Bildung und Erziehung*. Recent publications include "Education in Eastern Europe and the Former Soviet Union in a Period of Revolutionary Change: An Approach to Comparative Analysis," in D. Phillips and M. Kaser, *Education and Economic Change in Eastern Europe and the Former Soviet Union* (Triangle Books, 1992), and "Educational Issues in the Multicultural Society of Germany," in D. Ray and H. Poowassie, *Education and Cultural Differences: New Perspectives* (Garland, 1992).

David H. Monk is Professor of Educational Administration at Cornell University. He earned his Ph.D. at the University of Chicago and has taught in a visiting capacity at the University of Rochester and the University of Burgundy in Dijon, France. He is the author of *Educational Finance: An Economic Approach* (McGraw-Hill, 1990) as well as numerous articles in scholarly journals. He is a Senior Research Fellow for the Consortium for Policy Research in Education and serves on the editorial boards of *Educational Evaluation and Policy Analysis, The Economics of Education Review,* and the *Journal of Research in Rural Education.* He consults widely on matters related to educational productivity and the organizational structuring of schools and school districts and is the immediate past president of the American Education Finance Association.

David N. Plank is Associate Professor in the School of Education at the University of Pittsburgh, where he teaches in the program in Policy, Planning, and Evaluation. His publications on educational policy and educational finance have appeared in journals including *Economics of Education Review, Comparative Education Review, Journal of*

Education Finance, and *Revista Brasileira de Estudos Pedaogicos.* He is the editor, with Rick Ginsberg, of *Southern Cities, Southern Schools: Public Education in the Urban South* (Greenwood, 1990). He is now editing a second book (with Rick Ginsberg) on the politics of "blue-ribbon" commissions in U.S. school reform in the 1980s and is completing a book manuscript on the political economy of public education in Brazil. His current research focuses on the role of the World Bank and other international aid agencies in the formulation of educational policies in Africa, with a focus on Mozambique.

Peter Ribbins is Professor of Educational Management in the School of Education, University of Birmingham. He has undertaken research in a variety of aspects of education and its management at the system and school levels in the United Kingdom. He is editor of *Educational Management and Administration* and his most recent books include *Developing Educational Leaders, Delivering the National Curriculum, Greenfield on Education Administration,* and *Improving Education.*

Craig E. Richards is Associate Professor of Educational Administration at Teachers College, Columbia University. He has published widely in the area of incentives, school effectiveness, and accountability. He is currently coeditor of policy articles for the *Journal of Educational Finance* and coeditor of *Direktor,* the first independently produced Russian educational journal for school administrators.

Hywel Thomas is Professor of Economics of Education in the School of Education, University of Birmingham. The principal focus of his work has been the internal efficiency of the education system and the application of ideas from economics in ways that seek to take account of organizational and management contexts. He has published several books including *Financial Delegation and the Local Management of Schools* and *Education Costs and Performance: A Cost-Effectiveness Analysis.*

Manfred Weiss is Senior Researcher in the Department of Economics at the German Institute for International Educational Research and part-time lecturer in the Faculty of Educational Studies at the University of Frankfurt. In 1987 he was a visiting professor at the State University of New York at Buffalo. His main research interests involve the economics of education, educational planning and policy, and international developments in education. Recent publications include

Prospective Trends in the Socio-Economic Context of Education in European Market Economy Countries, with Hasso von Recum and Peter A. Döring (UNESCO, 1991), and *Recent Trends in Eastern European Education,* with editors Wolfgang Mitter and Ulrich Schaefer (German Institute for International Educational Research, 1992; also published in German by Lang).

PART I

Reform Initiatives
in the United States

ONE

School Reform in the United States
PUTTING IT INTO CONTEXT

SUSAN H. FUHRMAN

RICHARD F. ELMORE

DIANE MASSELL

The chapters in this volume focus on "a decade of school reform." Since the 1983 publication of *A Nation at Risk,* the National Commission on Excellence in Education's stirring call to arms, *reform* has become the byword of education policy discussions. Of course, education reform predates 1983. The United States has had numerous previous reform surges (Firestone, 1989; Ginsburg & Wimpelberg, 1987), and traces of the current interest in improvement were noticeable prior to *A Nation at Risk* (McDonnell & Fuhrman, 1986). Nonetheless, the large volume of reform and continued policymaker attention to reform issues, despite economic ups and downs, distinguish this last decade.

AUTHORS' NOTE: The material in this chapter is excerpted from two sources: the Consortium for Policy Research in Education's *Technical Proposal for Center on Education Policies and Student Learning,* New Brunswick, New Jersey, and S. H. Fuhrman and D. Massell's "Issues and Strategies in Systemic Reform."

Reforms of the Past Decade

An assessment of the educational reform in the past decade suggests that it has been broad, but not very deep; that it has involved multiple interventions, but a high level of incoherence among interventions; and that it entails high expectations for student learning, but as yet has had limited influence over the factors that directly effect learning.

Broad, but not deep. The educational reforms of the 1980s involved an unprecedented volume of policymaking on a broad range of subjects, accompanied by a significant shift in the locus of policymaking to states and localities. As part of a so-called first wave of reform focused on state standard setting, at least 45 states changed high school graduation requirements, either by raising academic course requirements or by introducing state requirements for the first time. In a number of instances, these reforms were accompanied by significant increases in state-level curriculum controls and state-mandated testing. In some cases, state curriculum policies deal with the actual content, sequence, and pacing of instruction. But in most cases, state policies mandated minimum required content coverage by subject area. In some states, students are required to pass minimum competency tests as a condition of graduation, though the standards on these tests are typically set at eighth- or ninth-grade levels. In other states, tests are used to assess student progress against state and local goals. In a small number of states, tests reflect state-mandated curriculum frameworks. Most states that mandate testing use commercial standardized tests (Firestone, Fuhrman, & Kirst, 1989).

Virtually all states made significant changes in policies affecting teachers during the 1980s. By one estimate, states considered at least 1,000 pieces of legislation to change teacher policy during the first 5 years of the reform decade (Darling-Hammond & Berry, 1988). The number of states requiring some form of testing as a condition of teacher certification increased substantially between 1983 and 1986, from 28 to 46. A few states introduced recertification tests for veteran teachers. Others have ventured further, by requiring formal on-the-job assessment of teachers prior to licensure. A handful of states adopted policies to change teachers' working conditions, such as career ladder, master teacher, and merit pay programs (Firestone et al., 1989).

As the education reform decade progressed, a number of states and districts launched programs intended to change the traditional administrative structure of schools or to alter the incentives under which schools operate. As part of a so-called second wave of reform focused on school-level change, several states and local school districts launched school-based management initiatives, designed to devolve some degree of control over curriculum, budget, or staffing to principals, teachers, and parents (Clune & White, 1988). Likewise, a number of local districts undertook concerted efforts to improve the quality of teaching and learning in schools by encouraging school-level planning and instructional improvement (David, 1989; Elmore & McLaughlin, 1988). In addition, at least half the states have initiated some kind of state-level policies designed to increase parent and student choice in the selection of educational programs (Fossey, 1992; Nathan, 1989).

The reform decade, then, has been one of unprecedented education policymaking in states and localities. But it is a mistake to equate increased policymaking activity with increased influence over teaching and learning (Fuhrman, Clune, & Elmore, 1988; Fuhrman & Elmore, 1990). The evidence thus far suggests that, while reforms have been broad in coverage, they have been shallow in their effects. Graduation requirements, for example, have increased the proportion of academic courses offered in high school curricula, but it is unclear whether they have increased the actual exposure of students to academic content or their learning of academic subjects (Clune, 1989). Changes in state curriculum and testing requirements have increased the state presence in local decision making, but the connections between policy in curriculum and testing and instruction in classrooms remain erratic (Schwille et al., 1988). Changes in teacher policy have altered the conditions of entry to teaching in many states, but there is little evidence yet that they resulted in significant improvements in the level of knowledge that teachers bring to the classroom (McCarthy, 1990). Changes in administrative structures have occurred in a number of local districts, but there is little evidence yet on how these changes are related to improvements in the quality of educational programs or student learning (Elmore, 1990). In other words, education reform has generated a high level of activity, but it has yet to exert much influence over the processes of schooling related to student learning.

Multiple interventions, low coherence. The unprecedented volume of policymaking activity in the 1980s signaled that learning of academic subjects was a high priority among state and local policymakers. Reform policies differ significantly across states. They embody very different views on curriculum and student learning. In some states, policies focus on minimum curriculum standards and basic academic skills, while in others the focus is on standards at the leading edge of current curriculum and teaching practice and on higher levels of understanding in academic subjects. Within states, some policies focus on compliance with minimum standards, while others encourage schools to develop ambitious new approaches to teaching and learning. Education reform, then, is not a single set of policies focused on a single conception of student learning but a variety of policies that embody very different ideas about student learning. While education reform has given student learning of academic subjects much more prominence as a policy objective, it has also increased the complexity, and reduced the coherence, of the policies under which schools operate.

Schools develop their approaches to teaching and learning within complex systems of influence emanating from a number of sources—community interests, district administrative structures, state and local financial constraints, as well as local, state, and federal policy requirements across a number of areas. With increased policymaking activity at all levels of government over the last 25 years, the policy environment of schools has become increasingly crowded, and the signals that policies send to schools have become increasingly uncoordinated, dissonant, and less coherent. Each new policy initiative, whether from the federal, state, or local level, is added to the previous ones, and none are taken away. Schools are expected to resolve these competing expectations of various generations of reform (Cohen, 1982; Elmore & McLaughlin, 1988; Fuhrman et al., 1988).

As the level of incoherence in the policy environment increases, districts and schools are forced into a difficult set of trade-offs. Should they layer new curriculum and testing requirements over the top of existing ones, or should they attempt to rationalize new ones and old ones in a new structure? Should they add increasingly specialized teaching and support staff, or should they attempt to accomplish new policy goals with existing staff? Should they divide students into increasingly more specialized groups, based on the objectives of policies, or should they attempt to provide special attention in less differentiated settings? Should they create new administrative roles to oversee new policy objectives, or should they add these objectives to the workload of existing administrators? Some districts and schools respond to these trade-offs by exercising considerable entrepreneurial skill, making a coherent mission from a collection of disparate and conflicting policies (Fuhrman et al., 1988). But many schools and districts respond to an increasingly incoherent policy environment by transferring the incoherence of policy into their daily operations. They react to new curriculum standards by layering them over the top of existing course content, producing a mix of instructional approaches that often makes little sense in the classroom. They respond to new testing requirements often by trying to figure how to teach to specific test items, usually without a clear conception of whether the test content reflects a clear picture of what students ought to know. They respond to new policy demands by giving teachers specific in-service training on the requirements of new policies, usually without a connection to the broader tasks of teaching or the cumulative effect of past policies.

Furthermore, policymakers and institutional actors often operate somewhat independently of each other, without a clear education reform agenda. State legislatures mandate greater attention to academic instruction in schools, but teacher education institutions often conduct preservice or professional education based on different conceptions of what teachers should know. Business leaders and elected officials articulate high expectations for the quality of academic learning in schools, but state and local agencies test students and teachers for low-level rote learning. Ambitious new curricula are adopted school by school and district by district in a number of states, while statewide curriculum guides and testing often represent older, more conventional conceptions of curriculum.

Finally, over the past 25 years, many policies have been implemented by what might be called the "project method" of organization and management, in which specific pots of money are allocated to specific activities over a limited period of time for selected groups of teachers and students. The effect of multiple waves of these policies over time has been to fragment school organization into a variety of specialized activities and to increase the complexity of teachers' and students' work in schools. For some time, reformers have urged policymakers to focus on improving the performance of whole schools, treating all students as if they can meet high expectations for learning, and increasing the coherence of teachers' and students' engagement in learning. While there are persuasive examples of whole-school approaches to improvement, these examples have had little effect on the overall policy environment in which schools operate.

The reforms of the 1980s have focused public attention on academic learning, and they have created the expectation that schools will teach academic content at a high level of understanding to all students. They have, however, done little to decrease the conflicting policy demands that operate on schools and they have contributed to an increasing incoherence in the policy environment of schools.

Increasing expectations, limited influence over student learning. The reforms of the 1980s focused educational policy on a very important goal: academic learning for all students, regardless of race, social class, or cultural background. It is now increasingly common to hear elected officials, members of the business community, and educators alike voice the expectation that all students will need a high level of understanding of academic subjects, a capacity for problem solving, and an ability to apply knowledge in concrete situations to function effectively in an increasingly demanding economy and society (see, for example, National Council of Teachers of Mathematics, 1989; National Governors' Association [NGA], 1986).

Yet evidence of progress on this goal is distressingly meager. There are many inspiring examples of schools and districts that have used educational reform to improve conditions for teachers and students. But by virtually all aggregate indices of performance, schools have shown little improvement since the beginning of the current period of reform. Academic achievement does not seem to have improved significantly over the past decade by most measures (National Center for Education Statistics [NCES], 1989, pp. 10-11, 14-15, 26-27). Even on those measures of academic achievement where some groups of students have shown improvement on basic skills, performance is extremely weak on the higher level problem-solving tasks that reformers value (Dossey, Mullis, Lindquist, & Chambers, 1988; Mullis & Jenkins, 1990). Dropout rates and rates of retention in grade have been stuck at unacceptably high levels for more than a decade (Frase, 1989; NCES, 1989, pp. 24-25; Shepard & Smith, 1989). Indices of students' attachment to school, such as engagement and membership in school activities and workforce participation, show a high level of alienation among significant portions of school-aged children (Wehlage, 1989; Wehlage, Rutter, Smith, Lesko, & Fernandez, 1989).

So, while education reform policies have set ambitious goals for student learning, there is not much evidence that the current array of reform policies is working toward those goals. There is reason for concern about whether the existing array of reform policies is the appropriate means of meeting the expectations of reformers.

The Next Stage of Education Reform

Pressure for better results from U.S. schools, and more consistent performance for different types of students, will continue to mount. Economic pressures, both internally and internationally, will continue to increase. The economic message is increasingly clear. To maintain, or increase, our standard of living, we will have to increase significantly the basic problem-solving knowledge students acquire in school, increase the capacity of individuals to acquire new knowledge over a lifetime, and increase individuals' ability to apply knowledge to complex practical tasks. Political pressures will also continue to mount. Education constitutes a large, and increasingly problematic, share of state and local expenditures. Policymakers at the state and local levels will be under increasing pressure to show results for these expenditures. Former President Bush and the governors showed a willingness to enter the policymaking arena in new ways, through the formulation of national goals for education. These goals send a strong signal to educators that schools should return to the core of the enterprise and evaluate policy, structures, and practices in terms of their relationship to student learning. Education, in short, will continue to be a highly visible item on the policy agenda at the federal, state, and local levels.

Responding to these economic and political pressures will require a new look at policy design. The new approach must remedy the problems of superficiality, fragmentation, and frailty that plague education policy. To create some sense of coherence out of the current chaos of education reform, leaders in California pioneered a novel reform strategy in the 1980s. They called for ambitious, common goals of student learning and achievement and the close coordination of various elements of the policy infrastructure around the outcome expectations. Similarly, Connecticut began to develop a Common

Core of Learning and related assessments. Several other states also
began to redesign policy in this fashion.

The new approach to reform, one that attempts to combine the
"first" and "second" waves into a "third" way, has been termed
systemic reform. This path would pair ambitious, coordinated state
policies with restructured governance (Smith & O'Day, 1991b). The
reform strategy would work by simultaneously

> increasing coherence in the system through centralized coordi-
> nation and increasing professional discretion at the school site.
> Thus while schools have the ultimate responsibility to educate
> thoughtful, competent, and responsible citizens, the state—
> representing the public—has the responsibility to define what
> "thoughtful, competent, and responsible citizens" will mean in
> the coming decade and century. (Smith & O'Day, 1991b, p. 254)

Since the late 1980s when "systemic reform" ideas began to circu-
late, a national movement under that rubric has been launched.
Numerous players at all levels of government as well as associations,
foundations, and other independent organizations advocate and support this change (e.g., Business Roundtable, 1991; National Council
on Educational Standards and Testing [NCEST], 1992; NGA, 1991).
Involved are dozens of states as diverse as Arkansas, Arizona, Vermont, and Kentucky; national agencies including the National Science
Foundation and the U.S. Department of Education; and organizations
including the Business Roundtable, the Education Commission of the
States, and the National Governors' Association. The National Education Goals Panel's plan to establish national standards foresees a
similar process of using standards as an anchor for assessment, professional development, and other instructional policies (NCEST,
1992). Systemic reform is a natural experiment of sizable proportions.

The policy efforts to set outcomes and reinforce them with integrated instruments are only a portion of the movement toward upgraded instruction. Larger developments in the culture surround and
support systemic reform, improving the destiny of policy approaches.
For example, disciplinary associations, such as the National Council
of Teachers of Mathematics (NCTM), have begun to reach consensus
on very challenging student outcomes. Spurred by the establishment
of national education goals, similar efforts are under way in other
subject areas. Business leaders, represented on panels like the Secre-

tary's Commission on Achieving Necessary Skills (SCANS, 1991), are also participating in efforts to establish competency goals for students. Such activities provide support for the notion of challenging, communally identified outcomes. Surrounded by such broad, societal backing, policy efforts to establish and reinforce such outcomes take on increased authority and leverage (Fuhrman, 1993).

Diverse political, economic, and legal traditions; policy cultures; and notions of best practice shape the ways states approach reform. Although they answer the questions that arise in different ways, states face a common set of challenges in crafting new reform strategies. The balance of this chapter highlights issues and strategies that characterize the unfolding of systemic reform in the nation.

Reform vision and scope. While the words *systemic reform* take on many meanings, depending on the users, two themes predominate. Some use the term to refer to comprehensive change that is focused on many aspects of the system. Others stress the notion of policy integration, coordination, or coherence around a set of clear outcomes.

States have long experience with comprehensive policy efforts that touch upon multiple components of schooling, often in the form of omnibus education legislation. In the 1980s, legislatures passed omnibus reform bills that exacted more stringent graduation requirements, professional standards, and discipline policies; raised teacher salaries; extended school days and years; and more. Although often undertaken with broad objectives to improve academic achievement, decision makers analyzed each program or policy instrument independently. As a result, no common, core goals united the diverse policy and program areas (Firestone et al., 1989; Firestone, Rosenblum, Bader, & Massell, 1991).

Coordinated efforts, by contrast, assemble policy reforms to undergird a more focused set of policy goals. Explicit goals that articulate the meaning of more rigorous academic standards are critical. In recent years, many states have crafted goal statements for the entire education system in general as well as for curriculum in particular. Once goals are established, integrated strategies focus on coordinating various aspects of policy so they reinforce the goals and one another. For example, California's curriculum frameworks and guidelines underpin the state's testing program (California Achievement Program), staff development, textbook adoption, school evaluations, and publicly disseminated accountability reports.

While California focuses on integrating policies that provide guidance about instruction (see Cohen & Spillane, 1992, for a discussion of "instructional guidance"), other states include a broader range of policies in the systemic strategy. The Kentucky Education Reform Act of 1990 (KERA) is an example of more comprehensive reform. It includes not only integrated reforms of key instructional policies but also restructuring of the state department, school governance, and the organization of schools in addition to a plan for a network of Family or Youth Resource Centers, which would focus on coordinating such social services as child care, health services, and drug and alcohol abuse counseling.

The past failures of fragmented policy suggest that "integration" is critical to reform that is truly "systemic." The political system, however, is more accustomed to the "comprehensive" notion. Typically, legislatures build coalitions by bundling together many discrete programs. With omnibus or comprehensive approaches, many policymakers can share credit and satisfy diverse constituencies. More integrated approaches require trade-offs and difficult choices among policy options. Therefore achieving and maintaining coherence presents political challenges.

No matter how many policy elements states include in reform efforts, state policymakers must be aware of the many factors that can work to frustrate attempts at coordination. Systemic reform implies simultaneous alterations in two or more spheres. As state departments of education across the country have been cut back, these agencies often lack the resources or technical staff to accomplish reform. Furthermore, staffs traditionally divide along programmatic lines, such as Chapter 1, gifted and talented, and the like. Time schedules for the completion of one task often compete with others, resulting in uncoordinated changes or in one policy mechanism driving changes that it was intended to follow. By shifting organizational resources and priorities, and building an institutional base for long-term development, some of these obstacles may be tackled.

In addition, the technology for change sometimes lags behind the intended reform vision. This is nowhere so evident as in the new authentic assessments embraced by many states. Despite much publicity, the fact is that full development of reliable and valid authentic assessments is several years away. So, in the interim, states rely on other tests to fulfill political demands for statewide accountability. And even if states develop and connect their own relevant policy instruments, they face the challenge of local tests or other factors that compete with the new direction.

On another level, mobilizing a particular policy sector into overall state reform may be difficult. For example, states often find it hard to garner the political support for teacher in-service training programs that link what teachers know to what students are expected to know, as such programs are very expensive on a large scale and many policymakers and citizens view staff development as a special bonus for teachers rather than a real means of improving instruction. Staff development is, however, key to the success of efforts to upgrade classroom content, so policymakers are seeking strategies for alternative kinds of staff development, including teacher networks and teacher participation in the creation of new state frameworks and assessments.

Teacher education, subject to the separate governance systems of higher education, is particularly difficult to coordinate with expectations for student learning. In California, state department officials reported that efforts to substantively change the course work offered in teacher education programs bumped up against academic freedom issues and the tenure system. Nevertheless, some states are attempting reform in this area using such strategies as guidelines that would approve teacher education programs on a results-oriented basis, using portfolios; licensure and relicensure that focuses on teacher competence; or using professional recommendations for student competencies, such as those developed by the National Council of Teachers of Mathematics, in the determination of desired teacher competencies.

Finally, states have not linked school finance to systemic reform strategies. If states were to integrate finance with systemic reforms directed at teaching and learning, they might consider a number of strategies, including providing funding directly to schools to support school-level decision making and providing a committed, continuing source of funds for professional development linked to new expectations for students (Odden, 1991). They might also redesign teacher compensation systems to reward teacher knowledge and skills instead of the proxies currently used in experience- and education-related pay scales (Odden & Conley, 1991; Firestone, 1992). Finally, we need better knowledge than currently exists about the components and costs of high-quality instructional programs aimed at the achievement of challenging outcomes (Clune, 1992).

Professionals, the public, and politics. It can be argued that providing coherent guidance to instruction is as much a cultural effort as a policy reform task (Cohen & Spillane, 1992). Employers, college officials, and parents must come to understand and value challenging notions of learning if they are to reinforce school reform. Professionals, teachers, and administrators must understand and value new forms of teaching and learning if they are to make instruction more challenging. One way to educate the public and professionals, to enlist their important insights and expertise, and to grant them ownership of the reform enterprise is to involve them in the development of standards for students.

States have used a variety of mechanisms for public and professional involvement (Massell, 1992). Beliefs about the best ways to secure consensus and develop support for the state's new curriculum goals and documents shape decisions about who participates and when. Strategies used by different states range from those rooted in disciplinary perspectives and created by experts in these disciplines to those that are organized around technical and life skills and focus on seeking lay citizen support and consensus. These different beginnings will likely yield different strategies to achieve their goals and form different public and professional constituencies.

For most states, it is too early yet to see how these various agenda-setting processes enable a more relevant and demanding course of studies, foster political and professional consensus, or facilitate local implementation. We can make some observations, however. California, for example, had success gaining support among professional educators through the development of high-quality frameworks, but it can also be observed, from the experiences of other states, that, while public participation is desirable, it can be difficult to sustain.

In addition to participation in curriculum goals and frameworks, states have other mechanisms for professional involvement in reform. In Connecticut, Maine, Kentucky, and Vermont, for example, volunteer teachers pilot the new assessments and help to score them. In addition, some of Connecticut's science and mathematics teachers participate in an interstate compact that allows them to work with other people also engaged in these tasks.

Teacher participation may be seen as a form of professional development around the new content expectations. Ultimately, the answer to the question of whether or not schools have the capacity to respond to state policies about ambitious instruction comes to rest on teacher professional development. As noted previously, this unquestionably important aspect of reform is not necessarily politically popular. Fiscal stress makes it particularly vulnerable.

Teacher networks seem to provide one particularly promising approach that has emerged in the last few years (Adams, in press). Successful programs have shown that staff development is greatly enhanced by daily preparation periods involving networks of teachers and long summer workshops and that meeting people who are influential within their own discipline, in industry, or in local, state, or national policy enhanced teachers' sense of the possible and helped them to recognize expertise and incorporate this into their teaching. As teachers extend themselves professionally, they expand their own understanding of their role. Teacher empowerment rests not simply on greater decision making but on decision making that rests on subject matter knowledge, knowledge of the broader professional community, and knowledge of education policy (Lichtenstein, Mc-Laughlin, & Knudsen, 1991).

Beyond gaining the support of the public and professionals, states must also build and maintain political support for systemic reform. The fragmentation of education policy and reform in this nation is the natural result of our political system's divided governance structures, single issue candidates, and interest-group politics. Electoral politics place a premium on distinguishing one policymaker's efforts from another's to enhance visibility at the polls. Over the years, as states have become more active in school finance, the administration of federal programs, and in other areas of school policy, interest groups and lobbyists at the state level have mushroomed. These factors result in policy driven by compromise and bargaining rather than any uniform vision of change (Fuhrman, 1993).

In some states, partly as a consequence of increased responsibilities and tighter budgets, we have seen increased partisanship in education as well as competition between education and other social services. Policymakers have become lightning rods for partisan issues that divide and disperse, rather than integrate, reform ideas.

Systemic reform entails a fundamentally different way of thinking about and strategizing for school change. It requires a generalists' knowledge of education and enough understanding of various policy instruments to coordinate and link them to the central goals. Even in states that have strong leaders with the personal charisma and authority to insulate the broader vision of school change from the political tendencies toward fragmentation, the momentum for reform then becomes highly vulnerable to turnover in leadership.

One approach to encouraging sustained coordinated policymaking is broadening the jurisdiction, and hence the constituent base, of governmental structures. While all policy areas feed off the same budget and the appropriations process forces trade-offs, substantive integration across committees is rare. Consolidating the structure or work of existing entities could expand their scope and provide a basis for improved coordination. Short of mergers, the various bodies could hold regular joint meetings and hearings and set up special offices within departments to encourage collaboration.

Entirely new governmental structures could also improve coordination and the political viability of systemic reform. An entirely new body, charged with the responsibility to monitor and fine-tune the reform act over time, could cause legislators to become vested in its progress and may be less likely to forge off in totally new directions. Such a strategy could avert the shifts in emphasis and proliferation of projects that occurred in many states during the 1980s.

In South Carolina, one of the oversight agencies created by reform legislation includes diverse members of the business, education, and legislative communities. Consequently, it provides a forum for negotiating across interests and reaching consensus before policy recommendations enter the political arena. The Business-Education Subcommittee functions much like a reform task force; it holds hearings, develops recommendations, seeks compromise, and tries to build support for the resulting policy. It is not ad hoc in the manner of task forces, however; it is a standing forum that functions as a permanent arena for consensus prior to the deliberation of political bodies.

Might such an entity representing key constituencies interested in improving student achievement—teachers, university experts, parents, administrators, business and political leaders—serve to preserve political momentum for systemic reform? States that are establishing broad-based, continuing curriculum/assessment committees may be moving in such a direction. Whether these kinds of entities are able to protect the coherence of their approach over time will probably depend on a number of factors, including their membership and scope of concern.

The entity's recommendations would take force from the expertise and representativeness of the membership. Bringing political leaders into the deliberations may give suggestions a better chance of surviving authorization and appropriations processes. Involving practitioners will improve the likelihood that their recommendations reflect the realities of teaching and learning and enlist teachers' support. In effect, the standards developed by such an authority would influence educators much as design standards influence engineers; they would carry the "best practice" seal of approval granted by professional leaders (Fuhrman, 1993).

Such a group would not only set standards but also refine them over time, providing a mechanism for ensuring the incorporation of new knowledge and for adjusting to feedback provided by experience. With such flexibility in mind, it might be advantageous to avoid codifying standards by formal enactment and to rely instead on the continuing authority of a well-constituted and legitimate standards entity. The broader the scope of the entity, the greater the foundation for policy coordination. For example, in addition to subject matter content standards, they also might consider inter- and cross-disciplinary implications. As in the case of California's framework writing committees, deliberations could encompass the array of policies that should be aligned in support of outcome recommendations.

Combining bottom-up and top-down reform. The approaches to systemic reform described thus far have been deductive; that is, coordination begins at the state level. Another way of approaching systemic reform is through more inductive, bottom-up methods, which begin at the local school level and look "up" through the system to assemble the resources and support for coherent change. A challenge is how to replicate the effort across new sites and whether states can reasonably accommodate and tailor their policies to the individually identified needs of each site. The United States might learn some lessons from Australia in this regard. In that nation, a national-level curriculum mapping exercise seeks to distill a common core curriculum from various, existing state curricula. There might be parallels between that process and what could occur between local and state governments in this nation.

Even in the states that initiate reform with state standards and coordinated policies, there is discussion of granting simultaneous school flexibility. Many leaders believe that the state should set broad goals and policies but that schools should specify the details of curriculum and instruction, much as Smith and O'Day (1991b) argued.

The difficulties of combining "top-down" and "bottom-up" reform should not be underestimated, however. A number of contradictions and missed opportunities indicate that this area of reform will be among the most challenging to accomplish. For example, in Kentucky, schools are to be self-governing, yet KERA requires schools to elim-inate grade-based classrooms in K-3. A number of states have re-structuring programs to support school decision making but school councils are not explicitly encouraged to focus their activities on meeting state instructional goals. Even though school choice is very compatible with systemic reform, many discussions pit choice against state policy improvement, as if market control and coherent state guidance were antagonistic. Systemic reform might enhance choice, for the state curriculum frameworks would establish a protective structure to ensure that all schools were providing challenging con-tent and examinations would provide valid data to guide decisions (Smith & O'Day, 1991b). But, while public school choice is increas-ingly on state policy agendas, policymakers are not linking choice and state instructional guidance by combining them in reform ap-proaches.

How to allocate responsibilities among levels of decision makers is a perennial question in this nation and others, across areas of public policy and in the private sector as well (Clune & White, 1987; Hanna-way & Carnoy, 1993). Two current dilemmas facing policymakers indicate how difficult it is to sort out responsibilities in the system.

The first quandary concerns the degree of detail states should specify in curriculum standards. State frameworks or curriculum guidelines vary in the extent to which they specify course content. No state curriculum effort determines the exact content or timing of daily lessons, as occurs in France or other European countries (Smith, O'Day, & Cohen, 1990, 1991). In the United States, these documents are intended to serve as guidelines for coordinating other state poli-cies and local curriculum development. But the variation in specific-ity—from those that have an extensive rationale and philosophy, as well as numerous examples illustrating standards of achievement, to those that describe what students should know and be able to do but that do not begin with the subject matter disciplines and are relatively less detailed—provides interesting contrasts.

Less specific documents provide greater latitude for local decisions on curriculum. Some reformers believe that the more local flexibility the better. Although the true test of these arguments will come in research that focuses more strongly on the enactment of curriculum in schools and classrooms (Elmore, Sykes, & Spillane, 1992), evidence suggests that more specific documents, supported by many examples of teacher lessons, may be more enabling for schools and teachers (e.g., Hannaway, 1993). Although states do not want to infringe upon hallowed traditions of local curriculum development, the fact is that the capacity of many local schools and districts to create their own curriculum has declined steadily over the years (Walker, 1990). Furthermore, the degree of centralization of the curriculum has not been shown to produce a strong difference in teachers' sense of personal efficacy and job satisfaction (Archbald, 1991).

Furthermore, the notion of school-by-school creation of curricula is vastly complicated by high student mobility in urban areas. In single courses, only 30% of a class may be enrolled for one entire semester while only a small minority of students might take a complete sequence in the same school. The ultimate significance of this situation for policy remains to be explored: Does high mobility make a standard curriculum necessary?

A subset of the specificity issue concerns the establishment of state standards as generic versus subject matter-specific skills and competencies. In a number of states, policymakers are debating how best to express outcomes. Some assert that generic competencies are most likely to support interdisciplinary studies or that the "content wars" about which topics to include or exclude should be fought at the local level. Business leaders, too, tend to express work-related skills in more generic terms. On the other side are those who believe that skills are embedded in content and that subject-specific standards give more concrete guidance to teachers trying to implement them. As noted in the previous section, the process established to determine standards can interact with the content/generic skill debate.

The second issue concerns the fate of traditional regulation of practice, given new state emphasis on outcomes rather than process. Much reform discussion centers on anchoring accountability around outcomes; schools and districts would be accredited, rewarded, and/or sanctioned based on student performance and other measures such as student attainment. Schools would have utmost flexibility in organization and delivery of instruction, so that they could maximize achievement on the outcomes in ways tailored to the needs of their own students. No longer would states regulate practice, such as class size or amount of instruction in various subjects.

Deregulatory efforts to date indicate the complexities of process deregulation. First, current deregulatory programs do not shed much light on the type of wholesale deregulation envisioned by the outcome accountability scenario. Some states are contemplating broad-scale deregulation, but at the moment a number of states use deregulation, or eligibility for waivers, as a reward for higher achieving and/or consistently highly accredited schools. Although school improvement research teaches that autonomy or flexibility is a likely precursor to improvement, many programs deny discretion to schools most needing improvement (Fuhrman, 1989).

Second, recent experience indicates that removing regulation will not in and of itself turn tradition-bound schools into exemplars of creativity. A range of policies—such as teacher professional development and assistance to schools—might be needed to help schools take advantage of the flexibility and maximize achievement. Deregulation does provide a stimulus to change by encouraging schools to examine and address barriers to improvement, including but not limited to regulation. Studies in South Carolina and Washington suggest that automatic exemption from a number of rules, in contrast to rule-by-rule waivers on local request, is particularly promising (Fry, Fuhrman, & Elmore, 1992; Fuhrman, Fry, & Elmore, 1992). Deregulation, however, will disappoint those who view rules as the primary enemy of school improvement; removing the rules will not be sufficient stimulus for reform.

Furthermore, deregulatory programs still leave many regulations on the books. Adequate levels of health and safety, adequacy of physical plant, and financial accountability must be assured. Categorical programs, which typically include requirements to assure that services are targeted to meet special needs, are an important continuing source of regulation; many practitioners in currently deregulated schools find their flexibility hampered by such special program rules.

Finally, it is incumbent on the system to assure that all students have an opportunity to meet new outcome standards, to learn the expected content and skills. Assuring equitable access to well-qualified teachers, high-quality instructional materials, and various instructional offerings may require some degree of regulation. Many argue that opportunity to learn can be measured or tracked without setting standards or constraining practice. Others assert that some regulation of practice is essential for at least some districts, particularly in instances where taxpayer support needs extra leverage or where corrupt practices exist.

The difficulty of resolving dilemmas about the desired degree of state guidance and the necessary degree of regulation suggests that reform rhetoric about "outcome accountability and process deregulation" needs serious examination. Within the categories of "outcomes" and "process" are many discrete policy instruments. One interesting finding from a study of decentralized schools in two districts illustrates the complexity of control issues. Unlike typical schools where teachers work isolated and relatively autonomously in their classrooms, teachers in the study schools are brought out of their individual classrooms and expected to interact with colleagues and administrators in planning, implementing, and evaluating their educational programs. The consequence is that teacher behavior is more highly controlled in decentralized settings, but the control process is not a bureaucratic one based on rules and regulations or an economic one based on incentives; it is a process of social and cognitive control (Hannaway, 1993).

Reform and equity. One of the reasons more and more policymakers are attracted to systemic reform is the hope it offers for greater equity. Emphasis on basic skills instruction and improved social and economic conditions contributed to a narrowing of the achievement gap between minority and white students, and to some extent between students at different levels of economic advantage, between 1960 and the mid-1980s (Consortium for Policy Research in Education [CPRE], 1991; Smith & O'Day, 1991a). To continue such improvement, despite recent reverses in social and economic trends, it would be beneficial to have a common set of high-quality standards for curricular content and student performance. A structure that reinforces challenging outcomes for all students, in all schools, would promote equity (O'Day & Smith, in press).

An integrated structure and clearly articulated standards would provide a basis for comparing the quality of educational inputs, such as the quality and appropriateness of curricular materials, and the adequacy of teacher preparation and so on. Such comparison is more educationally relevant than a simple comparison of fiscal resources; it speaks to how resources are allocated rather than simply to amounts of dollars. Schools spending equal dollars could vary enormously in the equity of opportunity. Some could educate all children comparably; some could offer a strongly differentiated curriculum. If we had common challenging standards, policy support in the way of well-trained teachers and materials, and accountability tied to achievement of the standards, schools would be pressured and supported in developing programs that maximize achievement for all students.

A number of challenges arise in linking challenging standards to greater equity. One is striking a balance in constructing the standards between the common culture and needs of the society as a whole and the diverse perspectives, needs, and histories of individuals and subgroups within that society. To do this, states are trying to construct standards as a core set of expectations that themselves contain some choice and flexibility and that may be supplemented by schools and teachers responding to community concerns. In addition, the dialogue about what belongs in the common core, as contentious as it may be in some subjects and some settings, can be a constructive experience for the public and professionals alike.

A second challenge concerns the meaning of ambitious content for students of different ability and prior achievement. The idea of challenging standards is higher expectations for all students; nevertheless, students come with different levels of preparation. There is the danger that adjusting to different needs means watering down expectations for some students.

An associated issue concerns the relationship between upgrading of the general curriculum through systemic reform and programming for special need students. At this early stage in systemic reform efforts, it seems that special-need programs are largely left in place while reform efforts focus on the curriculum for mainstream students. Perhaps because of concerns about federal requirements (some of which may be overinterpreted by states, districts, and schools), and worries about student service needs and legal rights, discussions of systemic reform rarely touch on how students with special problems may be educated under common standards. If systemic reform efforts bypass those students, including many in large cities where funding from categorical programs drives much of what happens in schools, they will neither produce reforms nor be systemic.

Resources for reform. Finally, in these times of financial uncertainty, we must ask whether the development of systemic reform strategies can withstand state financial stress. The financial outlook for state budgets in the near future is bleak. Despite massive budget cutting and tax increases in fiscal 1991 and 1992, by the middle of this fiscal year, 35 states were forced to cut $5.7 billion. Rather than maintaining the usual 5% budget reserves, these balances are expected to drop to .8% of total expenditures and rebound only to 1% during fiscal 1993. At the same time, all states in general are increasing spending by 5% on average (still below the average of 7.4%) but even faster for the enrollment-driven budgets in education. Additional monies for school reform will come into increased competitions with other state services (Harp, 1992). No doubt, state fiscal problems are slowing the pace, if not the intent, of systemic reform in states where it has gotten a toehold.

Short of great influxes of new cash, states can continue to move toward systemic reform in a fiscally conservative fashion. Through interstate networks like the Connecticut Multi-State Performance Assessment Coalition Team (COMPACT) funded by the National Science Foundation, states can share knowledge and pool resources. Coordinating textbook adoptions with other states may leverage publishers into both providing a greater variety of options and books at lower cost. California strategizes to coordinate outside project dollars to support its reforms, such as Eisenhower monies for staff development linked to the curriculum frameworks. Enlisting broad teacher support in the development of assessments and curriculum, as mentioned above, at the same time builds support and understanding to help in implementation. With fiscal constraints, focusing resources on the full development of curriculum goals and guidelines or other mechanisms that implement what students should know and be able to do will at minimum provide guidelines for local districts and others to begin to mobilize their own testing and curriculum around the goals.

Conclusion

Putting the pieces of reform together so that policy provides strong, coherent support for school improvement is a complex undertaking. Systemic reform ideas seem to require unprecedented efforts to integrate separate policies, new strategies of policy sequencing, novel processes to involve the public and professionals in setting standards, challenges to traditional politics, complex efforts to balance state leadership with flexibility at the school site, extraordinary investment in professional development, and creative approaches to serving the varied needs of students. To compound the challenge, states are facing these extremely demanding issues at a time of severe fiscal difficulty.

Nonetheless, policymakers are crafting strategies to deliberate, develop, and implement more coherent policy that supports ambitious teaching and learning. Even at this early stage of state efforts, some approaches seem quite promising. The promise is amplified by the broader, societal movement toward consensus on challenging student outcomes that surrounds these early policy activities. Both the difficulty of the problems facing systemic reform efforts and the promise of a number of intriguing state strategies suggest the need for continued study of systemic reform over the next several years.

References

Adams, J. (in press). *Policy implementation through teacher professional networks: The case of Math A in California.* Unpublished doctoral dissertation, Stanford University, Palo Alto, CA.

Archbald, D. (1991). *Emerging state/district systems of curriculum control: Tradeoffs between content standardization and teacher autonomy.* Paper presented at the annual meeting of the American Educational Research Association, Chicago.

Business Roundtable. (1991). *The nine essential components: Putting policy into practice.* New York: Author.

Clune, W. (1992). New answers to six hard questions from Rodriquez: Ending the separation of school finance and educational policy by bridging the gap between wrong and remedy. *Connecticut Law Review, 24*(3), 1-42.

Clune, W., & White, P. (1987). Institutional choice as a theoretical framework for research on educational policy. *Educational Evaluation and Policy Analysis, 9*(2), 117-132.

Clune, W., & White, P. (1988). *School-based management: Institutional variation, implementation, and issues for further research.* New Brunswick, NJ: Center for Policy Research in Education.

Clune, W. (with White, P., & Patterson, J.). (1989). *The implementation and effects of high school graduation requirements: First steps toward curricular reform.* New Brunswick, NJ: Rutgers University, Center for Policy Research in Education.

Cohen, D. K. (1982). Policy and organization: The impact of state and federal educational policy in school governance. *Harvard Educational Review, 52*(4), 74-99.

Cohen, D., & Spillane, J. (1992). Policy and practice: The relations between governance and instruction. In G. Grant (Ed.), *Review of research in education* (pp. 3-49). Washington, DC: American Educational Research Association.

Consortium for Policy Research in Education. (1991). *Equality in education: Progress, problems and possibilities* (CPRE Policy Briefs). New Brunswick, NJ: Author.

Darling-Hammond, L., & Berry, B. (1988, March). *The evolution of teacher policy* (JRE-O1). Santa Monica, CA: RAND.

David, J. L. (with Purkey, S., & White, P.). (1989). *Restructuring in progress: Lessons from pioneering districts.* Washington, DC: National Governors' Association.

Dossey, J., Mullis, I., Lindquist, M., & Chambers, D. (1988). *The mathematics report card: Are we measuring up? Trends and achievement based on the 1986 national assessment.* Princeton, NJ: Educational Testing Service.

Elmore, R. F. (Ed.). (1990). *Restructuring schools: The next generation of educational reform.* San Francisco: Jossey-Bass.

Elmore, R. F. (1991). *"Would choice + competition yield quality education?" Voices from the field: 30 expert opinions on "America 2000." The Bush administration strategy to "reinvent" America's schools.* Washington, DC: William T. Grant Foundation Commission on Work, Family and Citizenship and Institute for Educational Leadership.

Elmore, R. F., & McLaughlin, M. W. (1988). *Steady work: Policy, practice, and the reform of American education* (R-3574-NIE/RC). Santa Monica, CA: RAND.

Elmore, R. F., Sykes, G., & Spillane, J. (1992). Curriculum policy. In P. Jackson (Ed.), *Handbook of research on curriculum* (pp. 185-215). New York: Macmillan.

Firestone, W. A. (1989). Educational policy as an ecology of games. *Educational Researcher, 18*(7), 18-24.

Firestone, W. A. (1992). Teacher incentives: Mixing intrinsic and financial. In B. A. Jones & K. Borman (Eds.), *The new American schools: Alternative concepts and practices.* Norwood, NJ: Ablex.

Firestone, W. A., Fuhrman, S. H., & Kirst, M. W. (1989). *The progress of reform: An appraisal of state education initiatives.* New Brunswick, NJ: Rutgers University, Center for Policy Research in Education.

Firestone, W. A., Rosenblum, S., Bader, B., & Massell, D. (1991). *Education reform from 1983 to 1990: State action and district response.* New Brunswick, NJ: Consortium for Policy Research in Education.

Fossey, R. (1992). *School choice legislation: A survey of the states* (CPRE Occasional Paper). New Brunswick, NJ: Consortium for Policy Research in Education.

Frase, M. J. (1989). *Dropout rates in the United States: 1988* (NCES 89-609). Washington, DC: Government Printing Office.

Fry, P., Fuhrman, S. H., & Elmore, R. F. (1992). *Schools for the 21st century program in Washington State: A case study.* New Brunswick, NJ: Consortium for Policy Research in Education.

Fuhrman, S. H. (1993). *Designing coherent education.* San Francisco: Jossey-Bass.

Fuhrman, S. H., Clune, W., & Elmore, R. F. (1988). Research on education reform: Lessons on the implementation of policy. *Teachers College Record, 90*(2), 237-257.

Fuhrman, S. H., & Elmore, R. F. (1990). Understanding local control in the wake of state education reform. *Educational Evaluation and Policy Analysis, 12*(1), 82-96.

Fuhrman, S. H. (with the assistance of Fry, P.). (1989). *Diversity amidst standardization.* New Brunswick, NJ: Center for Policy Research in Education.

Fuhrman, S. H., Fry, P., & Elmore, R. F. (1992). *Kentucky's program for educationally deficient school districts: A case study.* New Brunswick, NJ: Consortium for Policy Research in Education.

Ginsburg, R., & Wimpelberg, R. (1987). Educational change by commission: Attempting "trickle down" reform. *Educational Evaluation and Policy Analysis, 9*(4), 355-358.

Hannaway, J. (1993). Decentralization and two school districts: Challenging the standard paradigm. In J. Hannaway & M. Carnoy (Eds.), *Decentralization and school improvement* (pp. 135-162). San Francisco: Jossey-Bass.

Hannaway, J., & Carnoy, M. (1993). *Decentralization and school improvement*. San Francisco: Jossey-Bass.

Harp, L. (1992). Report documents new round of state fiscal lows. *Education Week*, *11*(32), 17.

Lichtenstein, G., McLaughlin, M., & Knudsen, J. (1991). *Teacher empowerment and professional knowledge*. New Brunswick, NJ: Consortium for Policy Research in Education.

Massell, D. (1992). *Achieving consensus: Setting the agenda for state curriculum reform*. New Brunswick, NJ: Consortium for Policy Research in Education.

McCarthy, M. (1990). Teacher-testing programs. In J. Murphy (Ed.), *The educational reform movement of the 1980s: Perspectives and cases* (pp. 189-214). Berkeley, CA: McCutchan.

McDonnell, L. M., & Fuhrman, S. H. (1986). The political context of school reform. In V. Mueller & M. McKeown (Eds.), *The fiscal, legal, and political aspects of state reform of elementary and secondary education* (pp. 43-64). Cambridge, MA: Ballinger.

Mullis, I., & Jenkins, L. (1990). *The reading report card, 1971-88: Trends from the nation's report card*. Princeton, NJ: Educational Testing Service.

Nathan, R. (1989). The role of the states in American federalism. In V. Horn (Ed.), *The state of the states*. Washington, DC: Congressional Quarterly Press.

National Center for Education Statistics (NCES). (1989). *The condition of education 1989: Vol. 1. Elementary and secondary education*. Washington, DC: Government Printing Office.

National Commission on Excellence in Education. (1983). *A nation at risk: Imperative for educational reform*. Washington, DC: Government Printing Office.

National Council of Teachers of Mathematics (NCTM). (1989). *Curriculum and evaluation standards for school mathematics*. Reston, VA: Author.

National Council on Educational Standards and Testing (NCEST). (1992). *Raising standards for American education: A report to Congress, the secretary of education, the National Goals Panel, and the American people*. Washington, DC: Government Printing Office.

National Governors' Association (NGA). (1986). *Time for results: The governors' 1991 report on education*. Washington, DC: Author.

National Governors' Association (NGA). (1991). *From rhetoric to action: State progress in restructuring the education system*. Washington, DC: Author.

O'Day, J., & Smith, M. S. (in press). Systemic reform and educational opportunity. In S. Fuhrman (Ed.), *Designing coherent policy*. San Francisco: Jossey-Bass.

Odden, A. (1991). School finance in the 1990s. *Phi Delta Kappan, 73*(6), 455-461.

Odden, A., & Conley, S. (1991). *A new teacher compensation system to promote productivity* (USC Center for Research in Education Finance [CREF] Policy Brief). Los Angeles: University of Southern California.

Schwille, J., Porter, A., Alford, L., Floden, F., Freeman, D., Irwin, S., & Schmidt, W. (1988). State policy and the control of curriculum decisions. *Educational Policy, 2*(1), 29-50.

Secretary's Commission on Achieving Necessary Skills. (1991). *What work requires of schools: A SCANS report for America 2000*. Washington, DC: U.S. Department of Labor.

Shepard, L. A., & Smith, M. L. (1989). *Flunking grades: Research and policies on retention*. New York: Falmer.

Smith, M. S., & O'Day, J. (1991a). Educational equality: 1966 and now. In D. Verstegen & J. G. Ward (Eds.), *The 1990 American Finance Association yearbook: Spheres of justice in education* (pp. 53-100). New York: Harper & Row.

Smith, M. S., & O'Day, J. (1991b). Systemic school reform. In S. Fuhrman & B. Malen (Eds.), *The politics of curriculum and testing* (pp. 233-267). Bristol, PA: Falmer.

Smith, M. S., O'Day, J., & Cohen, D. K. (1990, Winter). National curriculum, American style: Can it be done? What might it look like? *American Educator,* pp. 10-17, 40-47.

Smith, M. S., O'Day, J., & Cohen, D. (1991). A national curriculum in the United States? *Educational Leadership, 49*(1), 74-81.

Walker, D. (1990). *Fundamentals of curriculum.* Saddlebrook, NJ: Harcourt Brace Jovanovich.

Wehlage, G. G. (1989). Engagement, not remediation or higher standards. In J. Lakebrink (Ed.), *Children at risk* (pp. 57-73). Springfield, IL: Charles C Thomas.

Wehlage, G. G., Rutter, R., Smith, G., Lesko, N., & Fernandez, R. (1989). *Reducing the risk: Schools as communities of support.* Philadelphia: Falmer.

T W O

Cooperative Performance Incentives in Education

CRAIG E. RICHARDS

DANIEL FISHBEIN

PAULA MELVILLE

Currently, two approaches to financial incentives for educational performance predominate: incentives to individuals, that is, students, teachers, or administrators, and incentives to groups, that is, departments, divisions, schools, or districts. Performance incentives to individuals, particularly merit pay plans, have been studied extensively and their problems have been reported widely in the literature (Cohen & Murnane, 1985; Johnson, 1986; Kienapfel, 1984; Richards, 1985). The less than promising track record of merit pay plans has prompted researchers and policymakers to urge states to experiment with cooperative performance incentives (CPIs) to schools rather than with incentives to individuals (Richards & Shujaa, 1990).

While CPIs make for novel policy in education, they have been widely used in the private sector for more than 25 years (Lawler, 1971). CPIs are designed to encourage cooperation on tasks that are highly group interdependent and cannot be satisfactorily performed unless employees use teamwork. The use of CPIs to encourage school-level problem solving is of growing interest in the field of education precisely because school tasks are highly group interdependent (Boe, 1990; Picus, 1991; Richards & Shujaa, 1990).

CPIs in the current discussion are restricted by two substantial parameters: The award must be given to a group, such as a school, department, or grade; and the award must be material and substantive, not merely symbolic, although financial and other material rewards also carry significant symbolic and psychological import. Within these two parameters, this chapter discusses (a) the economic rationale for incentives, (b) the research literature on group incentives in business and education, (c) a case study of the application of group incentives to public schools in South Carolina, and (d) policy implications for the use of CPIs in education.

The Economics
of Collective Choice

What does economic theory have to say about group incentives? Kenneth Arrow's General Possibility Theorem has been credited with establishing an academic field of specialization known as social choice theory. The central problem in social choice theory is this: How can many individuals' preferences be combined to yield a single collective choice? The mechanisms or combination rules for accomplishing a collective decision are called "aggregation devices." The crux of Arrow's theorem is that no rational aggregation device exists. If we accept Arrow's theorem as correct, then it is not possible to maximize the collective utilities of a group. Arrow's theorem has two important implications—first, for economics generally, because the entire field of consumer choice is predicated on the notion that individual consumers maximize their individual utilities. Such utilities are reflected in their preferences. Thus, only in the instance where every group member has exactly the same preference schedule can a rational aggregation device be constructed. The second implication is for CPIs, because the theorem suggests that an optimal collective good can only be defined by a group in which someone is comparatively worse off. CPIs are likely to be inefficient because they encourage some group members to work against their own self-interest. A group reward, however, can itself be considered a collective good. When the reward is won, all members of the group share equally in the reward, independent of individual contributions to its attainment. While the reward is a potential collective good, exertion of extra effort is individual and voluntary (excluding peer pressure).

Solving the problem of Arrow's theorem, however, creates another. For example, given that participation is voluntary, why wouldn't one teacher choose to "free ride" on the hard work of other teachers? Each teacher, student, and administrator makes an independent decision to provide the extra effort required to improve a rewarded performance outcome according to individual assessment of the relative trade-offs and risks involved. The structure of CPIs does not fit into the social choice framework as this critique suggests. The free-rider problem and related challenges to the efficacy of CPIs will be discussed next.

Will Higher Incentive Payments Lead to Increased Effort?

Two types of problems can overwhelm CPI plans. The first has to do with the economic and theoretical problems of collective incentives, the most important of which are *the free-rider problem* and the *income-leisure*[1] *substitution effect.* The second class of problems is primarily associated with program design and implementation, that is, overcoming the role of risk and uncertainty in the model design and avoiding perverse incentives. These problems are directly related to three basic assumptions about organizational performance embedded in most CPI plans:

- *Cooperative performance deficit*: The assumption here is of a significant gap between the current work effort and the capacity of the group to engage in productive work.
- *Organizational performance constraint*: The assumption is that existing social, psychological, and organizational constraints prevent the desired higher levels of effort and performance.
- *Incentives motivate cooperation*: This assumes that correctly designed and implemented CPI plans will motivate additional productive work effort.

The Free-Rider Problem

Game theory has been most often used to analyze strategic interdependence among members of a group. The most popular version of the game is the single episode prisoner's dilemma. It shows that rational, self-interested individuals will not act to achieve their common or group interests, as Mancur Olsen wrote in *The Logic of Collective Action* (1965). In fact, in his later work, Olsen argued that entire social systems decline because of the tendency of special interests to free ride on the system (Marwell & Ames, 1979).

As many critics of education observe, a single salary schedule and tenure provisions encourage educators to free ride. The positive economic incentive of a wage is virtually guaranteed in those states where teachers are protected either by tenure or by the convention that a job has vestment rights. If there is no individual or group sanction for a merely adequate performance, then the temptation to do a merely adequate job may be overwhelming. If teachers are paid equally for adequate efforts and best efforts, what encourages some teachers to work to capacity on behalf of the children they teach?

In large groups, free riding is more likely because the primary difficulty in such groups is coordination. If the contributing behavior of others is difficult to predict with assurance, contributions will fall even if the incentive to free ride is not dominant. In experimental studies of the free-rider problem, the findings of Gerald Marwell and his coauthors (Alfano & Marwell, 1980; Marwell & Ames, 1979, 1980, 1981) mount the strongest challenge to the free-rider hypothesis. They report: "People voluntarily contribute substantial portions of their resources—usually an average of between 40 to 60 percent—to the provision of a public good" (Marwell & Ames, 1981, p. 307).

Runge (1984) found that interdependent choice situations create incentives for group members to create institutions that coordinate expectations based on rules of fair-mindedness. In the presence of such coordinated expectations, voluntary contributions to public goods may be utility-maximizing strategies. He noted, "We observe substantial voluntary contributions to public goods without outside enforcement" (p. 157). Thus the state has the option to provide an institutional setting sufficiently supportive that participants perceive assessment and reward provisions as fair-minded.

Whenever benefits and costs are a function of the total actions of the group, it seems implausible that decisions to contribute are unaffected by expectations of the decisions of others (Runge, 1984, p. 160). Where such interdependencies are very high, the players' most preferred strategy is this: "I'll give my share if you give yours." In this sense then, fair-mindedness simply describes a preference for equal contributions. It is neither altruistic nor selfless. The expressed desire for coordinated action is called the "assurance preference," which can be either in favor or against a contribution depending upon the expected actions of others. The expected contribution of the other players determines the contribution of the first player. With very little information, the first player is not likely to have very much confidence in his or her ability to predict the behavior of others. The institution contributes at this juncture by providing assurances (information) that each member will, in fact, make a reasonable contribution to the cooperative effort of the group. When faith in the institutional assurance is high (largely a function of institutional history), then expected effort should approximate actual efforts. Thus the legitimacy of institutions providing the assurance is a critical determinant of the success of a group incentive. Where the probability that others will contribute is estimated to be high to begin with, assurance that this estimate is correct will reinforce the propensity to match voluntary contributions to work effort.

Institutional legitimacy can provide a critically supportive organizational context for voluntary contributions of additional work effort. Whether the trade-offs involved result in a positive cost-effectiveness ratio is an empirical, not a theoretical, question. In sum, a CPI does not require maximization to be justified. It must simply meet the cost/benefit test that it improves employee performance more efficiently than simply raising salaries (cost less per unit increased performance).

The Income-Leisure Substitution Effect

In addition to the free-rider problem, the incentive effect of CPI may be diminished by the declining ratio of the incentive to base salaries. If the award is a fixed sum and schools continue to acquire greater income as a result of seniority, inflation, and promotions, eventually the employee's utility will be higher if he or she does not respond to the incentive. The difference in the effort supplied at two different income levels is called the "income effect." The substitution effect occurs when an increase in earnings predisposes the employee to purchase more leisure (discretionary effort). Note that the income and substitution effects have opposite impacts on effort when the incentive rate is raised. Thus productivity may rise or fall with an increase in the size of the incentive payment. It will fall if productive work effort does not increase more than the cost of the incentive plan. Whether it does or not can only be resolved by empirical research (see the South Carolina case study later in this chapter).

Economists generally agree that the labor supply curve is backward bending: At low wages, workers are willing to increase the number of hours worked (effort) as wages are increased. If the analogy to work effort is valid, the substitution effect should dominate the income effect. The opposite relationship holds at the highest levels of income: The income effect should dominate, and the supply of increased effort will be backward bending, implying that employees will not respond to the incentives offered. The lesson in this for CPI plans is that, everything else being equal, schools where teachers earn very low salaries are more likely to be motivated by school performance incentives than schools where average salaries are relatively high, unless the incentive is very large.

Risk and Uncertainty

Our discussion assumed that performance incentives will increase proportionately with increases in productive effort. What happens when uncertainty or risk is introduced? For example, consider the impact of risk on performance if employees are uncertain whether their additional productive effort will actually be recognized by those who provide the incentives or whether CPIs reward on an all-or-nothing basis rather than in direct proportion to the degree of success.

Another factor that can influence the level of risk and uncertainty is poor information. It occurs when employees do not clearly understand the conditions under which a performance incentive is attainable. Strictly because of poor information, their increased effort may be misdirected.

When risk is introduced into the calculations schools must make to decide whether to increase effort, the efficiency of performance awards as an inducement to higher effort is weakened. As risk increases, larger incentive payments will be required to induce increased effort. To the extent that teachers are risk adverse, and not merely risk neutral, the relationship between the size of the incentive will have to increase. To summarize, it is difficult to make cooperative incentives work when the expected ratio of the incentive to salary is small or when risk and uncertainty are high. Further, when school staff expect that they will have to undertake relatively large increases in effort to attain relatively small increases in the selected outcome indicators, the cooperative incentive plan will not be successful even when the incentive is large.

Avoiding Perverse Incentives

Perverse incentives occur when the wrong behavior is unintentionally rewarded. For example, the state and federal governments currently pay schools according to how many children they maintain on compensatory education rather than for their success in raising student performance to grade level. One of the most important design issues of CPIs is that they must reward the appropriate performance outcome.

CPIs in schools can reward two basic types of accomplishment: net gains from one time period to a subsequent time period—*value-added performance*—or competitive ranking in a given time period—*ranked performance*. A CPI that rewards net improvement would probably compare students' pre- and postperformance results. A CPI plan that rewards ranked performance would evaluate each school against the performance of other schools. Both can be performance-based systems where a selected percentage, such as the top 20%, would be eligible to receive the award. In both cases, schools that satisfied the criteria would earn a school performance award.

South Carolina's School Incentive Reward Program

South Carolina's CPI was established by the Education Improvement Act of 1984: the state's omnibus education reform legislation. Schools compete for awards within comparison bands. This provision is regarded as one of the most important aspects of the CPI. According to the policymakers who designed the CPI plan, the bands mitigate the influence of background factors and increase the validity of the CPI among teachers and administrators in schools with low-income children.

Three performance criteria determined a school's eligibility to receive an award: student achievement gain, teacher attendance, and student attendance. Student achievement gain is the essential measure. To illustrate, Hillary Smith, a hypothetical sixth-grade student, attained a score of 728 in reading and 699 in mathematics on the Comprehensive Test of Basic Skills (CTBS) last year in the fifth grade. Hillary's scores this year on the sixth-grade Basic Skills Assessment Program (BSAP)[2] are compared with the scores of all students in the state who scored exactly 728 and 699 last year in reading and mathematics, respectively. The mean for this group of pupils on the reading scores of BSAP was 786.6. Hillary scored 780, or 6.6 points below her expected score. The discrepancy score is calculated in this fashion for each student in South Carolina for whom two consecutive years of test scores are available. The School Gain Index (SGI) is the median of all the standardized discrepancy scores (both reading and mathematics) in the school. An SGI value of 0.0 indicates that the school's median actual performance and its median predicted performance are equal. A positive SGI value indicates better-than-expected performance and a negative SGI indicates less-than-expected performance.

South Carolina provides each district with a school performance report. The school performance report provides two types of comparisons. First, all of the data (BSAP scores, CTBS scores, teacher attendance, student attendance, and dropout rates) are compared with those of all other schools in the state at each grade level. Second, achievement test scores (BSAP and CTBS) are compared within a group of schools with similar characteristics. As a rule, the number of award recipients represents approximately 25% of the schools in the state.

Examining South Carolina's CPI over 3 years, Richards and Sheu (1992) found weak predictive ability for student-teacher ratios, average years of teacher education, local tax effort, and expenditure per pupil. They concluded that organizational factors may be more significant than background variables in contributing to differences in school gain scores. All of the available background variables together only explained about 11% of the variance in school gain scores. When Richards and Sheu considered the values for mean levels of school achievement, however, they discovered that background variables explained from 2 to 2½ times as much of the variance. Effective schools research suggests that out-of-school contributions to student achievement have less influence on student gain scores and more influence on absolute differences. It is argued that, while schools are not responsible for the variations in the wealth of the children who come to them, they should be able to demonstrate comparable gains in student achievement, independent of student background characteristics.

Considerable debate exists about whether the measures and the incentives in school awards should be based on performance, value-added improvement, equality of outcome, or some policy mix (Edmonds, 1979; Holmes, 1989; Mann, 1991; Richards, 1990). Richards and Sheu found that significantly different schools would win awards if achievement rankings were used rather than gain score rankings. The use of gain scores, rather than performance outcomes, does benefit the poorest schools, but this effect was less pronounced than one might have expected.

In theory, the exclusive use of gain scores may tend to discourage high-performing schools who are unlikely to achieve large year-to-year gains in student achievement. The findings of Richards and Sheu (1992) suggest, however, that even with gain scores the wealthiest schools received a larger share of the available funds than the poorest schools. School incentive programs that distribute rewards about equally between value-added improvement and performance still shifted some funds away from the poorest schools. This occurred, even when coupled with a banding system that protects disadvantaged districts from competing directly with advantaged districts on performance. This problem could be solved by dividing available dollars into equal parts for each band.

Finally, Richards and Sheu found that withdrawal of the banding system would be likely to have a severely adverse impact with respect to perceptions of distributive justice, even though the underlying regression equations are quite weak. One major criticism of the South Carolina CPI plan was the restricted set of outcomes for which rewards were forthcoming. Linking financial incentives to an appropriate array of desired outcome measures focuses organizational resources and effort on a broader band of student outcomes. Thus the harmful narrowing of curriculum recently criticized by the National Science Foundation is reduced. Which outcome measures are to be used and how they are to be implemented are topics of great concern to teachers.

Motivating Teachers

School CPIs should include adequate salary, participatory decision making, and released time for collegial relationships, sabbaticals, and major project involvement as well as a system of supervision that recognizes strengths and assists improvement with formative evaluations. Research demonstrates that teachers need a variety of interaction with peers, students, and administrators: professional, personal, and extracurricular (Sederberg & Clark, 1990). Because teaching is not piecework, the benefits of learning that occur on one grade level may not fully present themselves until the student is at an entirely different grade level. Rewards should suit the concentric, nonlinear nature of teaching (Hannaway, 1991; Lawler, 1971).

From 10 to 12 states are now experimenting with a variety of CPIs. Experts have recommended that school CPIs should be directly linked to school improvement plans to make those programs more effective. Little evidence exists, however, that CPIs are being tied to more fundamental changes in teacher professionalism, governance, and accountability (Picus, 1991; Richards & Shujaa, 1990; Watson, Poda, & Miller, 1988). While CPIs do not guarantee teacher commitment, as our earlier discussion of the theoretical literature indicated, Hannaway (1991) concurs that peer pressure would be likely to discourage free riders. The benefits of collegial interaction would more than make up for less energetic staff members. Perhaps the greater problem is the size of the reward. If school rewards are not based on a quota system, and research warns that they should not be, the problem of adequate compensation for all participants still exists. Many participants receiving small amounts of money "may appease a number of constituencies otherwise antagonistic to the plan, but it undermines the distinction of winning a performance award" (Richards & Shujaa, 1990, p. 136).

Conclusion and Policy Implications

We have reviewed a diverse literature in an effort to inform educational policymakers about the limits and possibilities of CPIs as policy instruments. Some convergence between the literature in business and education seems particularly noteworthy from a policy perspective. Perhaps most important, cooperative incentives do work. This observation is consistent in a variety of business applications, with students in cooperative groups and with schools as organizational units. Second, cooperative incentives appear to overcome many of the obstacles engendered by individual incentives plans, that is, performance bonuses and merit pay, particularly in work settings where cooperation is vital to the performance of the organization.

These few remaining pages speak to policymakers contemplating the introduction of cooperative incentives. Extrapolated from a heterodox and multidisciplinary literature, our policy recommendations are divided into five categories: (a) ethos, (b) decision support systems, (c) models, (d) implementation, and (e) evaluation.

Ethos

Most of the organizational literature we reviewed made a consistent point: CPIs are most helpful when they are consistent within a larger set of organizational values. To put the point bluntly, they will be of little value to an organization dominated by rigid bureaucratic structures or organizational climates characterized by symbolic and ritual performance. Conversely, they seem to work best in organizations devoted to an open exchange of information, participatory management, and a culture of organizational learning. Thus, as an isolated policy instrument, CPIs are of marginal value. Incentives are only one element in a broad set of commitments to educational performance. With an emphasis on teacher professionalism, participatory governance structures, and authentic accountability, CPIs are more likely to reinforce a consistent vision of the organization. It may not be so much a matter of increasing organizational effectiveness as decreasing the bureaucratic impediments to that goal that have been widely cited in the literature (Feldman & Arnold, 1991; Galbraith, 1977; Kanter & Summers, 1987).

Decision Support Services

The Achilles' heel of CPIs is the crude accountability mechanisms widely used by educators to evaluate organizational performance. Far too much of the effort lies in the area of regulatory compliance. Most compliance efforts are directed at minimum acceptable standards for inputs, teacher credentialism, building codes, and Carnegie units. The single major exception is test scores. Indeed, school systems are inundated with test score data. These data are seldom organized to facilitate school or classroom problem solving or organizational learning. Indeed, few teachers understand how to assess trend data, stanines, grade-level equivalents, standard deviations, or other basic indicators of differences between students, classes, and schools. While important work is under way beneath the tent of "authentic assessment," prodigious difficulties with standardization, cost, and administrative complexity remain.

At a minimum, states or school districts contemplating the introduction of CPIs must require a decision support system that will permit schools to compare their performance by several standards, including (a) previous performance (value added), (b) national norms, and (c) state norms. Three- to five-year trend data would also be quite valuable, as would comparison with a random sample of schools with similar profiles, such as comparing all elementary schools with 50% of the students on free lunch. Such information should be published and widely available to parents, teachers, students, and other interested parties. The outcomes should include, in addition to test scores, other indicators of school performance.

Models

CPIs can be applied to diverse educational settings. They may be used with groups of students, departments, schools, or even districts. They have also been proposed to reduce the length of time that students stay in compensatory education programs. However varied the applications, successful programs must meet the following minimal conditions:

- Cooperative staff input in all phases to gain staff ownership and support of the plan
- Clear and credible standards of eligibility and performance; consistent and credible administration of the program
- Protection of the program from budgetary and political turmoil
- A reasonably level playing field so that groups with widely dissimilar students and resources are not competing unfairly

- A group reward commensurate with the level of additional effort required to attain it

Although most school CPIs to date have been the result of state
initiatives, this is not a necessary condition. Certainly school districts
could design cooperative incentive plans consistent with their overall
mission and managerial style.

Implementation

Cooperative incentive plans require a significant commitment of
resources, organizational effort, and persistence. It may take 3-5 years
to fully implement a school incentive plan, as the South Carolina
experience has shown. And even in the case of South Carolina, the
plan is subject to shifting political climate, financial exigencies, and
technical adaptation. Thus implementation should be seen as part of
a broader reform effort. It would be best if such efforts were supported
by a wide political and professional consensus so that reform tran-
scends the political interests of a specific party or personality. Fishbein
(1992), for example, has found that lack of local support from the
teachers' union was sufficient to undo a student incentive program in
one New Jersey experiment.

Evaluation

More demonstration projects, evaluation studies, and basic research are needed. The research experience in the private sector has
been under way for over 25 years. In education, most CPIs have had
a life span of less than 5 years. In the private sector, such plans have
been a part of a global corporate vision of culture and strategy, such
as the participatory management approach of the Scanlon Plan. We
have yet to see comparable integrative approaches in public education, nor have most been subjected to ongoing research and evaluation.

Clearly, a confluence of policy experiments in site-based management, professionalization of teaching, cooperative learning strategies,
accountability, and CPIs is occurring. What we have not yet attempted
in public education is a systematic effort to combine the best theory,

policy, and practice of each into a coherent, synergistic reconstruction of public education. Students confront a future requiring lifelong learning and a deep capacity for cooperative problem solving and invention. Yet the conventional educational practice of teachers and administrators is seldom cooperative. If cooperative learning and problem solving is the preferred pedagogy of the future, then it must also become the preferred organizational ethos of the present. One reinforcing element of that ethos is the CPI.

Notes

1. In the present discussion, it is more accurate to replace the conventional economic term *leisure* with *discretionary work effort*. By the latter term, we mean the range of effort between the amount necessary to keep one's job and the amount required to reach one's capacity.

2. The BSAP is a South Carolina criterion referenced test.

References

Alfano, C., & Marwell, G. (1980). Experiments on the provision of public goods by groups. III. Nondivisibility and free riding in "real" groups. *Social Psychology Quarterly, 43*(3), 300-309.

Boe, E. (1990). *Teacher incentive research with SASS.* Washington, DC: National Center for Education Statistics. (ERIC Document Reproduction Service No. ED 275 064)

Cohen, D., & Murnane, R. (1985). The merits of merit pay. *The Public Interest, 80,* 3-30.

Edmonds, R. (1979). Effective schools for the urban poor. *Educational Leadership, 37*(1), 15-23.

Feldman, D., & Arnold, H. (1991). Recent innovations in reward systems. In D. Organ (Ed.), *The applied psychology of work behavior* (pp. 190-198). Boston: Richard D. Irwin.

Fishbein, D. (1992). *Student monetary incentive programs: An evaluation.* Unpublished doctoral dissertation, Teachers College, Columbia University.

Galbraith, J. (1977). *Organization design.* Reading, MA: Addison-Wesley.

Hannaway, J. (1991). *Higher order skills, job design, and incentives: An analysis and proposal.* Unpublished manuscript, Stanford University, Stanford, CA.

Holmes, M. (1989). From research implementation to improvement. In M. Holmes, K. Leithwood, & D. Musella (Eds.), *Educational policy for effective schools* (pp. 3-30). New York: Teachers College Press.

Johnson, S. M. (1986). Incentives for teachers: What motivates, what matters. *Education Administration Quarterly, 22*(3), 54-79.

Kanter, R., & Summers, D. (1987). Doing well while doing good: Dilemmas of performance measurement in nonprofit organizations and the need for a multiple-constituency approach. In W. W. Powell (Ed.), *The non-profit sector* (pp. 154-166). New Haven, CT: Yale University Press.

Kienapfel, B. (1984). *Merit pay for school administrators.* Arlington, VA: ERS, Inc.

Lawler, E. (1971). *Pay and organizational effectiveness: A psychological view.* New York: McGraw-Hill.

Mann, D. (1991). *Killing school reform.* Unpublished manuscript, Teachers College, Columbia University, New York.

Marwell, G., & Ames, R. E. (1979). Experiments on the provision of public goods. I. Resources, interest, group size, and the free-rider problem. *American Journal of Sociology, 84*(6), 1335-1360.

Marwell, G., & Ames, R. E. (1980). Experiments on the provision of public goods. II. Provision points, stakes, experience, and the free-rider problem. *American Journal of Sociology, 85*(4), 926-937.

Marwell, G., & Ames, R. E. (1981). Economists ride free, does anyone else? Experiments on the provision of public goods. IV. *Journal of Public Economics, 15*(3), 295-310.

Olsen, M. (1965). *The logic of collective action.* Cambridge, MA: Harvard University Press.

Picus, L. (1991). *Using incentives to stimulate improved school performance: An assessment of alternative approaches.* Los Angeles: University of Southern California, Center for Research in Education Finance.

Richards, C. (1985). The economics of merit pay: A special case of utility maximization. *Journal of Education Finance, 11*(2), 176-189.

Richards, C. (1990). The meaning and measure of school effectiveness. In J. Bliss, W. Firestone, & C. Richards (Eds.), *Rethinking effective schooling: Policy and practice* (pp. 28-42). Englewood Cliffs, NJ: Prentice-Hall.

Richards, C., & Sheu, T. (1992). The South Carolina school incentive reward program: A policy analysis. *Economics of Education Review, 11*(1), 71-86.

Richards, C., & Shujaa, M. (1990). School performance incentives. In P. Reyes (Ed.), *Teachers and their workplace* (pp. 115-140). Newbury Park, CA: Sage.

Runge, C. F. (1984). Institutions and the free ride: The assurance problem in collective action. *Journal of Politics, 46*(1), 154-181.

Sederberg, C., & Clark, S. (1990). Motivation and organizational incentives for high vitality teachers: A quality perspective. *Journal of Research and Development in Education, 24*(1), 6-13.

Watson, R., Poda, J., & Miller, C. (1988). State-mandated teacher incentives and school improvement plans: Problems and connections. *ERS Spectrum, 6*(1), 21-24.

THREE

"Professionalizing" Teaching by Expanding Teachers' Roles

BETTY MALEN

During the 1980s, clarion calls to enhance the quality of teaching captured attention. Signs of a "crisis in teaching" and a "crisis in schooling" triggered a rapid-fire proliferation of state legislation in virtually every domain of "teacher policy" and a noticeable escalation of district action in these areas as well.[1] While such patterns are subject to different interpretations, a common observation is that, during the "first wave" of education reform, state and local governments addressed concerns through "bureaucratic controls" but shifted, during the "second wave," to "professional controls" (McDonnell, 1989, 1991; Rowan, 1990). This shift was presumably sparked by shrill indictments of "bureaucratic controls" (i.e., the rules and regulations developed by public officials or their designated agents). For example, critics argued that "bureaucratic controls" operate to denigrate and deskill teachers, routinize and trivialize teaching, standardize and stultify learning, dampen or deaden local initiative, and otherwise impede rather than promote instructional improvement (Darling-Hammond & Wise, 1985; McNeil, 1986; Rosenholtz, 1987). Critics also argued that teaching is a complex process that involves continuous invention and adaptation and hence requires substantial discretion and judgment (Lieberman, 1992; Shulman, 1991). By these accounts, quality controls based on professional tenets (e.g., expert knowledge, collegial interaction) could make teaching a more attractive occupation and schools more effective organizations (Rowan, 1990).

Purpose and Perspective

This chapter examines a prominent subset of policies to "professionalize" teaching and improve schooling by expanding teachers' responsibilities in the broad area of organizational decision making and the more focused area of staff development/peer assistance. It outlines a framework for assessing these policies, synthesizes information on select impacts, and highlights policy implications.

Orienting Framework

Rowan's conception of these policies as examples of a "network structures" strategy frames the analysis (Rowan, 1990). This perspective assumes that "network structures" can expand teachers' authority and influence in the workplace, enhance motivation and morale, foster collegial interaction, capitalize on and contribute to teachers' expertise, and operate to improve instruction, engender satisfaction, and otherwise enhance commitment and improve performance. While network structures can take several forms (Lichtenstein, McLaughlin, & Knudsen, 1992; Louis, 1992), the establishment of councils or committees to involve teachers in school-level policymaking and the creation of leadership positions to address staff development/peer assistance represent prevalent manifestations of this approach. Consistent with the "work redesign" and "quality of work life" movement in corporations, the strategy is both promising and problematic (Louis, 1992; Rowan, 1990).

On the promising side, features of the workplace can have profound, albeit not altogether predictable or even, effects on employee commitment and organizational performance (Hackman & Oldham, 1980; Lawler, 1991; Rowan, 1990). A range of organizational factors including opportunities to participate in decision making, be involved in frequent, stimulating collegial interactions, and develop knowledge/skills are all related to a sense of control over, dedication to, and accomplishment of work (Hall, 1986; Louis, 1992; Rowan, 1990). On the problematic side, because numerous organizational factors (e.g., task characteristics, social relations, resources to carry out responsibilities) interact with individual characteristics to shape responses, restructuring work roles is an exceptionally complex strategy that begets markedly mixed reviews (Hackman & Oldham, 1980; Hall,

1986; Kushman, 1992). There are cases of "successful implementation," marginal gain, and "outright failure" across organizational settings (Hall, 1986, pp. 284, 285). More precisely, there are tendencies, if not propensities, for "countervailing forces" to arise and offset the intended effects (Kushman, 1992). Because the strategy requires organizations to *replace* hierarchical structures with alternative forms of coordination/control and develop different norms of interaction, it is also an ambitious, expensive strategy. Crisply put, "Only rather affluent organizations can attempt redesign efforts" (Hall, 1986, p. 285). While some would soften this statement, many maintain that the strategy requires substantial fiscal/technical support.

When augmented by literature on the prominent organizational characteristics of schools and the dominant features of policy provisions, this brisk review of the "network structures" notion suggests the strategy may be difficult to install and sustain in schools for several reasons. First, schools tend to be pressure-packed places, "street-level bureaucracies" (Lipsky, 1980) wherein people are continuously confronted with multiple, competing demands, chronic resource shortages, intense client interactions, diverse constituency expectations, incessant pressures to make consequential decisions, and intermittent challenges to their physical and emotional safety. Under these conditions, innovative policy of any sort tends to be converted into familiar practice, not because individuals are lazy, inept, or recalcitrant but because the pressures of the workplace overpower the provisions of policy.

Second, schools are lodged in a multitiered, hierarchical governance system. Because school-based "network structures" sit inside broader, hierarchical structures that they cannot replace by might or magic, professional controls coexist with bureaucratic controls, interact with them, and are mediated by them (McDonnell, 1989; Weick & McDaniel, 1991; Weiss, 1990). Because bureaucratic features may constrict or support what professionals seek to do (Carnoy & MacDonell, 1990; Moore, 1991; Rowan, 1990), they condition what "network structures" can accomplish.

Third, the approach may have especially rough sledding because it challenges deeply ingrained "privacy-equality-civility" norms (Bird & Little, 1986). In most schools, administrators and teachers subscribe (behaviorally, if not rhetorically) to these norms. As a result, teaching is usually carried out in isolation; differences in teachers' knowledge and capabilities are not often acknowledged, appreciated, or accommodated; and concerns for harmony and camaraderie tend to constrain critical, collegial conversation (Griffin, 1985; Little, 1982, 1987, 1990). Policies that violate these norms usually encounter reticence, if not resistance.

Fourth, schools are not affluent organizations. They receive a favorable portion of state budgets and augment these allocations with local revenues and supplemental funds. Still, fiscal resources are often in short supply, particularly when assessed in terms of the claims made upon them (Nasser, 1992). On balance, the fiscal circumstances of schools are captured more by the notion of austerity than the presumption of abundance (Corcoran, 1990).

Finally, policies that permit or require the establishment of school-based network structures appear to be blunt mechanisms for instituting such a complex strategy in such a pressure-packed context. The policies tend to rely heavily on vague structural adjustments rather than more robust options, such as blends of structural adjustments and capability-building provisions (Malen & Ogawa, 1992; Wohlstetter & Odden, 1992).[2] The assumption seems to be that existing resources can be reconfigured or that modest inducements are sufficient to install and sustain this strategy in schools.

Application of Framework

The orienting framework embodies highly complex constructs and relationships that can only be partially and primitively treated, given the nature of policy provisions and the limitations of available data. It is used here to highlight dimensions for gauging and perspectives for interpreting policy effects.

In terms of dimensions of assessment, the framework directs attention to the authority transferred to and conferred upon teachers. While authority is rooted in personal as well as positional attributes, in social interactions as well as structural arrangements, it can be at least partially gauged by examining the formal authority granted teachers and, where data permit, by examining perceptions of teachers' ability to exercise influence. The framework directs attention to motivation (i.e., the willingness to expend effort on job-related tasks), morale (i.e., the attitudes group members hold toward one another, themselves, and their tasks), collegial interaction, and collective problem solving (i.e., frequent, rigorous discussions of salient organizationwide or classroom-specific matters that capitalize on the expertise of teachers). It also directs attention to instructional adaptations (e.g., adjustments in the overall program or in individual classrooms) and job satisfaction (a summative judgment of rewarding/distressing aspects of work). The intent, then, is to examine polices in terms of their impact on these dimensions. It is not to determine whether the effects constitute "professionalization" or "improvement."[3] Because the framework posits that webs of factors may shape responses to these policies, the intent is to array key factors but focus on those most amenable to policy influence.

Data Sources and Limitations

This chapter draws on case studies and district evaluations of policies seeking to create network structures that increase teachers' responsibilities in the broad area of organizational decision making and the more focused area of professional development/peer assistance.[4] The chapter also draws on related literature, notably syntheses of current studies and reviews of previous attempts to install versions of the network strategy in schools. Since the focus is on policies to engender "professional controls," initiatives more aligned with the broader notion of "community control" (e.g., the Chicago reform) or spawned by localized grassroots movements are not included.

The data are severely limited. First, the case studies and district evaluations encompass a small number of sites in different stages of the implementation process. Second, the works tend to be exploratory investigations, guided by or interpreted in light of varied conceptual lenses. As a result, data sources address different versions and dimensions of network structures. Third, because the investigations tend to concentrate on reputedly exemplar sites in a particular setting during a particular period, it is difficult to gauge the extent to which teacher roles are fundamentally different and/or the extent to which "impacts" can be attributed to new policy provisions, "halo effects," or other confounding factors. Recognizing that data are thin and efforts to aggregate information regarding diverse forms of "network structures" in diverse contexts risk distortion as well as generate insight (Cotton, Vollrath, Froggatt, Lengnick-Hall, & Jennings, 1988; Moore,

1991), the chapter focuses on cross-cutting themes, acknowledges exceptional patterns, and underscores the suggestive nature of the inferences drawn.

Expanding Roles: Network Structures
for School-Level Decision Making

Policies that seek to expand teachers' roles in school-level decision making have many origins and take many forms but embody similar stated aims.[5] Essentially, they seek to extend teachers' decision-making authority and influence to new areas (e.g., budget, personnel, and program) and broader arenas (i.e., the school as well as the classroom) and to capitalize on the potential benefits of employee participation in organizational decision making.

Impact on decision-making authority and influence. Although signs of exceptional cases are present, prominent patterns indicate these varied policies may not be fundamentally altering teachers' decision-making authority and influence. First, policy provisions tend to define "new" decision-making arrangements in ambiguous or familiar terms. In most cases, vague references to greater latitude, opportunities to propose experimental projects to district officials or state agencies for approval, and options to offer "input" are more pronounced than clear depictions of increased authority (Kelly, 1988; Malen, 1992; Malen, Ogawa, & Kranz, 1990; White, 1992; Wohlstetter & Odden, 1992). Most plans grant teachers greater responsibility for completing certain tasks (e.g., preparation of school improvement plans, organization of in-service sessions) and implementing policy decisions made in other arenas (e.g., development of plans to accommodate budget crunches or to institute state/district initiatives). But few appear to grant teachers greater formal authority to initiate and formulate policy in the central domains of budget, personnel, and program (Conley, 1991; Kelly, 1988; Malen, 1992; Malen et al., 1990; Smylie & Tuermer, 1992; Zeichner, 1991). Perhaps that is why, in some settings, the majority of teachers report they have insufficient "wiggle room" to make major changes at the school site; curricular changes are "largely central office dictates . . . rather than school-initiated efforts" (DeLacy, 1990, pp. 6, 30) and school councils function more as forums to rally support for/reduce resistance to policies made elsewhere than as forums to forge policies for schools in schools (Hanson, 1991; McLeese, 1992). Perhaps that is why some proximate observers conclude that "examples of token authority . . . are far more common than examples of meaningful decentralization [of decision-making powers]" (David, 1991, p. 13).

Second, where provisions noticeably alter formal decision-making arrangements, the adjustments are frequently confined to select domains (e.g., discretionary funds, aspects of personnel or program) and sharply circumscribed by the rules and resources of the broader system (Carnoy & MacDonell, 1990; DeLacy, 1992; Hanson, 1991; Malen et al., 1990; Stevenson & Pellicer, 1992). Thus the formal policymaking powers lodged at the school remain fairly narrow in scope and piecemeal in character, and the related influence resources (e.g., time, information) of teachers are not noticeably altered (Malen & Ogawa, 1992; Wohlstetter & Buffet, 1992).

Third, despite the presence of "new arrangements," the traditional patterns—wherein site-based councils operate as ancillary advisers or pro forma actors, principals control building-level decision making, and teachers control classroom-level decision making—tend to persist, even in settings that have extensive experience with and long-standing commitments to teacher participation in school-level decision making (Berman, Weiler Associates, 1984; Malen, 1992; Mc-Leese, 1992). The pronounced tendency for shared decision making to be characterized by regular but restricted occasions for teacher input on a narrow band of issues (White, 1992) or a ready and robust mechanism for teacher assistance in averting or absorbing the contention associated with divisive retrenchment decisions or curricular requirements is present (Conley, 1991; Malen, 1992; Malen et al., 1990; McLeese, 1992). The prevalent promise of shared decision making as a means through which teachers might exercise significant influence on significant issues may be approximated in some settings (Carnoy & MacDonell, 1990; DeLacy, 1992; Hanson, 1991; Malen, 1992) but this pattern seems to be more the noteworthy exception than the dominant feature of current and previous efforts to expand teachers' roles in school decision making (Berman, Weiler Associates, 1984; Conley, 1991; Corcoran, 1990; Duke, 1984; Elmore, 1991).

Impact on motivation and morale. Opportunities to be involved in school decision making appear to have an initial, energizing, elevating effect on some. Although many are skeptical, some are eager to tackle the

tough problems facing their schools and optimistic about their capacity to do so (Carnoy & MacDonell, 1990; Corcoran, 1990; DeLacy, 1992;
Smylie & Tuermer, 1992; Weiss, Cambone, & Wyeth, 1992). They
appreciate the opportunity to voice concerns, offer suggestions, and
develop solutions. They view the opportunity as a recognition of their
expertise, an affirmation of their worth (White, 1992). But these initial
effects tend to be offset by a host of countervailing forces.[6] To illustrate,
teachers involved in various school-based management/shared decision-making ventures report they are excited by the prospects but
exhausted by the pressures. Many express concerns about their ability
to "keep up the pace" as workdays and workweeks are voluntarily
but necessarily extended to accommodate the demands of organizational decision making and the demands of other aspects of their
work roles and private lives. Teachers report that the intensification
of work (which at times translates into 12- to 16-hour workdays and
6- to 7-day workweeks) imposes personal as well as professional costs
(Carnoy & MacDonell, 1990; DeLacy, 1990, 1992).

Echoing the findings of previous efforts to involve teachers in
decision making, both recent district evaluations and case studies of
current efforts indicate that, in some settings, the "initial enthusiasm"
for shared decision making is followed by "exhaustion and burnout,"
an "appreciable drop in the degree of involvement," and an increase
in absenteeism that seems related to, if not fully explained by, the
intensification of the workload in schools piloting school-based man-
agement/shared decision making (Collins & Hanson, 1991; Morris,
1991, pp. 11, 12) and that about half the teachers are, by their own
estimation, "under extreme stress," about 40% "feel bogged down
rather than empowered," and approximately 60% tend to agree that
"it is more important to me to use my out of class time to plan for
upcoming classes" than to participate in school-based decision making (DeLacy, 1990, pp. 27, 12, 4). While teachers in these settings are
not ready to relinquish involvement in decision making, here as
elsewhere, the signs of strain are apparent; the risks of overload are
evident; the seeds of disillusionment are present (Carnoy & Mac-
Donell, 1990; Conley, 1991; Lichtenstein et al., 1992; McLeese, 1992;
Zeichner, 1991).

Impact on collegial interactions. Various shared decision-making policies may direct attention to aspects of schoolwide planning and
collaborative problem solving in some settings, but that impact does

not appear to be widespread (Berman, Weiler Associates, 1984; David & Peterson, 1984; McLeese, 1992). Some joint planning and collective problem-solving processes do not appear to capitalize on either the expertise of teachers or the benefits of group interaction. Plans get assembled, in isolation, by principals, district administrators, or individual teachers. The lack of time to address difficult issues, the concern for harmony and civility, the tendency to "paper over differences" (Weiss et al., 1992, p. 355), and the absence of relevant information combine to constrict both the quantity and the quality of collegial interactions and collective problem-solving exchanges (Berman, Weiler Associates, 1984; David & Peterson, 1984; DeLacy, 1990, 1992; Malen et al., 1990; Weiss et al., 1992). Some teachers may be actively and continuously engaged in collaborative interactions in some schools (Carnoy & MacDonell, 1990; DeLacy, 1990, 1992), but this outcome does not appear to be broadly or dependably realized.

Impact on instructional adaptations. Whether teacher involvement in school-level decision making can engender instructional adaptations remains an open question. The prominent patterns suggest that most school councils do not spend much time talking about the instructional program except in the context of budget reductions and program cutbacks (DeLacy, 1990; Hanson, 1991; Malen et al., 1990; McLeese, 1992). As one study captures it, shared decision making appears to be focused more on "how to avoid bankruptcy" than on how to improve instruction (Smylie & Tuermer, 1992). As other studies depict it, immediate issues associated with the day-to-day operation of schools dominate meeting agendas (Berman, Weiler Associates, 1984; Malen & Ogawa, 1988). While there are some exceptional instances, involvement in schoolwide decision making does not seem to foster the development and implementation of major instructional changes in most school settings (Carnoy & MacDonell, 1990; DeLacy, 1990; Glickman, 1990; Hanson, 1991; McLeese, 1992). In some instances, it may weaken rather than strengthen the instructional component as teachers take on activities that consume their time, drain their energies, and limit their abilities to be, by their own estimates, adequately prepared for class (DeLacy, 1990, 1992). In some instances, involvement in schoolwide decision making may be creating the "organizational antecedents" (e.g., increased communication among teachers) of major changes in school governance and classroom instruction (DeLacy, 1990, 1992; Smylie & Tuermer, 1992). Whether these antecedents will become the ingredients of significant organizational changes remains an unanswered, empirical question.

Impact on job satisfaction. Teachers seem more ambivalent about than satisfied with involvement in schoolwide decision making. Their responses indicate that involvement in decision making can both contribute to and detract from satisfaction with work. Individuals acknowledge these mixed responses and groups vary in their "on-balance" appraisals. As recent program evaluations illustrate, the number of teachers reporting that site-based management/shared decision making contributes to a more satisfying work environment held steady in some settings but declined sharply in other locations (DeLacy, 1990, 1992; Morris, 1991); the number of teachers calling for adjustments that might make their roles more manageable as well as more meaningful is sizable in all cases (Bredeson, 1992; Collins & Hanson, 1991; DeLacy, 1992; Weiss et al., 1992).

Network Structures: Professional Development, Peer Assistance

Provisions that grant teachers greater responsibility for staff development/peer assistance have numerous sources and take various forms but reflect similar stated aims.[7] Essentially, the provisions seek to augment the salary/status of select teachers and provide opportunities for professional development through activities that might enable teachers to acquire new knowledge and skills, develop collegial relationships/collaborative problem-solving processes, and otherwise strengthen instructional support systems/services (Bird, 1986; Little, 1990; Malen, Murphy, & Hart, 1988).

Impact on Teachers' Authority and Influence

It is difficult to determine the extent to which this genre of policies enhances the authority and influence of teachers for several reasons. First, the policies tend to define the "new" positions in fairly ambiguous or conventional terms. Most include peer observation and assistance, staff development and curricular improvement responsibilities, as well as classroom teaching duties. The positions, however, "rarely . . . entail formal authority for personnel or program matters" (Little, 1990, p. 301; Little & Long, 1985; Popkewitz & Lind, 1989). While such positions may modify formal authority relationships, the way these "new positions" differ from existing arrangements is difficult to discern. For decades, teachers have held leadership posts as department chairs, grade-level coordinators, program directors, team leaders, and the like. In some contexts, the new provisions may be essentially renaming existing arrangements (Hatfield, Blackman, Claypool, & Mester, 1985; Malen & Hart, 1987) or defining roles "within the boundaries of familiar roles and functions" (Little, 1990, p. 304) by having teachers take on projects they carry out in isolation or assume the duties of administrators whose posts were eliminated when budgets were cut (Hanson, 1991; Little, 1990). In other places, teachers' work may be more markedly redesigned (Amsler, Mitchell, Nelson, & Timar, 1988; Firestone, 1991; Firestone & Bader, 1991). Second, the policies rarely endow the "new" positions with substantial doses of critical resources (e.g., discretionary funds, substantial released time, sizable, stable reductions in classroom teaching assignments, up-front training) that teacher leaders might deploy to enhance their influence. In some settings, the lead teachers' classroom assignment is partially reduced, their work year is extended, and several days are added so other teachers can access the services of lead teachers. In other places, these rather modest adjustments are not made. Hence the influence of lead teachers tends to rest on the "personal credibility" individuals bring to the position, not enhancements derived from the position (Little, 1990; Malen et al., 1988). Although there are settings where expanded responsibilities may have enhanced the status of lead teachers and engendered respect for faculty members (Malen et al., 1988), the "modal response" appears to be one in which lead teachers "discount the status distinctions," "discount their special expertise," and otherwise discredit the potential sources of influence lodged in leadership positions (Little, 1990).

Impact on Motivation and Morale

Whether conceived as opportunities for many teachers to take on projects on a "fee for service" basis or as opportunities for select teachers to assume positions on a fairly permanent or more short-term, rotated basis, the chance to take on additional responsibilities seems to have an initial, energizing, elevating effect on some teachers. Case studies indicate teachers applied for and received support for projects. Although some report they felt "pressured" to participate (i.e., they did not want to be perceived as "less committed" than their colleagues), most note they appreciated the option to acquire some institutional acknowledgment and financial support for the "extra work" they were already doing and/or for other tasks they wanted to pursue (Malen et al., 1988; Popkewitz & Lind, 1989). Although extra projects can prompt teachers to document what they are currently doing, individuals claim they "learned a great deal" from the projects and that others benefited as well, especially where projects generated instructional resources or strategies that teachers could use (Malen et al., 1988; Popkewitz & Lind, 1989). Case studies also indicate teachers applied for formal positions and appreciated the professional recognition embodied by them, the salary supplements attached to them, and the activities associated with them (Firestone, 1991; Hart & Murphy, 1990; Little, 1990; Malen et al., 1988). Though subjected to "collegial sanction," teacher leaders enjoyed the opportunities to observe and coach other teachers, develop in-service programs, conduct workshops, do demonstration lessons, create instructional materials, and otherwise lend assistance and support. Teacher leaders report they "learned a great deal" from those experiences and that other teachers also valued the chance to share ideas and accumulate resources for classroom instruction (Firestone, 1991; Firestone & Bader, 1991; Hart & Murphy, 1990; Little, 1990; Malen et al., 1988).

These positive sentiments are tempered, however, by disconcerting comments regarding the escalation of work pressures and the creation of role conflicts. Teachers who took on "special projects" indicate that these can be draining and distracting. In some cases, teachers end up with less time to prepare for their classes and less energy to dedicate to students (Malen et al., 1988). Teachers who assumed formal positions report they are frustrated by the ambiguity of their assignments, distressed by the "collegial censure" they feel and fear, exhausted by the demands of the additional responsibilities, and torn by the demands to handle their classroom assignments and the expanded duties. Teachers talk candidly about the inability to "do both jobs well" and state directly that they may be compromising their teaching and shortchanging their students (Little, 1990; Malen et al., 1988). Thus there are signs of strain and conflict as well as signs of enthusiasm and endorsement (Bird, 1986; Bredeson, 1992; Duke, 1984; Firestone, 1991; Firestone & Bader, 1991; Smylie & Denny, 1990).

Impact on Collegial Interactions and Instructional Adaptations

While opportunities for individuals to take on special projects could stimulate collegial interaction, collaborative effort, and organizational innovation (McDonnell, 1989), case studies indicate that projects tend to be individually designed, sporadically diffused, and loosely tied to instructional priorities (Malen et al., 1988) and that projects may be "intensifying the work of teaching rather than redefining its conditions to make them more intellectually and socially satisfying" (Popkewitz & Lind, 1989, p. 591). The emphasis on extra work and the creation of a structure that expects additional work can make it more, rather than less, difficult for teachers to engage in substantive conversations regarding the goals as well as the means of the instructional program, the aims as well as the "techniques" of teaching (Popkewitz & Lind, 1989). Moreover, when project demands collide with classroom demands, teachers perceive themselves to be less prepared, if not ill-prepared, for class. Given the pace and pressure of life in schools, it is plausible if not probable that extra projects could make teaching more frenetic and fragmented, collegial interaction less likely, and school environments busier but not better places for teachers to work and students to learn (Duke, 1984; Griffin, 1985; Malen, 1992; Popkewitz & Lind, 1989). In settings that emphasize formal positions, responses indicate that teachers have been exposed to new skills and have become more aware of their teaching styles and more receptive to discussions of alternative strategies. In some settings, the positions provide structures through which teachers can share ideas, tackle immediate problems, produce materials, and expand their repertoire of knowledge/skills (Malen et al., 1988; Smylie & Denny, 1990). But these general assessments of perceived benefits are tempered by recurrent references to patterns that suggest collegial interaction and instructional innovation may be more desired aims than actual outcomes. Several examples will illustrate.

First, there is a strong tendency for mentors to "stress matters of comfort over issues of competence" (Little, 1990, p. 342). In some instances, the emphasis on interpersonal relations may be more a substitute for than a complement to an emphasis on instructional analysis (Little, 1990). Second, the opportunity to observe and interact with teachers on a regular, let alone frequent basis is constrained by both time schedules and ingrained norms. Because lead teachers tend to have classroom assignments, many simply are not free to observe or coach their peers during the school day. When they are free, other responsibilities may take precedence so that only a relatively small portion of the limited time allotted is used for activities that include direct interaction with other teachers (Bird, 1986; Smylie & Denny, 1990). Further, the tendency to view classroom teaching as a private matter and classroom observation as an unwelcome interference interact to make it hard for lead teachers to "go where they are not invited" and move conversations about day-to-day teaching to critical inspections of those processes (Little, 1987, 1990; Little & Long, 1985; Malen et al., 1988). Finally, the impact of these collegial interactions on classroom behaviors is hard to gauge, in part because teachers' decisions about classroom instruction are shaped by a wide range of factors such as personal preferences, prior experiences, knowledge of subject, tacit treaties with students, anticipation of parental responses, and the like (Powell, Farrar, & Cohen, 1985; Little, 1990); in part because patterns of rigorous, sustained collaboration have been difficult to engender; and in part because collegial interaction may be a supportive but not a sufficient ingredient of instructional improvement (Little, 1987).

Impact on Job Satisfaction

Teachers' responses are characterized more by ambivalence than satisfaction. The financial supplements are usually modest but appreciated, since they signal some recognition of the additional effort teachers tend to expend whether they are paid for it or not. The added responsibilities are, for some, intrinsically rewarding because they provide opportunities to pursue interests, acquire knowledge, and interact with others. But those effects are not universal or dependable. Given that added responsibilities engender frustration and exhaustion as well as fulfillment and satisfaction, teachers struggle to determine whether the positions are "a blessing or a burden" (Little, 1990, p. 338; Smylie & Denny, 1990).

Interpretations and Implications

When conceptualized as examples of a more general "network structures" strategy, policies that seek to expand teachers' roles in the broad area of organizational decision making and the more focused area of professional development/peer assistance beget mixed reviews. There are signs of gains along some if not all dimensions of interest, but these gains are neither certain nor consistent. Formidable "countervailing forces" (e.g., stress, anxiety, overburden, exhaustion) arise and operate to substantially offset, if not fully overshadow, the more consonant effects. Efforts to account for these mixed reactions illustrate both the complexity of the strategy and the difficulty of getting such an ambitious strategy installed and sustained in the pressure-packed settings that characterize most schools. As the literature on "network structures" would predict, a wide array of factors seems to be shaping effects. While a veritable web of factors that are more or less amenable to policy influence may be operating, several policy adjustments might function to buffer the countervailing forces and bolster the consonant effects. Thus this section highlights the webs of factors, recommends policy revisions, and encourages more careful, comprehensive assessment.

Webs of Factors

Among the many factors shaping effects, one set relates to individual predispositions. Simply put, some teachers respond more favorably to the prospects of expanded roles than others (Conley, 1991; Hart & Murphy, 1990; Malen et al., 1990). Apparently some have a penchant for participation in more collaborative activities while others have a preference for more independent work (Conley, 1991; Miskel & Ogawa, 1988; Rowan, 1990). Apparently some have experiences that prompt them to greet these "new" policies with caution, at times skepticism, while others are more inclined to greet them with optimism and enthusiasm (Conley, 1991; Johnson, 1990). Like other occupational groups, teachers have different orientations that mediate the response to and impact of efforts to alter work roles and relationships (Hackman & Oldham, 1980).

A second set relates to the credibility of participants. Where credibility is high—that is, when teachers perceive that the individuals involved in school-level decision making and professional development activities are capable, conscientious, and sincere, they responded more positively (Conley, 1991; Malen et al., 1988; McLeese, 1992). The converse also seems to hold.

A third set relates to the quality of existing relationships and the strength of ingrained norms. That is, in settings where teacher-teacher and teacher-administrator relationships are characterized by mutual trust, respect, and regard, efforts to establish network structures are more readily embraced. Where relationships are already strained, the expanded roles and responsibilities exacerbate these tensions and meet stronger resistance (Bredeson, 1992; Malen et al., 1988; Smylie & Tuermer, 1992). And as all studies vividly illustrate, the pressure to accommodate ingrained "privacy-equality-civility" norms affects how teacher roles in school-level decision making and staff development are conceived, conducted, and received (Little, 1990; Malen & Ogawa, 1988; Malen et al., 1988; Smylie & Denny, 1990).

Other sets of factors more amenable to policy influence are also apparent. There is rather consistent, hence convincing, evidence that ambiguous provisions and resource shortages both constrain the ability of school-based network structures to engender the desired effects and contribute to the creation of "countervailing forces" that threaten the ability of this strategy to register large and lasting gains along the dimensions considered. Whether attention to these matters would maximize the consonant effects and minimize the countervailing effects is an open, empirical question. That neglect of these matters will diminish if not deny the promise of the network structures strategy is a tentative but tenable proposition.

Recommended Policy Revisions

Clarification of Authority Relationships

The literature reviewed here indicates that vague policy provisions support the pronounced tendency to translate policy options into familiar practices (Little, 1990; Malen & Hart, 1987) and contribute to the confusion, skepticism, frustration, overburden, and exhaustion so apparent within and across sites. Efforts to clarify what authority has been delegated to and distributed among teachers at the school site and how that translates into greater discretion, given the rules and resources of the broader system, might enhance the efficacy and integrity of school-based network structures strategies by revealing what "bureaucratic controls" have been relaxed or replaced, what "professional controls" have been added or augmented, and whether other adjustments might be warranted (DeLacy, 1992; Hannaway, 1992; Malen, 1992). There is suggestive evidence that efforts to clarify formal authority relationships may be alleviating some concerns and enhancing teachers' ability to influence school policy decisions and professional development activities in several settings (DeLacy, 1992; Hannaway, 1992; Smylie & Tuermer, 1992). Thus clarifying authority relationships may help (Little, 1990; Malen, 1992).

Provision of relevant resources. The shortage of key resources, notably time to carry out the added responsibilities, appears to substantially restrict the ability of network structures to achieve their aims and consistently contribute to the presence of side effects that threaten the viability and durability of the strategy. All studies document that time constraints limit the opportunity of teachers to engage in the collaborative problem-solving processes that lie at the heart of the strategy and intensify the pressures associated with the approach.

   Clearly, the time issue is a tough issue. It is hard to know how much time is needed and it is hard to secure the fiscal resources and political consensus required to support a view of teaching that puts organizational decision making and professional development on par with classroom interactions, a view that builds these responsibilities into the "regular day" rather than adds them on to an already full day (Malen, 1992). While a number of districts have tried to "create time" in various ways (e.g., added days for schoolwide planning, arranged released time, staggered schedules), these "stop-gap" measures seem insufficient (Malen, 1992). More encompassing changes (e.g., hiring additional teachers so classroom duties are permanently reduced, extending the school year across the calendar year) may be required. Making these adjustments would increase the price of the strategy, but avoiding such investments may deny the benefits of the strategy. Moreover, the time issue is not the only resource issue to be faced. Shortages of other critical resources, such as information, technical assistance, instructional materials, training, and the like, also condition the impact of network structures. Rather, intensive, comprehensive efforts to infuse resources so that schools can cope with the added responsibilities of network structures strategies and the pressure-packed conditions of street-level bureaucracies may be necessary.

Broader Policy Assessments

Given the complexity of the network structures strategy, the uncertain connections between policy provisions and actual effects, and the limitations of existing data, a good bit of work must be done before firm judgments regarding the strategy's ability to professionalize teaching and improve schooling can be rendered. This chapter took a narrow cut. It examined school-based network structures along select dimensions and outlined revisions that might bolster their consonant effects. In so doing, the analysis underscores the need for focused work (e.g., continuous, systematic empirical assessments) to determine the conditions under which school-based network structures might more closely approximate their stated aims. Equally important, it highlights the need for comparative work that examines alternative forms of network structures (e.g., content-centered collaboratives, broad-based professional networks), particularly because preliminary evidence suggests "knowledge-based" collaboratives may be an important complement, if not a more robust approach, to teacher empowerment (Lichtenstein et al., 1992; Louis, 1992). Perhaps most important, it highlights the need for comprehensive work that examines how the plethora of "teacher policies" interact, how alternative forms and combinations of control (e.g., professional, bureaucratic, community) play out, and whether efforts to professionalize teaching enhance as well as effect, improve as well as intensify the quality of life and learning in schools.

Notes

1. Profiles of cohorts entering and incumbents leaving teaching, reports of actual and anticipated teacher shortages, and surveys of teachers' views of work indicated teaching was not an attractive occupation, at least not one the most academically able were eager to enter and reluctant to leave (Corcoran, 1990; Schlecty & Vance, 1982; Soder,

1986a). These and other signs of crisis fueled policy action (Darling-Hammond & Berry, 1988; Rowan, 1990).

2. In some settings, these policies were financed by "seed money" (e.g., small planning grants), "supplemental funds" (e.g., modest categorical aids), or "soft money" (e.g., foundation grants) that locales secured (Carnoy & MacDonell, 1990; Malen & Ogawa, 1992). In some cases, additional resources were not allocated. In other cases, resources were cut back (Hanson, 1991; Malen, 1992).

3. Both notions are complex, contested concepts (Soder, 1986a, 1986b). While policies address aspects of professionalization (e.g., granting teachers greater control over policies that affect their work or knowledge required to carry out their work), these may (or may not) be the most critical components. While policies produce outcomes (e.g., collegial interaction, instructional innovation), these may or may not be improvements (Hargreaves, 1991; Moore, 1991). Establishing criteria for judgments on these matters goes beyond the scope of this chapter.

4. Case studies of relatively recent and long-established school-based management ventures in several states (e.g., Utah, California, Minnesota, Florida, Washington), district evaluations of school-based management in Dade County, Florida, and Bellevue, Washington, evaluations of shared decision-making arrangements in unspecified school settings, and related literature reviews are used to gauge the impact of efforts to expand teacher involvement in school-level decision making. Case studies that focus on the implementation of California's mentor teacher program, components of Utah's career ladder statute, Missouri's career ladder legislation, Wisconsin's master teacher policy, and other comparable state statutes or contractual provisions in five unnamed settings as well as program evaluations of Dade County's efforts to alter teacher roles and synthesis of other program evaluations and related literature sources are used to gauge the impact of efforts to expand teacher roles in staff development/peer assistance.

5. There are, for example, district-initiated provisions that permit principals to decide the level of teacher involvement on an issue-by-issue basis, contractual agreements that render principals and teachers "equal partners" with "equal power" in school policy, state statutes that mandate teacher representation on school councils, and pilot projects that encourage shared decision making (Conley, 1991; Malen et al., 1990; Wohlstetter & Odden, 1992).

6. These include the confusion, anxiety, and contention generated as people try to decipher ambiguous provisions, define roles, and work on complex problems; the "rifts" that develop between teachers who participate and those who don't; the dissonance created as committee assignments compete with classroom responsibilities; the resentment generated when participants perceive they have modest influence on marginal matters; the cynicism engendered as issues get recycled through an endless series of circuits or overturned by principals, district administrators, or school boards; and the frustrations imposed by fiscal constraints (DeLacy, 1992; Hanson, 1991; Malen et al., 1990; Morris, 1991; Weiss et al., 1992).

7. Some are embedded in various "career ladder" statutes (Malen et al., 1988; Rowan, 1990). Some are embodied in various state- or district-sponsored "mentor teacher" or "lead teacher" policies, and others are part of local collective bargaining agreements (Conley, 1991; Firestone & Bader, 1991).

References

Amsler, M., Mitchell, D., Nelson, L., & Timar, T. (1988). *An evaluation of the Utah career ladder system*. San Francisco: Far West Laboratory for Educational Research.

Berman, Weiler Associates. (1984). *Improving school improvement: A policy evaluation of the California school improvement program*. Berkeley, CA: Author.

Bird, T. (1986). *The mentors' dilemma*. San Francisco: Far West Laboratory.

Bird, T., & Little, J. (1986). How schools organize the teaching occupation. *Elementary School Journal, 86*, 493-511.

Bredeson, P. (1992, April). *Responses to restructuring and empowerment initiatives: A study of teachers' and principals' perceptions of organizational leadership, decisionmaking and climate*. Paper presented to the American Educational Research Association, San Francisco.

Carnoy, M., & MacDonell, L. (1990). School district restructuring in Santa Fe, New Mexico. *Educational Policy, 4*, 49-64.

Collins, R., & Hanson, M. (1991). *Summative evaluation report: School-based management/shared decisionmaking project 1987 through 1989-90*. Miami: Dade County Public Schools, Office of Educational Accountability.

Conley, S. (1991). Review of research on teacher participation in school decision making. In G. Grant (Ed.), *Review of research in education* (pp. 225-265). Washington, DC: American Educational Research Association.

Corcoran, T. (1990). Schoolwork: Perspectives on workplace reform in public schools. In M. W. McLaughlin, J. Talbert, & N. Bascia (Eds.), *The contexts of teaching in secondary schools: Teachers' realities* (pp. 142-166). New York: Teachers College Press.

Cotton, J., Vollrath, D., Froggatt, K., Lengnick-Hall, M., & Jennings, K. (1988). Employee participation: Diverse forms and different outcomes. *Academy of Management Review, 13*, 8-22.

Darling-Hammond, L., & Berry, B. (1988). *The evolution of teacher policy*. Santa Monica, CA: RAND.

Darling-Hammond, L., & Wise, A. (1985). Beyond standardization: State standards and school improvement. *Elementary School Journal, 85*, 315-335.

David, J. (1991). What it takes to restructure education. *Educational Leadership, 48*, 11.

David, J. L., & Peterson, S. M. (1984). *Can schools improve themselves? A study of school-based improvement programs*. San Francisco: Bay Area Research Group.

DeLacy, J. (1990). *The Bellevue evaluation study: Studying the effects of school renewal*. Seattle: University of Washington, Institute for the Study of Educational Policy.

DeLacy, J. (1992). *The Bellevue evaluation study* (2nd report). Seattle: University of Washington, Institute for the Study of Educational Policy.

Duke, D. (1984). *Teaching: The imperiled profession*. Albany: SUNY Press.

Elmore, R. (1991, May 3-5). *Innovation in education policy*. Paper prepared for the Conference on Fundamental Questions of Innovation, sponsored by the Governor's Center at Duke University.

Firestone, W. (1991). Merit pay and job enlargement as reforms: Incentives, implementation and teacher response. *Educational Evaluation and Policy Analysis, 13*, 269-288.

Firestone, W., & Bader, B. (1991). Professionalism or bureaucracy? Redesigning teaching. *Educational Evaluation and Policy Analysis, 13*, 67-86.

Glickman, C. (1990). Pushing school reform to a new edge: The seven ironies of school improvement. *Phi Delta Kappan, 72,* 68-75.

Griffin, G. (1985). The school as a workplace and the master teacher concept. *Elementary School Journal, 86,* 1-16.

Hackman, J., & Oldham, G. (1980). *Work redesign.* Reading, MA: Addison-Wesley.

Hall, R. (1986). *Dimensions of work.* Beverly Hills, CA: Sage.

Hannaway, J. (1992, April). *Decentralization: Multiple forms, multiple effects.* Paper presented to the American Educational Research Association, San Francisco.

Hanson, M. (1991, April). *Alteration of influence relations in school-based management innovations.* Paper presented to the American Educational Research Association, Chicago.

Hargreaves, A. (1991). Contrived collegiality: The micropolitics of teacher collaboration. In J. Blase (Ed.), *The politics of life in schools* (pp. 46-72). Newbury Park, CA: Sage.

Hart, A. W., & Murphy, M. (1990). New teachers react to redesigned teacher work. *American Journal of Education, 93,* 224-250.

Hatfield, R., Blackman, C., Claypool, C., & Mester, F. (1985). *Extended professional roles of teachers in the public schools.* East Lansing: Michigan State University, Department of Teacher Education.

Johnson, S. M. (1990). Teachers, power and school change. In W. Clune & J. Witte (Eds.), *Choice and control in American education* (Vol. 2, pp. 343-370). New York: Falmer.

Kelly, T. (1988). *Small change: The comprehensive school improvement program.* New York: Educational Priorities Panel.

Kushman, J. (1992). The organizational dynamics of teacher workplace commitment: A study of urban elementary and middle schools. *Educational Administration Quarterly, 28,* 5-42.

Lawler, E. (1991). *High-involvement management.* San Francisco: Jossey-Bass.

Lichtenstein, G., McLaughlin, M. W., & Knudsen, J. (1992). Teacher empowerment and professional knowledge. In A. Lieberman (Ed.), *The changing contexts of teaching* (pp. 37-58). Chicago: University of Chicago Press.

Lieberman, A. (1992). Introduction: The changing context of education. In A. Lieberman (Ed.), *The changing contexts of teaching* (pp. 1-10). Chicago: University of Chicago Press.

Lipsky, M. (1980). *Street-level bureaucracy.* New York: Russell Sage.

Little, J. W. (1982). Norms of collegiality and experimentation: Workplace conditions of school success. *American Educational Research Journal, 19,* 325-340.

Little, J. W. (1987). Teachers as colleagues. In V. Richardson-Koehler (Ed.), *Educators' handbook: A research perspective* (pp. 491-518). New York: Longman.

Little, J. W. (1988). Assessing the prospects for teacher leadership. In A. Lieberman (Ed.), *Building a professional culture in schools* (pp. 78-106). New York: Teachers College Press.

Little, J. W. (1990). The mentor phenomenon and the social organization of teaching. In C. Cazden (Ed.), *Review of research in education* (pp. 297-351). Washington, DC: American Educational Research Association.

Little, J. W., & Long, C. (1985). *Cases in emerging leadership by teachers: The school-level instructional support team.* San Francisco: Far West Laboratory.

Louis, K. S. (1992). Restructuring and the problem of teachers' work. In A. Lieberman (Ed.), *The changing contexts of teaching* (pp. 138-156). Chicago: University of Chicago Press.

Malen, B. (1992, February). *"Finding our way forward": Teacher unions and education reform: The Bellevue (WA) case.* Monograph prepared for Project VISION, Claremont Graduate School, Claremont (CA), and the Bellevue (WA) School District.

Malen, B., & Hart, A. W. (1987). Career ladder reform: A multilevel analysis of initial effects. *Education Evaluation and Policy Analysis, 9,* 9-23.

Malen, B., Murphy, M., & Hart, A. W. (1988). Restructuring teacher compensation systems: An analysis of three incentive strategies. In K. Alexander & D. Monk (Eds.), *Attracting and compensating America's teachers* (pp. 91-142). Cambridge, MA: Ballinger.

Malen, B., & Ogawa, R. (1988). Professional-patron influence on site-based governance councils: A confounding case study. *Education Evaluation and Policy Analysis, 10*(4), 251-270.

Malen, B., & Ogawa, R. (1992). Site-based management: Disconcerting policy issues, critical policy choices. In J. Lane & E. Epps (Eds.), *Restructuring the schools: Problems and prospects* (pp. 185-206). Berkeley, CA: McCutchan.

Malen, B., Ogawa, R., & Kranz, J. (1990). What do we know about school-based management? A case study of the literature. In W. Clune & J. Witte (Eds.), *Choice and control in American education* (Vol. 2, pp. 289-342). New York: Falmer.

McDonnell, L. (1989). *The dilemma of teacher policy.* Santa Monica, CA: RAND.

McDonnell, L. (1991). Ideas and values in implementation analysis: The case of teacher policy. In A. Odden (Ed.), *Education policy implementation.* Albany: SUNY Press.

McLeese, P. (1992). *The process of decentralizing conflict and maintaining stability: Site council enactment, implementation, operations and impacts in the Salt Lake City School District 1970-1985.* Unpublished doctoral dissertation, University of Utah, Salt Lake City.

McNeil, L. (1986). *Contradictions of control: School structure and school knowledge.* New York: Routledge & Kegan Paul.

Miskel, C., & Ogawa, R. (1988). Work motivation, job satisfaction, and climate. In N. Boyan (Ed.), *Handbook of educational administration* (pp. 279-304). New York: Longman.

Moore, D. (1991, April). *Chicago school reform: The nature and origin of basic assumptions.* Paper presented at the American Educational Research Association, Chicago.

Morris, D. (1991, April). *Initial patterns and subsequent changes in staff characteristics of the sbm pilot 1 schools, relative to those of non-participating schools.* Paper presented at the American Educational Research Association, Chicago.

Nasser, H. El (1992, September 5). Education pie contains less dough: Administrators having to do more with less. *Seattle Times,* p. A3.

Popkewitz, T., & Lind, K. (1989). Teacher incentives as reforms: Teachers' work and the changing control mechanism in education. *Teachers College Record, 90,* 575-594.

Powell, A., Farrar, E., & Cohen, D. K. (1985). *The shopping mall high school.* Boston: Houghton Mifflin.

Rosenholtz, S. J. (1987). Education reform strategies: Will they increase teacher commitment? *American Journal of Education, 93,* 335-352.

Rowan, B. (1990). Commitment and control: Alternative strategies for the organizational design of schools. In C. Cazden (Ed.), *Review of research in education* (pp. 353-389). Washington, DC: American Educational Research Association.

Schlecty, P., & Vance, V. (1982). Recruitment, selection, and retention: The shape of the teaching force. *Elementary School Journal, 83,* 469-487.

Shulman, L. (1991). Teaching alone, learning together: Needed agendas for the new reforms. In T. Sergiovanni & J. Moore (Eds.), *Schooling for tomorrow* (pp. 166-187). Boston: Allyn & Bacon.

Smylie, M., & Denny, J. (1990). Teacher leadership: Tensions and ambiguities in organizational perspective. *Educational Administration Quarterly, 26,* 235-259.

Smylie, M., & Tuermer, U. (1992, February). *The politics of involvement versus the politics of confrontation: School reform and labor relations in Hammond, Indiana.* Report prepared for Project VISION, Claremont Graduate School, Claremont, CA.

Soder, R. (1986a). *Professionalizing the profession* (Occasional paper no. 4). Seattle: University of Washington, Institute for the Study of Educational Policy.

Soder, R. (1986b, November-December). Tomorrow's teachers for whom and for what? Missing propositions in the Holmes Group report. *Journal of Teacher Education,* pp. 2-5.

Stevenson, K., & Pellicer, L. (1992). School based management in South Carolina: Balancing state-directed reform with local decision making. In J. Lane & E. Epps (Eds.), *Restructuring the schools: Problems and prospects* (pp. 123-139). Berkeley, CA: McCutchan.

Weick, K., & McDaniel, R., Jr. (1991). How professional organizations work: Implications for school organization and management. In T. Sergiovanni & J. Moore (Eds.), *Schooling for tomorrow* (pp. 330-355). Boston: Allyn & Bacon.

Weiss, C., Cambone, J., & Wyeth, A. (1992). Trouble in paradise: Teacher conflicts in shared decision-making. *Educational Administration Quarterly, 28,* 350-367.

Weiss, J. (1990). Control in school organizations: Theoretical perspectives. In W. Clune & J. Witte (Eds.), *Choice and control in American education* (Vol. 1, pp. 91-134). New York: Falmer.

White, P. (1992). Teacher empowerment under "ideal" school-site autonomy. *Educational Evaluation and Policy Analysis, 14,* 69-82.

Wohlstetter, P., & Buffet, T. (1992). Decentralizing dollars under school-based management: Have policies changed? *Educational Policy, 6,* 35-54.

Wohlstetter, P., & Odden, A. (1992). Rethinking school-based management policy and research. *Educational Administration Quarterly, 28,* 529-549.

Zeichner, K. (1991). Contradictions and tensions in the professionalization of teaching and the democratization of schools. *Teachers College Record, 92,* 363-377.

FOUR

Decentralization and Community Control

G. ALFRED HESS, JR.

The last two decades of the twentieth century have seen extraordinary interest in public education, both in the United States and in countries around the world. Two competing themes have been present in many of the efforts to change public schooling: greater centralization and greater decentralization. Not infrequently, these two themes have both been advanced at the same time. Thus, in both Great Britain and the United States, there has been a movement toward the establishment of national goals and objectives, national standards of what children should be able to know and do when they complete public schools, national standards of acceptable teaching practice, and national means of holding school people accountable. At the same time, in both nations, there is a concerted effort to move decision making down to the school level, to decentralize practical decision making. Under both themes, the traditional loci of control, states and local school districts in the United States and Local Education Agencies in England, are losing authority both upward and downward along the "chain of command."[1]

After a decade of fits and starts in educational reform, with a number of divergent directions undertaken by various reform advocates and a clear bias toward diversity of approaches and decentralization of authority, a countermovement has emerged at the beginning of the 1990s that is oriented toward bringing improvement actions in the various levels of educational activity into a common alignment.

This countermovement is being spurred by leaders in the Consortium for Policy Research in Education, involving scholars from Harvard, Rutgers, Michigan State, Stanford, and Southern California (Olson, 1992, pp. 1, 31). This countermovement, making references to the proclaimed success of the education systems in several European countries, seeks to create a coherence between national goals and objectives for education, the patterns of teacher training, the criteria for certifying teacher competency, the educational curriculum offered in schools, and the programs of testing and accountability by which we can judge both student and school achievement.

At first blush, this "systemic reform" effort is in sharp contrast to the decentralization efforts that marked the 1980s. The early efforts toward decentralization were rooted in two research traditions. During the 1970s and 1980s, a series of researchers were identifying individual schools that could be considered "effective," particularly those that were effective with socially and economically disadvantaged young people.[2] The scholars involved in this research were identifying the characteristics that set "effective schools" apart from those that were ineffective, with the presumption that, if schools could change their behavior such that they matched the lists of "effective school" characteristics, they would be equally successful with their students. A second research strain examined the conditions under which educational innovations were successfully implemented (see Elmore, 1979; Mann, 1978). This innovation research emphasized the necessity of "teacher buy-in" if real change were to occur in public schools.

The 1980s decentralization movement was initially given impetus by actions of local teachers' unions affiliated with the American Federation of Teachers (AFT). In 1983 the Hammond Teachers Union proposed to rewrite its contract with the school system to create school improvement teams in every school that would share decision making with the principal in seeking to improve that city's public schools. A key element was the agreement to waive either union contract provisions or bureaucratic regulations that would hinder reform efforts. This initiative gained much higher visibility when adopted by the Dade County Public Schools, the nation's fourth largest school system. It has since been copied in several other school systems where teachers are affiliated with the AFT. Toward the end of the decade, the AFT's competitor, the National Education Association, launched its own shared decision-making program, Schools for the 21st Century.[3]

The effort to reform the Chicago Public Schools took a more radical form of the decentralization approach. Richard Elmore (1991) has described why he thinks the Chicago reform effort stands apart from others of the 1980s:

> First, it originated from a grass roots political movement, formed around a nucleus of business, philanthropic, and community organizations, in response to increasing evidence of chronic failure of schools to educate children. Most other reforms have originated from the action of policy makers, legislatures and governors, at the state level; and, at the local level, coalitions of superintendents, union leaders, and board members.
>
> Second, the Chicago reform is, more than any other, based mainly on the theory that schools can be improved by strengthening democratic control at the school-community level. Most other reforms have been based either on theories of regulatory control—increased standards for teachers and students—or professional control—investments in the improvement of teachers' competence and increased decision making authority at the school site. While the Chicago reform has elements of both regulatory and professional control, it is mainly based on a theory of democratic control.
>
> Third, the Chicago reform is probably more ambitious—some would say radical—than any other current reform in its departure from the established structure of school organization. The creation of 542 Local School Councils with significant decision making authority for schools is, by itself, an enormous departure from established patterns of school organization. The departure is even greater when democratic control is coupled with the other elements of the reform—commitments to reduce central administration, reallocation of resources to the school level, changes in school principals' roles and responsibilities, and the like. (p. vii)

As Elmore indicates, the core of the Chicago reform effort was the creation of Local School Councils at each school with the power to create and adopt a school improvement plan, to design and approve a local school budget to dictate spending to implement that plan, and to hire and fire the school principal, the leader charged to help conceptualize and lead the effort to improve each local school. In addition, there were a number of changes in the way in which the school district was organized and its resources were allocated. The reform legislation was enacted into law in December 1988, with initial implementation in the fall of 1989. At the midpoint in the envisioned 5-year initiation period, the Chicago Panel on Public School Policy and Finance released a report on progress in implementing the reforms (Hess, 1992a). A summary of the report is provided next.

School Restructuring, Chicago Style: A Midway Report

Reform was launched with the appointment of an Interim Board in May 1989. The Interim Board quickly extended employee contracts and reallocated the budget to move $40 million to the school level while cutting about 500 administrative positions. Local School Councils were elected in October 1989 with more than 300,000 votes cast for more than 17,000 candidates for the roughly 6,000 spots on these LSCs. Later that same year, the Interim Board signed employee contracts, which granted 7% raises plus a number of bonuses in each of the succeeding 3 years. With the granting of these contracts, the board faced budget deficits in excess of $200 million before schools could open in September 1991 and 1992. During the second year of reform implementation, the Illinois Supreme Court ruled the reform act was unconstitutional, requiring corrective legislation in both January and July 1991 to enable the reform effort to continue.

Real Reform: Change at the School Level

Chicago's reform effort has frequently been characterized as a change in governance, but that change was intended to provide the opportunity for changes to take place in the educational programs in schools. There are exciting instances of such changes, but more schools need to be focused in that direction. On the basis of systemwide observations and an ongoing intensive study of 14 representative Chicago schools, the Panel has found the following:

(1) LSCs have been established and, for the most part, function successfully.
LSCs were elected at all regular schools in October 1989. Despite initial
chaos concerning a place to meet and early expenditure decisions,
they successfully adopted school improvement plans and local school
budgets; they evaluated principals and selected their leadership for
the next 4 years. At 38% of Chicago schools, a new principal was
selected. LSC attendance varied from school to school but overall was
at about 70%, with principals attending most frequently. LSC chairs
and teacher representatives had attendance rates above 80%, while
those for community representatives and parents other than for the
chair were nearer 60%. Although LSCs spent nearly a third of their
agendas on organizational matters, they also devoted a third of their
topics to dimensions of the school program. Building, finance, and
personnel (primarily principal selection) dominated the remainder of
their discussions. Efforts to increase parent involvement were discussed infrequently.

*(2) School Improvement Plans have focused more on "add-ons" than on
altering the regular instructional programs of schools.* In the first year of
school improvement planning, most schools focused on solving practical problems such as overcrowding, discipline in the school, controlling gangs, and increasing attendance. About a quarter of the
observed schools planned quite significant changes in their instructional programs while another quarter approved very rudimentary
plans. An analysis of the revised plans adopted in the second year
showed curricular changes were most prevalent, pedagogical improvements next most frequent, and organizational and other changes
following. About a quarter of the studied schools were attempting
changes that would affect regular classroom instruction throughout
the school, while another quarter were planning changes in some
classrooms. More frequently, schools were favoring "add-on" programs such as additional classes (art, music, science, or computer
labs) and additional instruction (after school, preschool, or summer
school). Most add-ons can be implemented easily if money and new
staff are available. Initiatives that may affect the regular classroom
experiences of students require significant commitment and time on
the part of teachers. One elementary school is emblematic of efforts to
change regular classroom instruction. It is implementing Socratic
seminars in an attempt to improve the content and intellectual level
of classroom discussion, a literature-based reading program, exten-

sive use of hands-on learning in mathematics, an experimental approach to science, and an innovative schoolwide writing program.

(3) Principals have adopted new roles and are providing new leadership. As mentioned above, at least 38% of Chicago schools are now led by a principal who was not in that position when reform began. A similar percentage of schools in the Chicago Panel's study sample are now served by new principals. The selection process went smoothly in some schools, but others had a more difficult time keeping their incumbent evaluation process objective and separate from the launching of a search for a new candidate. In some schools, the principal selection process so dominated their agendas that they could not conduct other business such as revising their improvement plans or adopting a school budget. Principals during the initial years of reform found the time demands to be excessive. They found themselves playing new roles, not all of which seemed appropriate. One principal complained that she now had to be a PR figure, a referee between factions in her school, and a glorified clerk making lots of reports. But some principals also saw the reform effort as providing more opportunities, particularly relative to staff selection and to the additional support they received from more involved LSC members, parents, and teachers.

(4) Teachers have become increasingly involved and positive about reform. Based on two surveys and interviews with a series of key school-level teacher leaders, it appears that teachers are now quite involved in reform at most schools. A small survey taken before the first LSC elections showed teachers did not expect to be extensively involved in reform (Easton, 1989). They thought increased parent involvement was the primary strength of the reform effort but worried that such involvement might lead to greater classroom interference. A much more comprehensive survey of 13,000 elementary school teachers administered at the end of reform's second year (Easton et al., 1991) revealed that a majority of teachers had responded positively to questions about school reform. In 62 schools, teachers were very positive about reform, while, in another 241, they were moderately positive. In 89 schools, teachers were somewhat negative, while, in 9 schools, they were very negative. Teachers felt they were fairly represented on LSCs, that they had increased involvement in policymaking, and they said they were involved in implementing their School

Improvement Plans. Interviews in the Chicago Panel's 14 sampled schools indicated that teachers had a major role in determining their schools' improvement plans, which were generally accepted as proposed by teachers to the LSC. Although the survey indicated teachers were mildly optimistic that their schools would improve, fewer than half indicated their own instructional practices have changed or will change in the future.

(5) Resources have been increasingly focused on the schools, with the greatest increases in schools enrolling the highest proportions of disadvantaged students. Between the 1988-1989 school year, when the reform law was being enacted, and 1991-1992, the Chicago Public Schools increased revenues by $403 million, mostly from increased local property tax receipts (state aid increased by only $25 million). Most of this money was reallocated to schools (primarily through State Chapter I) while some 840 administrative unit positions were eliminated. At the same time, school staff increased by 3,365. For half of those positions, schools hired classroom aides; schools also added just over 1,000 teachers and other professional staff. Funds have been much more equitably allocated to schools to meet the needs of disadvantaged young people. In the year before school reform began, elementary schools with 90% to 99% low-income students averaged $500 less per pupil in expenditures than did schools with fewer than 30% low income. In 1991-1992, the schools with the heaviest concentrations of low-income students had nearly $1,000 more per pupil than those with the fewest disadvantaged pupils.

(6) National school improvement efforts have "marched on Chicago" to assist many schools. In 1988 there were few national school improvement efforts working in Chicago schools. In 1992 there were more than 170 schools listed under various national reform efforts then working in Chicago (see Hess, 1992a, appendix). While some of these efforts have a distinctly Chicago flavor (Paideia, the Illinois Writing Project, and the federally supported desegregation program, Project CANAL), others are products of major school reformers such as Ted Sizer (Coalition of Essential Schools), Hank Levin (Accelerated Schools Network), and James Comer (Comer School Development Program). These national efforts are providing valuable resources to schools and school staffs as they work to improve Chicago's schools. These efforts were largely unavailable to the city's schools prior to school reform.

(7) It is still too early to see any changes in student achievement. School reform efforts in Chicago, at the midway point in the initial focus period, had had little opportunity to manifest themselves in improved student achievement. The first year of the reform effort was designed to establish Local School Councils at every school and to develop improvement plans with supporting school budgets. Only in the second year did schools begin to implement changes; but during that year, half the schools were still involved in the process of evaluating their incumbent principals and making leadership decisions for the next 4 years. The achievement tests available at reform's midway point had been taken only 8 months into that second year and could not be expected to show any significant changes—and did not show any. Other measures, such as dropout rates, continue to reflect prior years of neglect, while students who have experienced major changes under reform are still several years from graduation. Attendance rates for elementary schools remain flat; at the high school level, they have declined slightly, reflecting closer recording scrutiny.

(8) The midway summary: School reform is successfully launched; some schools are beginning to change in significant ways; many more need to follow their lead. Despite the chaos created by fiscal mismanagement, the major elements of the Chicago School Reform Act have been successfully established. Local School Councils are functioning in almost every Chicago school. School Improvement Plans are being debated by nearly 12,000 people each month of the school year. In some schools, important efforts are under way to change the way in which instruction is carried on in regular classrooms. In other schools, important practical problems have been addressed and new pro-grams have been added to meet the special needs of some students. In some schools, little of significance has occurred. If student achieve-ment is to improve measurably, the Chicago Panel urged more schools to turn their attention to changing the ways in which regular students and teachers interact in the majority of the city's classrooms.

The Movement Toward
Decentralization in a Time of Sea Change

In Chicago, school reform is being advanced by shifting the locus of power away from a central bureaucracy and governing board to democratically elected councils at the local school level. Contrary to the professionalization forms of shared decision making, which primarily change the relationships of principals and teachers in exercising the power already located at the school site, significant powers have been devolved to the schools and nonprofessionals predominate in the membership of the new governing councils. These councils have real power over real resources and real jobs. Whether they will be successful in improving the achievement of the real students attending the city's schools is yet to be seen. What are the issues raised by the adoption of such a radical reform plan and why has such a concerted centralizing countermovement toward systemic alignment emerged in opposition?

Tom Carroll (1992) has very helpfully described the development of public schooling in the United States. He suggests the first American public schools were developed in small agrarian towns with homogeneous populations. Such schools were charged to preserve and transmit the fundamental truths on which the republic was founded; the truths were rooted in the heritage of Western civilization. These were the *common schools*, which still dominate the nostalgic images of schools and to which many reformers seek to return. As the United States became the home to many immigrants, a new purpose emerged: to incorporate the great diversity into a common culture. Schools were a *melting pot* in which diverse traditions could be blended into a homogeneous whole. As the nation received these immigrants and became more urbanized, it also industrialized. Communities were diverse and made up of strangers who brought different abilities to their work and social lives. New structures of stratification and specialization were devised for manufacturing and other social pursuits. Schools adopted the factory model to "sort, select, and certify individuals for participation in the larger society" (Carroll, 1992, p. 196). The *factory model* has dominated schooling throughout the twentieth century.

But Carroll, with many others, suggests that, as we move out of the manufacturing century into the *information age*, our models for organizing behavior and learning will change dramatically, and so will our conception of schooling. One way of explaining the unprecedented focus on restructuring public schools during the last two decades of the century is to see this as a period of sea change as the purposes of public education shift to meet the challenges of a new and different century.

Four Arenas of Change in Conceptions of Schools

There are at least four arenas in which major changes in the way we conceptualize public schools are taking place. These arenas are the battlegrounds on which the forces of decentralization and the forces of a new, more aligned centralization are contesting. They include the locus of control of schools, who will control schools, the functions schools undertake, and the images of what schools are.

Locus of control. Chicago's is the most radical form of school system restructuring that has devolved power and authority away from the local district board of education and its central bureaucracy downward to local schools. As indicated above, earlier efforts at decentralization had been initiated by teacher unions as a vehicle for their members to share managerial power that already existed at the school site; only infrequently did schools gain additional powers under these plans. Only in Chicago was significant new authority vested at the school site. Central authority was reduced to goal setting, monitoring, and contract negotiations. While central administrators fought a bitter delaying action, even purchasing and staff development resources were vested in the schools under the Systemwide Goals and Objectives reform plan adopted for 1992-1993. With control shifted to more than 540 local schools, great diversity can be expected to emerge, as school councils are charged to meet the specific needs of their enrolled students. With greater diversity, however, it can also be anticipated that a more open enrollment procedure will be required to allow students to escape program emphases that are not congenial to already enrolled students. Thus such decentralization is more attuned to community control than to systemic alignment.

But, at the same time, centralization at the national level has been gaining wide attention. For the first time, national goals for education have been adopted by a president and governors of the various states. The secretary of education has proposed a model school curriculum. Commissions have been established to develop common standards for teacher certification and national achievement assessments. Legislation was introduced in Congress to force equalization of funding among school districts within individual states. Reputable scholars are questioning the rationale for continued existence of local boards of education. Thus authority is moving away from the local school district in two directions: downward to the school level and upward, first to the state in added regulations introduced as part of statewide reform packages in the middle 1980s and more recently to the federal level through goals, curricula, certification standards, and testing.

Predictably, school district officials have reacted negatively to both of these efforts to usurp their previous authority. They have also reacted defensively to efforts to move control *outside* the system of public schools. Although there has been a tradition of home schooling in the United States that dates to pioneer days, recent publicity about the practice has led to regional superintendents attempting to use truancy laws to force children being home-schooled to return to the structured school monopoly. In one sense an extension of home-school privileges, which are now guaranteed by law in many states, vouchers have received even more intense opposition from public school advocates. Fearing that vouchers will primarily divert scarce resources from public schools to private ones, public school leaders are also leery of any related developments, such as greater enrollment choice among public schools or the new for-profit Edison Project schools being developed by Whittle Communications. Thus public school officials have resisted every effort to remove students from their control and give control over students' futures to their parents, with one major exception. The irony is that, while some regional and state officials try to compel home-schooled children back into structured schools, inner-city and rural school officials have done little to overcome or have even welcomed and encouraged the absence of chronic truants and other troublesome students from their schools. From this evidence, it would appear that school officials are more worried about losing their monopoly over the more affluent middle-class students than they are about exercising their responsibility toward lower-class inner-city and rural children.

Who controls? As Elmore (1991; see p. 68) has suggested, there are at least three competing theories about who should control what happens at local schools. One group of scholars and activists have focused on greater regulatory control. Thus the 1980s saw the development of wider systems of accountability with the development of statewide report cards on each school and the Department of Education's infamous "wall chart" comparing public educational statistics on the 50 states. The efforts of the teachers unions and the Carnegie Task Force on Teaching have emphasized professional control at the school site, with teachers sharing in the managerial decision making. The Chicago reform effort, the various enrollment choice programs, and home schooling have all emphasized parent control of schools and schooling. All of these movements have sought to wrest control away from school district bureaucrats, board members, and the political patrons related to those districts.

During the nineteenth-century era of the common school, schools were reflections of their communities. They embodied the community's cultural values and mores, which were generally quite homogeneous. As communities became diverse and the country urbanized, the nation's more than 40,000 school districts were consolidated into the 15,000 that now exist. A century ago, there were 51 different systems controlling the public schools that now all are governed by the Chicago Board of Education (Herrick, 1984). But these 15,000 districts represent very different ways of controlling schools. In some states, school districts are still quite synonymous with local communities; in Illinois, exclusive of Chicago, the average size of the state's 970 school districts is 1,350 students. Other states, particularly in the South, organize districts along county lines and these districts share the bureaucratic structures of the nation's large urban systems. As these bureaucratic school systems developed, control was removed from local communities and vested in the hands of "rational managers." Education was to be removed from the hands of the politicians and given its own professionalized leadership. Schools were also to be removed from the parochial concerns of communities dominated by divisive ethnic traditions so that their children could be blended together, could be Americanized. This was an integrationist philosophy focused on ethnic and national background rather than race. It was the failure of that philosophy in the face of racist intransigence that led racial and ethnic minority leaders to reject the melting pot imagery of America in favor of the images of a tapestry of diversity that is interconnected and whose beauty depends upon the interwoven connections. Not surprisingly, leaders of diverse communities had little confidence that centrist leaders could move beyond the melting pot images to foster diversity. Thus a movement toward community control began to reemerge in the late 1960s, highlighted by the events in Ocean Hill-Brownsville, which led to the establishment of 32 community boards of education to govern New York City's elementary schools (Rogers, 1968).

But a second trend was occurring at the same time. With huge post-World War II federal subsidies for road construction, commuter rail development, and sewer and water extensions, suburbs were established and the white middle class abandoned the central cities. Gradually the political and administrative leadership of cities and their governmental services were assumed by minorities. Many thought that, when minorities controlled these governments, including school boards, minority city residents and students would be better served. But conditions in cities and in city schools did not markedly improve as minority bureaucrats found they faced even tougher problems to solve than had faced their white bureaucratic predecessors. And like bureaucrats everywhere, of whatever color, these bureaucrats were no more willing to tolerate diversity than those who had gone before them.

Thus a new dimension of the "who controls?" controversy emerged. It was one thing for progressive local leaders to oppose the oppressive regimes that resisted desegregation of urban schools and instead funneled resources into schools still mostly attended by whites. But what was one to do when the white leaders were finally replaced and the oppression was not relaxed? What was one to do if the first black superintendent in a city sought to "teacher-proof" the curriculum and thereby reduced schooling to filling in blanks on a work sheet under the guise of a "mastery learning" abomination that was repudiated by the guru in that field? What was one to do if the second black superintendent used the same "blaming the victim" rhetoric to excuse ridiculously low student achievement levels as had his embattled racist predecessors? What was one to do if the newly emerging black political and civic leadership articulated a "service" philosophy that also turned inner-city children into "victims," victims needing the paid professional services of the newly emerging black middle class?

This social service approach disempowered students just as certainly as had the "blaming the victim" rhetoric. Centrists, whether malevolent seekers of political and economic privilege, or benevolent providers of presumed student needs, were both incapable of meeting the diverse needs of a student body composed of at least four major racial/ethnic groups and multiple economic levels.

Decentralization, whether in schools or public housing, was a strategy for wrenching power away from those who would impose singular solutions, whether of the political Right or Left, on diverse and divergent needs of students. Community control was now being offered to inner-city neighborhoods similar to that which had continued unabated in suburban and rural communities throughout the twentieth century in states like Illinois.[4] It is for this reason that the decentralizers look askance, in ways very similar to those of their local bureaucratic antagonists, at proposals to divert resources away from their schools (vouchers) and at proposals for centralizing national goals, curriculum, teacher preparation, and testing.

For many in the inner city and in rural areas, public education could easily be understood as a massive colonial enterprise, with schools as colonial outposts of a foreign and oppressive regime. Schools were regulated by distant state governments not responsive to the concerns and funding needs of inner-city and rural areas; these state governments were controlled by populations quite different than those living in inner-city and rural communities. The schools were staffed with professionals who drove in from outside the community and who left the area as soon as possible after completing their contracted labor. The only local residents granted jobs in these institutions held more menial positions, and even the best of these were reserved through union control for the lower levels of the colonial elite. Even when members of their own kind succeeded, through education in the colonial institutions of higher education, and assumed professional positions in inner-city and rural schools, and later were granted administrative leadership, they frequently expressed the same derision for the native children and excused their inability to improve these schools by asking, "What do you expect us to do when we have so many poor children enrolled in our schools?"[5]

Community control, on the other hand, starts from a different premise: the empowerment of local actors. Instead of focusing on the deficits of the disadvantaged, it emphasizes their capacities, some of which are frequently not valued in the larger cultural society. As Don Moore (1992), one of the architects of the Chicago reform effort, has argued, empowering parents establishes a different agenda than that established when professionals are in uncontested control. By placing parents in control of the decision-making process, school professionals must convince parents that proposals they are making will benefit the school's students, not just its staff. Only by assuming that all children have similar needs can centrists, whether at the national, state, or school district level, claim a similar focus on the needs of students. At the same time, it must be acknowledged that simply establishing parent or community control does not guarantee that local actors will, in fact, put the needs of students foremost. Still, it is self-evident that it is more likely that the needs of these students will be foremost if it is their parents who are making the basic decisions.

One of the questions faced in the Chicago reform effort was how to give parents real financial control. In the past, when new general purpose funds were made available to the school system, they tended to be absorbed in giving current employees higher levels of compensation. Without debating whether these higher levels of compensation are appropriate or not, one other important question is how to make additional assistance available to students under the decision making of parents. The vehicle for doing that in Chicago was the use of a portion of state aid that was generated through the poverty weighting in the state aid formula. Called State Chapter I, these funds were partially targeted to schools prior to reform on the basis of enrolled disadvantaged students but were used in a manner so as to supplant regular local funding efforts. Thus their compensatory effect was being negated. The reform act required these funds to be entirely targeted to schools on the basis of low-income enrollments and to become entirely discretionary over a 5-year phase-in period. The result was that, by the third year of reform, the average elementary school had $350,000 in supplemental funding whose use was entirely at the discretion of Local School Councils dominated by parents.

A related issue in parent-teacher relationships is the class status of each group. While it is tempting to think of teachers as insiders and parents as outsiders, thus having less power, economic class has a powerful effect on relationships between the two groups. The Chicago School Reform Act recognized the potential for professionals to co-opt parents in the school decision-making process (see Malen & Ogawa, 1988). Therefore parents were given a majority of seats on the Local School Councils (LSCs) and school professionals between them were given only three (two teachers and the principal). In inner-city systems, lower-class parents tend to look up to teachers. On Chicago LSCs, parents were "astounded" to realize that teachers were just regular people, with the same faults and blemishes they, themselves, had. On the other hand, more affluent parents frequently look down on teachers as less educated, protected, and impotent (not working at any important work). Affluent parents expect teachers to accommodate their desires for their children. Affluent parents have waged stiff battles (e.g., over censorship) among themselves to gain control over educators. Not infrequently, suburban school superintendents feel inordinately victorious when they are able to fend off the superordinate power of such parents.[6]

To this point, the argument has been conducted as if school control were only in the hands of one group or another and the question was which should have the control. In fact, none of the various advocates argued for sole party control. All see the necessity of involving all stakeholders in the decision-making process. Under the past century of primarily professional control, the role for parent participation has been consciously reduced and very nearly eliminated, to the point where one former state education commissioner could title a book about expanding parent participation, *Beyond the Bake Sale* (Henderson, Marburger, & Ooms, 1986). In this context, it was more likely that parents would be the stakeholders left out of decision making rather than teachers, principals, administrators, or politicians. Thus it is the decentralizers who are most radically changing the answer to the question, "Who should control the public schools?"

Shift in function. As with the efforts to shift control away from local districts in two different directions, there are two quite different proposals about what functions should be carried out in schools. On the one hand, there is an effort to return to the basics as the sole function of schooling. Under several different guises, this effort focuses on the instructional role of schools and suggests that other services provided by schools are either diversionary or simply "waste." In some cases, the "return to the basics" movement is simply a cover for eliminating some portion of the school's program with which a number of parents or citizens disagree, for example, sex education. In other cases, the claim is made that the school's program, both educationally and in terms of other services, has become so broad that there is no central focus; this diverts students from learning what they really need to know and be able to do. For others, such as Bruce Cooper (Cooper, Sarrel, & Tetenbaum, 1990; see also Hess, 1992c, in rebuttal), the issue is defined as waste. Anything not directly contributing to the interaction of teachers and students in direct instruction is a candidate for being labeled waste and for elimination in future school budgets. The controlling imagery behind these related efforts is a return to the "common school" of the nineteenth century.

The trend in the opposite direction is to build on the gradual accretion of services provided at the school site, from federally supported free and reduced-price meal programs, to social work geared to assure the best learning context for students, and to nursing services, which have begun to turn into health clinics. This trend is now being met with efforts to treat families more holistically in terms of all government-provided services. From this perspective, schooling is only one of the many services being provided to families, frequently in a disconnected and overlapping way. Instead of seeing families through the narrow lens of various social service categories (unemployment, housing, welfare, health, nutrition, education), holistic advocates suggest governments should treat families as wholes with interconnected problems. Schools are a logical site for bringing these various services together, because the one government service that reaches nearly every family, particularly those using governmental social services, is public education.

This emphasis on holistic treatment of families is complemented by those who would like to reintegrate schools into efforts at community building. The nineteenth-century common school was frequently at the center of the community. In many twentieth-century suburbs and rural small towns, schools still play that role. But in urban school systems, the schools are frequently closed 5 minutes after the last student leaves and they sit idle until school opens the next morning. The emphasis toward decentralization in urban school systems and bureaucratically organized county systems and toward more extensive use of school facilities also intersects nicely with efforts at revitalizing inner-city and rural communities.

One of the ironies of this moment in school restructuring, with its unprecedented support from the business community in the United States, is that the value of this community control is lost on many business advocates. Instead, they see only the "inefficiency" of the existence of so many small units. They focus their whole effort on reducing that local control by forcing consolidation in the name of saving tax dollars. They do not even consider the loss in effectiveness as control is moved further and further from the home and school site. In this sense, the business community, despite its commitment to decentralized decision making as touted by various business gurus (see Deming, 1982; Peters & Waterman, 1982), is a much closer ally of the centralizers than of the decentralizers.

Shifts in images of schools. As Carroll and others have noted, the primary image underlying the current organization of schools in the United

States is that of the efficient factory. Schools are places where large numbers of young people can be sorted and separated into appropriate batches, be manipulated by different persons with different specializations, and emerge as a product about which the workers can be proud. Unfortunately, in rural and inner-city areas, the product is not measuring up. When that happens, the workers throw up their hands, claim they have done their tasks as they have been trained to do, and blame the raw material as deficient. Less charitable critics and parents in the inner city have claimed that their children are being herded into "factories for failure."

Some reformers have proposed changes that could best be envisioned as efforts to improve the current inefficiencies in these factories. Some suggest narrowing the focus to the "essentials" so that schools may focus upon what is really important and thereby be more successful. Others have sought to correct the deficiencies in the raw materials by emphasizing early childhood education and even infant intervention through parenting training. Still others have simply sought to replace ineffective characteristics of schools with those that have proven to be associated with effective schools. Albert Shanker, the president of the American Federation of Teachers, once called this "goosing up the old structure to make it work a little better." He went on to suggest that more radical change would be required for schools to meet the challenges of the twenty-first century.[7]

Other reformers, sensing the long-awaited demise of the Thorndyckian model of efficient schools, which defeated the individualistic approaches advocated by John Dewey at the beginning of this century, have emphasized developing communities of learners in which each student is given special attention and concern. So Philip Schlechty (1990) can suggest:

> One need not be an admirer of America's corporate leaders ... to understand that in the information-based society, commitment to human development and creating the conditions of freedom, growth, and respect in the workplace are not simply ethical choices. Investing in people is simply good business, for in the information society, knowledge and the ability to use it are power. And those who have knowledge are the employees. (p. 40)

Still, one suspects that the demise of the Thorndyckian factory model of schooling will not be accompanied by a return to early twentieth-century individualism, though the information age will no doubt deal with more individualized instruction than factory model schools were able to provide. The long-awaited triumph of Dewey is still not likely, because the efficiencies developed during the twentieth century will still be required in the new information age. Instead of turning back the clock, it is more likely that a new synthesis will emerge that still sees schools as efficient organizations but focuses much more on individualized instruction and uses far more advanced technology than the books, blackboards, and chalk that are still the staples of many late twentieth-century public schools.

Decentralization or Centralization: How to Move Forward?

Decentralization, shared decision making, and school-based management emerged as central themes in the reform movement of the 1980s. It was a powerful critique of the rigid and stultified institution public schooling has become. It opened the way for an advocacy for individuals and for diversity as an alternative to standardized tests, measures, and curricula. It fit into a movement for community reempowerment.

But even before it had time to demonstrate whether it could or could not be a vehicle for improving student learning, it was challenged by a new centralism, strangely supported by both the political Left and the political Right. Centrists of both the Left and the Right recognize the challenge posed by those who would take authority away from the center and vest it in local control. Their counterattack is founded in the experience of other, smaller, less heterogeneous and more centralized nations. It appeals to the logic of alignment, that if we expect students to meet certain national goals and do well on assessments, whether standardized tests as we now know them or other more sophisticated measures developed in the future, it makes sense to assure that students are studying the materials to be covered in the tests and are taught by professionals who were trained in the same material and in methods of pedagogy appropriate to reaching those goals. This is a powerful position.

The problems to be addressed in the last decade of the twentieth century are whether this new centralism can accommodate the diversity affirmed by the decentralizers and whether the decentralizers can assure that the diversity they value can still be incorporated within a framework adequate to produce graduates capable of living and working within a common social milieu. This latter concern has heightened value in the decade that has seen political decentralization in Europe result in widespread chaos and bloodshed. But the greater question is whether, out of the struggle between the centralizers and the decentralizers, a new image of schooling can emerge that will result in a way of organizing schools appropriate to the emerging information age.

Notes

1. For a more detailed account of similarities and differences in school reform in Great Britain and the United States, see Hess (1992b).
2. While I have provided a brief review of this literature elsewhere (Hess, 1991, pp. 83 ff.), the best summary of this research is still to be found in Purkey and Smith (1983).
3. See Hanson, Morris, and Collins (1992) and Etheridge and Collins (1992) for an analysis of the implementation of these teacher-oriented decentralization efforts in Dade County and Memphis, respectively.
4. It should be noted, however, that neither the rural communities nor the urban ones had the resources to fully exercise local choices. Thus the rise of a new round of equity lawsuits was a means of regaining greater "local control." Ironically, state governments and rich suburban districts regularly used "local control" as a rational goal of states in defending currently existing inequities.
5. Chicago's Superintendent Byrd was frequently quoted to this effect during the period leading up to the enactment of the Chicago School Reform Act.
6. I am grateful to Michelle Fine, whose insights prompted several of these thoughts.
7. These comments were made in a small celebration to launch the Chicago Teachers Union's Quest Center in early 1992. The Quest Center provides staff assistance to competitively selected school faculties undertaking radical school restructuring.

References

Carroll, T. G. (1992). The role of anthropologists in restructuring schools. In G. A. Hess, Jr. (Ed.), *Empowering teachers and parents: School restructuring through the eyes of anthropologists* (pp. 189-206). Westport, CT: Bergin & Garvey.
Cooper, B., Sarrel, R., & Tetenbaum, T. (1990). *Choice, funding, and pupil achievement: How urban school finance affects students—particularly those at risk.* Paper presented to the American Educational Research Association, Boston.
Deming, W. E. (1982). *Quality, productivity, and competitive position.* Cambridge: MIT Press.

Easton, J. (1989). *Teacher attitudes toward school reform*. Chicago: Chicago Panel on Public School Policy and Finance.

Easton, J., Bryk, A., Driscoll, M., Kotsakis, J., Sebring, P., & van der Ploeg, A. (1991). *Charting reform: The teachers' turn*. Chicago: Consortium on Chicago School Research. (Reprinted in *Catalyst*, *3*, September)

Elmore, R. (1979). Backward mapping: Implementation research and policy decisions. *Political Science Quarterly*, *94*, 601-616.

Elmore, R. (1991). Foreword. In G. A. Hess, Jr., *School restructuring, Chicago style*. Newbury Park, CA: Corwin.

Etheridge, C., & Collins, T. (1992). Conflict in restructuring the principal-teacher relationship in Memphis. In G. A. Hess, Jr. (Ed.), *Empowering teachers and parents: School restructuring through the eyes of anthropologists* (pp. 89-102). Westport, CT: Bergin & Garvey.

Hanson, M., Morris, D., & Collins, R. (1992). Empowerment of teachers in Dade County's school-based management pilot. In G. A. Hess, Jr. (Ed.), *Empowering teachers and parents: School restructuring through the eyes of anthropologists* (pp. 71-87). Westport, CT: Bergin & Garvey.

Henderson, A., Marburger, C., & Ooms, T. (1986). *Beyond the bake sale: An educator's guide to working with parents*. Columbia, MD: National Committee for Citizens in Education.

Herrick, M. (1984). *The Chicago schools: A social and political history*. Beverly Hills, CA: Sage.

Hess, G. A., Jr. (1991). *School restructuring, Chicago style*. Newbury Park, CA: Corwin.

Hess, G. A., Jr. (1992a). *School restructuring, Chicago style: A midway report*. Chicago: Chicago Panel on Public School Policy and Finance.

Hess, G. A., Jr. (1992b). Chicago and Britain: Experiments in empowering parents. *Journal of Education Policy*, *7*(2), 155-171.

Hess, G. A., Jr. (1992c). Reorienting a school district's funding priorities by state mandate. *Network News & Views*, *11*(5), 70-80.

Malen, B., & Ogawa, R. (1988). Professional-patron influence on site based governance councils: A confounding case study. *Educational Evaluation and Policy Analysis*, *10*(4), 251-270.

Mann, D. (1978). *Making change happen*. New York: Teachers College Press.

Moore, D. (1992). The case for parent and community involvement. In G. A. Hess, Jr. (Ed.), *Empowering teachers and parents: School restructuring through the eyes of anthropologists* (pp. 71-87). Westport, CT: Bergin & Garvey.

Olson, L. (1992). Fed up with tinkering, reformers now touting "systemic" approach. *Education Week*, *12*(1), 1, 30.

Peters, T., & Waterman, R., Jr. (1982). *In search of excellence: Lessons from America's best-run companies*. New York: Harper & Row.

Purkey, S., & Smith, M. (1983). Effective schools: A review. *The Elementary School Journal*, *81*(1), 426-452.

Rogers, D. (1968). *110 Livingston Street: Politics and bureaucracy in the New York City schools*. New York: Random House.

Schlechty, P. (1990). *Schools for the twenty-first century: Leadership imperatives for educational reform*. San Francisco: Jossey-Bass.

FIVE

Negotiating Reform
PRELIMINARY FINDINGS

JULIA E. KOPPICH

CHARLES TAYLOR KERCHNER

Prior to collective bargaining, teachers did not speak for themselves; they were spoken for. Salaries, hours of employment, class sizes, and assignment and transfer procedures were set by school boards and enforced by administrators. Teachers generally had little influence over, and even less say in, establishing the conditions of their professional employment. "Meet and confer," collective bargaining's precursor, offered teachers only modest opportunity to assert their own interests, to lobby for their own professional and economic concerns.

The advent of industrial-style unionism in the 1960s and 1970s was a watershed event for public education. The bilateral contract, the central feature of collective bargaining, served to define teachers' conditions of employment and governed the principal relationship between union and management. In important ways, collective bargaining gave teachers new economic standing and a voice in shaping their professional lives.

Teachers took their cues from the unionism of industrial America. Unions of educators used patterns of bargaining transported wholesale from the nation's factories. Thus labor relations in many school districts became adversarial. The bantering and bargaining of contract negotiations, if not conducted in an atmosphere of outright hostility, at least was often not distinguished by an abundance of cordiality and good feelings between the parties.

While collective bargaining in education may have begun as the child of industrial unionism, in some quarters it is becoming quite a different adult. The development from meet and confer to full-scale collective bargaining represented one stage in an evolutionary process. The next stage of development—to negotiated policy and professional unionism (Kerchner & Mitchell, 1988)—is now beginning to take shape.

For 2 years, with funding from the Carnegie Corporation and the U.S. Department of Labor, and under the auspices of Claremont Project VISION, we have visited more than a dozen school districts. We have talked with superintendents and union leaders, eavesdropped on teachers' lunchroom conversations, and observed parent, community, and school board meetings. Our goal was to gain an intellectual purchase on the emerging nexus between education reform and the changes under way in school labor relations.

This chapter represents a partial report of our findings.[1] Specifically, we focus here on the issue of negotiating reform—how unions and school districts are reinventing the process of collective bargaining to serve new educational ends.

What we have found, in short, is that, as districts begin to shed the mantle of old-style bargaining and don the garments of a new vision of union-management interaction, collective bargaining is undergoing a profound metamorphosis in form and function. The contract is beginning to assume a new purpose. Bargaining is adopting new styles. Labor-management agreements are taking new forms. The contract itself becomes a flexible rather than a fixed document, greatly expanding the range of topics that are the subject of agreement between labor and management. In addition, the agreement ceases to be "the union's contract," held as a shield against management's willful flaunting of the new set of negotiated rules. Rather, the document becomes a joint powers agreement, in effect enabling legislation for both union and management, and an instrument of education reform.

Highlighting Public Purpose and Professional Responsibility

The collective bargaining agreement is evolving as a principal tool to move districts and unions down a joint path of education reform.

Rochester School Board President Kathy Spoto boldly declares, "The contract is part of our strategic [education reform] plan." Significantly, in the districts we studied, the contract is becoming a statement of purpose and an affirmation of professional responsibility. And there is a new spirit embodied in these agreements. Conventional collectively bargained contracts, negotiated under the tenets of industrial unionism, stress the primacy of individual welfare. The contract promotes the economic, and to a lesser degree the professional, self-interest of *individuals* covered by the agreement. New contracts, while maintaining the basic framework of "wages, hours, and working conditions," place a principal emphasis on the welfare of the institution and the clients that institution serves.

The preamble to the 1990 contract between the Rochester school district and the Rochester Teachers Association emphasizes union-district joint responsibility for fulfilling the educational needs of the school system:

The RTA and the City School District believe that fundamental to education reform is delineating extended expectations for all professional staff. The parties are dedicated to undertake the purposeful change necessary to restructure schools. A commitment to change means a willingness to reconsider and alter traditional relationships, organizational structures, and allocations of personnel, resources, time and space to advance student achievement and enhance the life of the school as a center of learning and productivity. The first professional commitment must be to advance student achievement.

The constitution of Glenview, Illinois, an invention that was substituted for the conventional contract, likewise uses the written labor-management agreement as an instrument of broad-scale change and a statement of mutual obligation and expanded purpose. Glenview's constitution shifts emphasis in the negotiated document from work rules to work goals, which outline professional responsibility for defined standards of practice. The constitution commits the union and the district jointly to the "growth of teaching as a profession" and to "holding ourselves and each other accountable for the educational process."

Collective bargaining and its outcome—the contract—thus become strategic tools in the battery of education reform techniques. Moreover, the contract itself recognizes the symbiotic connection, in a public enterprise, among union-management interaction, continuous school improvement, and obligations to the larger community.

As the contract changes purpose and becomes a statement of educational mission and professional standards of practice, an expanded range of issues come to be encompassed by the document. Here, again, is evidence of change. Where "scope" is a topic of wide debate in conventional education labor relations, it is barely an issue of consequence under the aegis of new-style collective bargaining.

Expanding Scope, Enabling Reform

Teachers and school management, operating under the rules of industrial-style bargaining, often spend considerable time and energy haggling over the topics the parties might "appropriately" raise for discussion. "Management prerogatives" and union historical precedent often come to delineate the parameters of the collective bargaining agreement.

Scope generally remains a fairly constricted affair and, throughout the course of bargaining initial and successor contracts, continues to be an issue of contention. The union maintains, in defense of expanding the scope of bargaining, that the welfare of its members requires broader participation in a wider array of decisions. Administrators, on behalf of the school boards that employ them, counter that broader negotiating scope would force elected officials to relinquish the responsibility and authority placed in their hands by the voters.

Both arguments miss an essential point. What a narrow scope of bargaining primarily succeeds in accomplishing is creating the fiction that, in the public enterprise of education, it is possible to separate the particulars of employee welfare from the substance of the work.

As the purpose of the contract comes to encompass the welfare of the institution, the steam goes out of the argument over scope. Under the umbrella of the new collective bargaining, the range of negotiable issues is, by necessity, greatly expanded. Topics formerly "off limits" now become standard, and accepted, fare for labor-management discussion, and scope disappears as a point of union-management contention. Peer review, career ladders, school-based management, and the development of systems of professional accountability all become subjects of bargaining.

Rochester: Taking the lid off scope. The 109-page contract in Rochester, New York, contains 55 provisions. Some are relatively standard— grievance procedure, work year and teaching hours, and class size. Yet also included between the covers of this negotiated agreement are a series of bold new education initiatives. Among Rochester's more innovative contract provisions are School-Based Planning, the Career in Teaching Program, and Home Base Guidance.

A single sentence in the 1987 contract triggered the movement of significant educational decisions to individual schools: "The Board and the Superintendent and the Association agree to cooperatively participate in the development of school-based planning at each school location." This is one example of Rochester's "agreements to agree." The specifics of site planning were developed by a joint union-management committee convened after the contract was ratified.

Rochester leadership describes school-based planning as moving collective bargaining to the school site. All schools participate. As one district official explained, "Pilot [programs] do not commit the organization." School-based planning teams comprise teachers (who form a majority of the team), administrators, parents, and (in high schools) students. Each school team negotiates with the district a set of targets for student performance and the resources necessary to achieve the school's targets. School-based planning teams are empowered to decide "anything that directly or indirectly relates to instruction and student performance."

Section 55 of Rochester's contract encompasses the Career in Teaching Program, a new compensation structure that reconfigures the teachers' salary schedule and begins to redefine teachers' professional responsibilities. A four-tier career ladder now takes the place of the conventional structure in which teachers typically advance in salary on the basis of years of experience and college credits earned. The goal of the Career in Teaching Program is to make it possible for teachers to assume enhanced professional responsibility and enjoy greater professional discretion without leaving teaching for administration.

The Career in Teaching (CIT) Program is directed by a ten-member panel, five members appointed by the Rochester Teachers Association and five by the superintendent. The chair rotates each year between teachers and administrators. Responsibilities of the CIT panel include delineating roles and responsibilities of each of the four career levels, selecting lead teachers, and redesigning the performance appraisal system for professional teachers.

Like School-Based Planning, Home Base Guidance is another of Rochester's "agreements to agree." Barely referenced in the contract, the details of Home Base Guidance emerged as the program was implemented.

A variation on the old, and in most schools abandoned, homeroom, Home Base Guidance is established to provide each middle school and high school student with a school-based caring adult. Each home-base teacher is assigned approximately 20 students, meets with them for 20 minutes each day, and serves as these students' adviser throughout their time in the school. Home-base teachers maintain ongoing communication with the home, monitor cognitive growth and student behavior, serve as a resource to help students solve academic and social problems, refer students for additional services as appropriate, encourage participation in extracurricular activities, and promote attendance.

To be sure, gaining teachers' acceptance for Home Base Guidance has been difficult. Although instructors generally agree that students have a range of needs beyond the purely academic, many are reluctant to assume the responsibilities entailed in helping to meet these needs. The comment most frequently heard is that "I'm not a social worker." Nonetheless, Home Base Guidance represents an inventive approach in an urban district whose clientele is beset by myriad social problems.

Miami: Home of contract-driven reforms. Miami's contract, in addition to including the standard collectively bargained provisions on salaries, transfers, and the like, also contains a one-page section titled "Professionalization of Teaching/Education." This provision outlines the Professionalization of Teaching Task Force, delineates the School-Based Management/Shared Decision-Making program, lists waivers granted to individual schools, describes the career ladder program and lead teacher designation, outlines the Dade Academy for the Teaching Arts, describes the program for satellite learning centers, and introduces the teaching internship arrangement.

This contract is fat, covering more than 250 pages of text. But it is not designed to be restrictive. There are, for example, no class size maximums. Instead, the contract establishes a procedure by which student enrollment drives the resource allocation formula. The number of daily instructional periods per teacher are specified, but hours of employment and the length of the school day are not specifically delineated. The teacher evaluation system is described, but so, too, is the establishment of a joint labor-management committee to bring evaluation into line with Dade's teacher professionalization initiatives.

The keystone of professionalization is Miami-Dade's boldly conceived School-Based Management/Shared Decision-Making (SBM/SDM) program. School-based management in Miami is intended to focus all of the system's resources, including budgetary authority, at the school level, where the resources can be applied directly to improve student learning. Initiated with a three-phase pilot project of 150 schools, the district now gradually is granting SBM/SDM powers to all schools.

Schools in the workplace, called Satellite Learning Centers, have been developed to serve the children of employees of cooperating companies or groups of businesses or institutions. To participate in this program, a company provides the facilities and overhead costs for the satellite school; the school district provides the teachers, materials, and educational program.

Dade Academy for the Teaching Arts is a joint union-management program designed to "enhance teaching as a profession and to afford a true professional status for teachers." Each year 80 high school teachers, called "externs," are released from their classrooms for 9 weeks of intensive professional development. They participate in seminars focused on current issues and research in mathematics, science, language arts, social studies, exceptional children, and developments in their subject areas.

The process of reform through the contract in Miami also follows the rule of noncoerciveness. Pilot ideas are tested before dissemination becomes widespread. The contract not only allows for and documents change but also sets the course for future change and keeps that course visible to teachers and the public.

Cincinnati, Glenview, and Greece follow suit. Cincinnati's 1985 contract included a number of provisions not typical of a collective bargaining agreement. In a deviation from the conventional set of class size limits, the agreement established a joint union-district Teacher Allocation Committee that redistributes dollars and staff among schools experiencing class size overages. In addition, the contract contained provisions to allow teachers to decide on student promotions, agreement to pilot-test a peer review program, and the right of the union to appoint all teachers participating in joint teacher-administrator committees.

The 1988 contract both improved traditional teacher work rule protections and expanded moves toward professionalization begun in 1985. It established the Career in Teaching program, a career ladder approach patterned after Rochester's, and formalized the Peer Assistance and Appraisal Program. In addition, the 1988 contract required that "nonteaching supervisory duties" be assigned to nonteaching personnel, expanded teacher involvement in recommending teaching assignments for the next school year, mandated significant increases in teacher preparation time, and limited the total number of students secondary teachers could see in a single day to 150.

The constitution in Glenview, Illinois, which replaced its standard contract, serves as a metaphor for change in the district. A legally binding, 3-year collective bargaining agreement, the constitution contains statements about missions and principles rather than enunciation of specific work rules. Conventional day and hour provisions are replaced by general statements of responsibilities. A set of "bylaws" addresses issues of work year calendar, teacher leave and transfer policy, grievance procedure, and compensation and benefits. Many of these items, however, have now become matters of shared district and school-based decision making outside the traditional bargaining structures.

Importantly, Glenview's constitution significantly and expressly expands the professional role of the classroom teacher. The document states, in part:

> The teaching role extends beyond a teacher's most important role, the interaction with students in the classroom. In addition to this role of teaching, a professional teacher in Glenview is expected to engage in activities such as those required for planning for instruction, site-based management activities, District committee work, parent/teacher conferences, and parent/teacher relationships through Curriculum Nights and Open Houses. A professional teacher's role also includes the requirement for continuing self development.

The contract in Greece, New York, addresses three topical areas: (a) increased participation by teachers in professional decision making,

(b) options to increase the flexibility of the contract to accommodate within-district variation, and (c) alterations in teacher roles and compensation. Within each of these sections is a set of fairly general goals and principles that suggest continuing or future reform directions. In addition, a specific section of Greece's contract focuses on forward-looking reform. Called "Commitments for the Future," the section identifies eight issues for future activity that address "the need for continuous improvement."

Pittsburgh and Louisville enlarge the contract outline. Pittsburgh's earliest reform contract launched the Teacher Professionalism Project. (The name was changed in 1988 to the Professionalism and Education Partnership, or PEP.) The agreement pledged mutual union-district effort toward the fulfillment of several objectives: expanded professional decision-making authority for classroom teachers, new roles for teachers in staff development, new career possibilities for teachers, and teacher involvement in the induction and professional socialization of new colleagues.

One particular goal of the 1985 agreement was the establishment of Instructional Cabinets at each school. Instructional Cabinets are the governance structure for Pittsburgh's school-based management system. Comprising teachers and administrators, cabinets review existing instructional policies, programs, plans, and procedures and develop, implement, and evaluate new ones. Cabinets deal with issues of curriculum including testing, curricular emphasis, and student and staffing concerns such as articulation, staff development, and school activities.

The contract in Louisville, Kentucky, seems the most typical, the most aligned with conventional collective bargaining agreements, except for Section K. Section K of the employee rights section of the contract establishes school-based participatory management: "Both Parties to this Agreement endorse participatory management at the school level." This single sentence anchors in the contract teacher participation in expanded professional decision making.

The agreement specifies some of the structures of site management: Two thirds of the employees at the school must vote by secret ballot to participate; deviations from the contract are allowed if approved by vote; and representatives to site-based management committees are to be chosen by employees at the school. The contract also calls for a district-level union-management oversight committee to resolve problems. The remainder of the details are left to the schools to determine. The contract thus provides the outline for change but allows local school sites to fill in the specifics.

The Connection Between
Resources and Reform

Rochester's 1987 collective bargaining agreement gave teachers a $4,500 across-the-board salary increase in the first year of the contract. By year two of the agreement, half of Rochester's teachers would be earning $45,000 per year. In all, Rochester teachers would enjoy a 40% salary increase over the life of the 3-year contract. One of Pittsburgh's early reform contracts boosted top salaries by 25% over 4 years, while starting salaries rose 40% over the same period. Other contracts provided significant, if somewhat less dramatic, salary advancements for teachers. Many education reform commentators were quick to link higher salaries with anticipated better results, a kind of educational quid pro quo—money in exchange for reform.

Union leaders bristle at the notion of this type of "trade-off." Higher salaries do not, they say, represent pay for performance. Rather, improved levels of compensation are simply a recognition that professionals deserve professional salaries.

Union leaders' protestations notwithstanding, it is possible to review emerging compensation structures as a strategic trade, concluding that districts are giving teachers added dollars in exchange for prospective educational change. But there is another way to view the redistribution of resources and the impetus for reform. That is, in the new collective bargaining relationships that are developing, districts and unions *jointly* hold and distribute resources. This is not a case of barter but of mutual distribution of valued resources to programs that move the reform agenda forward.

In Miami, by virtue of agreement between the union and the district, schools are provided with all of the dollars that formerly were housed at the central office. In exchange for fiscal discretion, which may be substantial, amounting to as much as $1 million per school, sites are expected to produce increased student achievement. Site-based management of nearly all salaries lets schools add and delete positions, including teachers, administrators, and classroom aides, according to school-determined needs. Some funds previously allocated through area offices, such as those for security and cafeteria monitors, are now allocated directly to school sites. Dollars saved during the year in the substitute teacher accounts may be converted to discretionary funds. Thus, in Miami, by contractual agreement, the district and union gather fiscal resources formerly held centrally and jointly distribute them to school sites.

In Poway, California, $100,000 in state lottery money was set aside by union-district agreement to implement the Poway Professional Assistance Project, a peer appraisal and support program. Union and management jointly agreed to target this substantial resource, which otherwise might have been applied to the teachers' salary schedule, for the benefit of teachers and teaching in the district rather than for the personal benefit of any employee.

Cincinnati's Teacher Allocation Committee, a joint union-management venture, also distributes resources, in this case for the specific purpose of resolving class size problems. In Cincinnati's case, "resources" include dollars and personnel. The specific resources available to the allocation committee to reduce class sizes at individual schools include (a) a reserve pool of 35 teaching positions, (b) up to 50 instructor assistants who can be placed in classrooms with above-formula enrollments when extra teachers are not available, and (c) direct overload payments made to teachers who do not get relief from extra teachers or instructional assistants. As a significant part of this agreement, the district agrees to leave decisions solely in the hands of this joint labor-management committee. The union agrees not to grieve the committee's decisions.

In reform efforts such as those represented by Miami's School-Based Management/Shared Decision-Making, Poway's peer review program, or Cincinnati's Teacher Allocation Committee, union and management together distribute resources in the name of education reform. Resources are attached to programs rather than to people. And resources take on additive, rather than subtractive, qualities. Management does not hoard dollars and positions. The union does not attempt to attach all fiscal resources to the salary schedule. Rather, the parties together find ways to expand the impact of always-limited resources. In so doing, they endeavor to implement the old maxim, "The whole is greater than the sum of its parts."

Bargaining Becomes More Continuous,
Conflict Decreases

As bargaining changes function, it also changes form. Longer term agreements and continuous union-management meetings become hallmarks of the new collective bargaining. In conventional bargaining, contract negotiations have definable beginning and ending points. The process goes something like this: The union develops a set of contract proposals, management unveils a counterset. Talks begin. Sometimes they proceed smoothly. Often they do not. Ultimately, the contract is "put to bed," and talks are considered concluded until the contract expires and the next round of negotiations is initiated on a successor agreement. Between formal contract negotiations, labor-management discussions of contract-related items usually are confined to grievance hearings, in which the union alleges management violation of the bilateral pact.

Bargaining in the districts that were part of our study is more continuous, with no clear lines between negotiations' beginning and end. In many districts, joint committees conduct much of the ongoing work.

Ongoing committees in the Greece school district, for example, address issues of instructional management, personnel management, resource management, and partnerships between the school district and other organizations. Moreover, a joint committee established by the contract section "Additional Responsibilities and Compensation" establishes a pilot project to change job definitions and compensation structures for middle school and high school teachers.

Pittsburgh also engages in a form of continuous bargaining. Pittsburgh's Steering Committee, key to labor-management reform efforts, meets approximately once a month. (More important, the committee does not meet unless both the superintendent and the union president are available.) The committee develops an annual statement of priorities and supervises the design and implementation of myriad teacher professionalization efforts. The Steering Committee and the 16 subcommittees it has spawned work throughout the year on issues such as school site management. The results of their efforts, in part, become recommendations for subsequent contract provisions.

Ongoing work in Rochester has been undertaken by the Career in Teaching Committee, which not only oversees the career ladder program but is now also engaged in developing the Performance

Appraisal Redesign for Teachers, the new professional accountability system. In Miami, too, much of the contract writing occurs within subcommittees of teachers and administrators long before the onset of actual collective bargaining.

As collective bargaining comes to encompass the full range of the educational enterprise, it becomes clear that, if the new labor relations, like the old, are viewed as a zero-sum game, both union and management emerge as losers. Given the expanded topics of discussion and the need for union-management conversation to be ongoing, the parties cannot afford the luxury of continual conflict. Both union and management in the districts we studied recognize that it is their mutual interest to reach a level of accommodation. Problems are too difficult, and the stakes are too high, to behave otherwise.

Collaboration thus becomes the new labor relations mantra. Collaboration for the union does not mean co-optation or capitulation. The union maintains its organizational identity. But it is able to make its points, assert itself, and gain a professional advantage for its members in ways other than ritual, or actual, saber rattling.

Methods for achieving this new labor-management detente are somewhat different district to district but constitute variations on the same basic theme. Glenview adopted the "strategic bargaining" approach. The intent of strategic bargaining is to place squarely on the table a set of organizational problems that are central to strategic planning in organizations, to focus attention, in other words, on the future of the organization rather than on the self-interests or concerns of individual parties.

Greece engaged in "win-win" bargaining. Developed by the Harvard Negotiation Project, the purpose of this format is to change bargaining from a win-lose proposition to a process of mutual advantage in which each side "wins" through a process of principled compromise. Here, too, negotiations focus on interests rather than on individuals, positions rather than people.

Cincinnati participated in "principled negotiations." A variant on the "win-win" approach, the goal of principled negotiations is a just settlement that enhances the position of both parties.

No matter the particulars of the program, new-style bargaining looks different than industrial-style negotiations. More people are involved in the bargaining process. Committees, subcommittees, and various teams of teachers and administrators develop contract proposals, massage contract language, and bring recommendations to the full bargaining teams. There often is no single spokesperson "at the table." Negotiations take on a more conversational tone. Rules are more informal. Procedures are often ad hoc. Information is shared freely between the parties.

Each of the bargaining processes, whether "win-win," strategic bargaining, or principled negotiations, is designed to dampen the potential for labor relations flare-ups and create a productive working atmosphere. New processes, however, do not imply the end of conflict. Union-management points of disagreement remain. But conflicts tend to be over different issues. Rochester is a case in point. The issue was accountability.

Accountability, the Contract, and Reform

Accountability was the centerpiece of Rochester's 1990 contract. In a clear break from tradition, union and management agreed that the collectively bargained contract would be used as the vehicle for determining who should be accountable to whom and for what, what students should know and be able to do, how student progress appropriately should be measured, and what might be reasonable incentives to promote enhanced student achievement.

To lay a foundation for the intended contractual agreement, the superintendent and union president jointly hosted a series of forums for parents, teachers, and Rochester school administrators. They also jointly appointed a Task Force on Shared Accountability for Improved Student Learning to make recommendations to the district and union bargaining teams. The task force report recommended that achievement be gauged on the basis of "authentic assessment" and further recommended a set of requisite enabling conditions, including smaller school units, reduced class sizes, and extended instructional time for students who require it.

Individual teacher accountability under the proposed new system would be based on a Professional Code of Practice, as per criteria articulated by the National Board for Professional Teaching Standards. A new teacher evaluation system emphasizing peer review and assessment based on structured professional portfolios would be developed, and salary increases could be withheld from teachers required to participate in the "intervention" component (designed for tenured teachers "in trouble") of the Career in Teaching Program.

Tentative agreement on a new union-district contract was reached in September 1990. The pact, which included accountability provisions patterned after the recommendations of the Shared Accountability Task Force, was approved by the school board on a split 4-3 vote. Then it was the teachers' turn.

By the time teachers met to vote, the newspapers had latched onto the proposed accountability system. Professional accountability had been labeled "pay for performance," and the negative rhetoric surrounding controversial, and usually ill-fated, merit pay plans had thus attached itself to the proposed contract. The pact went down to defeat.

Another contract was achieved in January 1991. In this new version of the negotiated agreement, merit pay was gone and in its place appeared a modified, more "user-friendly" professional accountability plan. The Career in Teaching program would incorporate a "remediation" component that would allow "full or partial salary withholding during the period of remediation." Teachers ratified the contract by a 97% margin. But this time, the school board rejected it. Public pressure persuaded the board that the agreement was too expensive. And the topic seemed politically too hot to handle.

Finally in May 1991, nearly a year after the previous contract had expired, a new contract emerged. The accord established a new accountability task force, under the auspices of the Career in Teaching panel. The CIT panel was empowered to withhold raises for teachers rated "unsatisfactory," and accountability was preserved as a central collective bargaining issue.

Of particular significance is that during the extended contract crisis—the periodic acceptance and rejection of proposed agreements by one side and then the other—neither the union nor the district attempted to eliminate accountability as a subject of bargaining. If this had been conventional bargaining, it is likely the union would have whipped accountability from the table at the first sign of trouble. But it did not. Both union and management were committed to a mutually agreeable system of professional accountability as part of Rochester's contract.

Rochester's public contract debate over accountability is also a lesson in political expectations and legitimation in an era of reform.

Once the union and district had declared their intentions to develop a bilateral agreement on standards of performance, neither could back down without risking the ire of the community. Jettisoning accountability would have sent precisely the wrong message to the public, namely, that neither union nor district was as serious about reform as they claimed to be.

From Contracts to Waivers to Trust Agreements

Contracts are pushing the envelope of change. Restrictions on the scope of bargaining are evaporating. Peer review, school-based management, and systems of professional accountability are becoming collectively bargained bilateral agreements. Union-management negotiations are becoming vehicles for working on commonly acknowledged education problems. The purpose of the contract increasingly is coming to focus on the districtwide reform agenda geared around improved student achievement. Enhanced teacher working conditions are becoming means, not ends, of contract talks.

Yet, despite the new flexibility and change of contracts, these documents alone have proven insufficient to expand the opportunity for change within the broad framework of collective bargaining. Thus collectively bargained contracts now are being supplemented by a variety of extracontract pacts in the form of trust agreements and waivers.

Trust Agreements

Trust agreements offer an outside-of-contract option that allows union and management to experiment with new programs and make midcourse corrections along the way. The idea, developed in California, was the subject of a 4-year pilot project involving 12 of the state's school districts (Koppich & Kerchner, 1990).

A trust agreement is a written union-management compact that sits outside the collectively bargained contract. It is designed to deal with issues that arguably are outside the scope of bargaining (particularly important when discussions of scope are likely to eclipse discussions of substance) or for issues that are better handled in an arena less formal than contract negotiations with a desired outcome less rigid than a contract.

Of the districts that were part of this study, two—Poway and Cincinnati—are making use of trust agreements. Poway's trust agreement focuses on peer review. The district and union established a three-tier system of peer assistance, support, and assessment for new teachers, tenured teachers "in trouble," and competent teachers, all of whom must, by state law, be periodically evaluated.

The program was initially supported by $100,000 from the California lottery. Union and management had contractually agreed that this money would be set aside for "joint projects of special value." Negotiating funds to "hold in trust" for new educational programs is one of the driving ideas behind the trust agreement concept, and it is exemplified in Poway's sequestering of lottery money.

Poway's trust agreement had the result of propelling union and management to redefine "good teaching," involving teachers in new professional roles, and speeding more broad-scale labor-management cooperation. In essence, Poway's trust agreement enabled the union and the district to solve a problem—teacher evaluation—about which both sides cared deeply.

Cincinnati's trust agreement exists as an addendum to the union-district contract. The agreement deals with education reform issues raised during the bargaining process, such as teacher recruitment and training (including exploring the concept of a professional practice school), early childhood programs, educational program initiatives (such as participation in the Coalition of Essential Schools), and an expanded range of professional service activities.

While Cincinnati's trust agreement had a relatively smooth birth, it has experienced a rocky infancy. Unlike Poway, in which the union and district found it to their mutual advantage to take seriously the trust agreement process and outcome, in Cincinnati, the superintendent became disengaged from the process. The agreement foundered, at least temporarily, on the shoals of management indifference.

Trust agreements offer the potential to continue to expand the envelope of change by facilitating collective union-management decisions about the structure and function of schools and districts as organizations. But the Cincinnati experience, in particular, also reinforces the notion that both union and management must be committed to the process and its outcomes if trust agreements are to produce positive results.

Contract Waivers

Contract waivers provide new flexibility, allowing teachers to tailor the contract and thus tailor instructional programs, to meet the needs of their particular students. Waivers generally allow deviation from the standard contract to implement school-specific programs. The goal is to keep strict contract language from impeding school-generated, school-specific reforms.

Miami's waivers constitute a specific section of its collectively bargained contract. Waivers in Miami cover topics ranging from evaluation to salary supplements, scheduling meetings beyond the regular workday, altering the grievance procedure, and the assignment of nonteaching duties. Waiver requests, which must be signed by the union steward, school principal, and school-based management chairperson, are subject to approval by the Professionalization of Teaching Task Force, a joint labor-management committee. The policy of the task force is to approve waivers as long as the school is able to show a relationship between the proposed waiver and student outcomes.

In Rochester, waivers are a key element in School-Based Planning. School teams are encouraged to request waivers from the contract, or other district policies and procedures, that constrain the ability to reach student performance targets. The burden of proof is on central office (and, when a contract provision is concerned, on the union) to find a compelling reason *not* to grant the waiver.

Greece, New York, also has a waiver provision in its contract. The district and union have granted waivers in the areas of compensation (changing stipends for summer or extra work), relaxing contractual restrictions on teacher planning time, and hiring part-time personnel.

Waivers send a message of trust to building-level professionals. They say that the union trusts teachers to make intelligent professional decisions that both protect the framework of the contract and expand their own range of professional discretion. Waivers also shift emphasis from the "center" (union and district headquarters) to the schools, focusing attention, resources, and program emphasis on schools and classrooms, and ultimately on student outcomes.

Waivers and trust agreements, then, provide new flexibility and expanded professional discretion for teachers. They are also recognition that challenges over which teachers and administrators struggle are not settled issues but are complex problems to be defined and redefined over the long haul. The answers to questions that surround efforts to make schools more effective for students cannot be memorialized in a contract because the answers remain uncertain. Waivers and trust agreements acknowledge that solutions are works in progress.

Forecasting the Future

Collective bargaining in education slowly is being transformed as contracts assume expanded purposes. Educational decisions rise to the fore as the scope of agreements is enlarged. New bargaining techniques that stress collaboration rather than conflict are being invented and implemented. Extracontract agreements provide added flexibility to union-management pacts.

In sum, collective bargaining, in multiple forms, is becoming an exercise in developing negotiated policy toward the joint operation of school systems. The union, through contracts and other bilateral agreements, legitimates reform, giving the organizational imprimatur to expansive experiments and potentially broad-scale change. And union and management are becoming increasingly sophisticated in distinguishing between structural obstacles to change and politically created barriers to altering district and school operations.

Having said that, it is important to add a caveat. Our study encompassed only a minute fraction of the nation's 15,000 school districts. Most districts continue to negotiate over a relatively narrow package of items. Most continue to function as if the consequences of collective negotiations are separate from the issues of school reform. In many locales, labor-management relations remain tense, if not outright hostile.

To assert that change is under way, to give form and substance to that change, to give it a name, is in large measure to engage in social forecasting. Yet we believe that unions and management will change because they must if they wish to survive. Teacher unions must learn to balance their traditional functions, establishing at least a baseline for constituents' wages, hours, and working conditions—while at the same time evolving new organizational roles. School administrators must reassess and reconfigure their obligations to the public the schools serve and their relationship to the employees who make the system work.

As negotiated policy becomes a more central feature of labor-management relations, unions and management must grapple with a new set of tensions, specifically those tensions that are the natural by-product of reconciling individual interest with institutional and social need. To the extent that they are successful in resolving these tensions, we believe unions and management can be a force for positive school change.

Note

1. A more complete treatment of this research constitutes *A Union of Professionals: Labor Relations and Educational Reform* by Charles Kerchner and Julia Koppich (New York: Teachers College Press, 1993).

References

Kerchner, C. T., & Mitchell, D. E. (1988). *The changing idea of a teachers' union*. New York: Taylor & Francis.

Koppich, J., & Kerchner, C. T. (1990). *Educational policy trust agreements: Connecting labor relations and school reform*. Berkeley: Policy Analysis for California Education.

SIX

Educational Choice
COMPETING MODELS
AND MEANINGS

BRUCE S. COOPER

The decade-long struggle to reform American education seems sud-
denly to hang on a single word: "choice." Just a generation ago, freedom
of choice was the rallying cry of those who clung to their self-proclaimed
right to attend single-race schools. These days, school choice is a crusade
with different meanings—and vastly wider appeal. Americans, it is
argued, should be given a far greater voice in selecting the schools their
children attend. Choice advocates are promoting this option from the
nation's most respected political and academic pulpits, driven by the
conviction that public schools are in deep trouble and that bold, creative
steps are needed to shake up a lethargic education system.

(ERNEST L. BOYER, 1992, p. 1)

A collective sigh of relief was almost palpable on Election Day 1992
from the "education community" in the United States. At last, many
were feeling, the nation had chosen a Democratic president, Bill
Clinton, who would likely stop advocating constantly for *school choice,
marketplace competition, decentralization, deregulation,* and even *privatization.* These terms, often packaged as forms of "restructuring," had
upset many educationists for nearly a decade—since the so-called

107

second wave of reform began with Secretary of Education William J. Bennett's preaching all that New Right "stuff" from the bully pulpit in Washington, D.C. (Clark & Astuto, 1986; Doyle, 1990; Finn, 1986). The fear of many school leaders was that 4 more years of Bush/ Reagan school "choice policies" might turn public schools into holding tanks for those less able, less rich, less wily students while the middle-class pupils "escaped" into private schools and better public magnet schools of choice funded by vouchers, tax credits, or open enrollment programs.

Even before the election, the Carnegie Foundation for the Advancement of Teaching released to the press the results of a study, *School Choice* (1992), but unfortunately not the whole report itself. Newspapers picked up the story, particularly because the "findings" purported to show that school choice "is not evenly available to families" and tends to work best for parents who are "most economically and educationally advantaged" (p. 17). And the results of private school choice, according to the Carnegie report, are disappointing: "Evidence about the effectiveness of private school choice, limited as it is, suggests that such a policy does not improve student achievement or stimulate school renewal" (p. 20). Overall, the report concludes that, at best, the impact of school choice is ambiguous because no clear correlations between choice and school improvement can be found statewide. Hence, months before Clinton assumed the presidency, "choice" came in for a beating. Opponents got their chance to chop at choice in education as unfair, expensive, and probably ineffective— the perfect blast at the Republican regime that had fought so long and hard to increase school choice.

The time seems right to assess the future of choice in education. Will it indeed disappear with Bush's exit from public life? Or is it so much a part of U.S. education that it will continue? This chapter has several findings: (a) "Choice" in education is far more varied and complex than reformers may realize, making its implementation difficult but its elimination unlikely. (b) Choice rests on four different theoretical foundations, each of which contains certain internal inconsistencies for implementing school reform. (c) The four "choice frameworks" can be both mutually supportive—if they can be brought together—or can be in conflict with one another, depending on how these plans are implemented. And (d) the four choice plans can be best aligned by understanding their "logics of action," the basic assumptions about how choice works in that situation. In defining choice in schools, this chapter calls on a wide range of definitions, actors, theories, and practices, which makes the picture more complicated than previously realized. The effect of this intricate set of choice concepts makes the future of choice in schools both more likely and more difficult to assess. Using the micropolitical concept of "logics of action" developed by Bacharach and Mundell (1993), we shall try to show how the concepts of choice fit together and how this newly formulated framework ("logics of action") may be applied to an analysis of an issue as complex as "choice" in education.[1]

The Many Faces of School Choice

Choice in education has had many meanings during the 1980s and early 1990s, as shown in Table 6.1. First, certainly, it included *parental choice*, granting families options as to where and what kinds of schools their children would attend in a kind of local education marketplace. For, as James S. Coleman (1990) explains, "Given the way modern society is organized, with production outside the household, and the future occupations of children different from those of their parents, one of the things parents can do for their children is to select for them the kind of environment which is best" (p. ix). The "marketization" of education sets in motion, according to advocates, a drive for clearer priorities, greater unity, and improved performance through school competition, specifically parents trying to get their children admitted (selected) and teachers and administrators trying to attract these "clients."

Thomas Jones (1990) wrote: "Underlying this shift in school models is a declining faith in the powers of government to improve schools through regulation or resources. There is a growing faith in the salutary effects of market competition among schools" (p. 241). Chester E. Finn, Jr., too, focuses on the effects of market forces on all schools, weak and strong. He explains the net results of consumer choice:

When such decisions [selecting a school] are aggregated across a community, we will find that some schools are attractive to a lot of people, others manifestly less so. In an unconstrained market, this would in time mean that popular schools would grow or replicate themselves while the unpopular schools would shrink and perhaps vanish. I cannot imagine a more suitable fate for a school that nobody would willingly attend than for it to close down. (Finn, 1990, p. 11)

Table 6.1. Theories of Choice in Education: Qualities and Concepts

Concept	Arena	Educational Examples
Public Choice Theory		
Consumer-producer relationships	Markets	Vouchers, magnet school Open enrollment, relocation
Exit options		
Constituent Choice Theory		
Voter choice	Elections	Local School Councils (Chicago)
Voice options		Community School Districts (NYC)
Organizational Choice and Autonomy		
Decentralization, loose coupling	School site	Local management, shared decision making, school site
Devolution of authority		goal setting, local governance of schools
Professional Choice and Autonomy		
Colleagueship, expert knowledge	School and professional groups	Teacher leadership; empower-ment; reconfiguring schools as places for professional control, practices, career ladders, na-tional advanced teacher certifi-cation and rewards

But choice has other faces as well. Thus, second, in public education systems, choice is also exerted by the "public" through the vote, as the electorate determines who will sit on various legislative bodies that set school priorities and policies. In the period of recent reform, *constituent choice* was extended to those closely related to a particular school: the parents, teachers, administrators, and community members. The so-called Chicago experiment is perhaps the best example in the nation of school reform tied to radical democratization of schools through the election of Local School Councils in every public school in the system.

As G. Alfred Hess (1991), one of the architects of the Chicago reform, explains, "On October 11 and 12, 1989, 313,000 persons voted to elect 5,420 members of Local School Councils to begin school-based man-agement at 542 Chicago Public Schools. This election was the climax of a movement to restructure the Chicago public school system radically" (p. 59). School improvement, the main goal of the Chicago restructuring effort, was believed best achieved not through market choice but through direct local democratic rule in each school. This electoral choice, like consumer choice, requires that individuals express their preferences by taking action: enrolling a child in school or casting a ballot for a candidate.

The third form of choice so prevalent during the 1980s and beyond was *organizational choice* created by site-based management and shared decision making. While acting as a voter or consumer is essentially an individual and personal activity, decentralized decision making is based on organizational redesign aimed at breaking the hegemony of the "central office" and empowering the school to take control of its own fate. Here "choice" is dispatched to the school through radical decentralization of control. As then Superintendent Joseph Fernandez (1990) of Miami-Dade County, Florida, public schools discussed about his extension of choice to those in the schools: "Our school system encourages collaborative planning and problem-solving among teachers, administrators, students, parents and other community members through its district-wide restructuring process" (p. 224). This kind of choice is mainly structural, a redesign of where power and authority are vested and of who participates in the process. Hence, while consumer choice is mainly a form of economic activity, and voter initiatives, a political act, school decentralization is a means of organizational change in structure and activity.

And a fourth form of choice, also very prevalent during the last 12 or so years, is *professional choice*. Teachers, primarily, have sought greater discretion in their jobs through new uses of the school schedule, activities, and decision making. "The new call for teacher leadership," Patricia A. Wasley (1991) explained, "is fueled by important and conclusive research conducted over the last 20 years that demonstrates that teachers, too long silent and isolated in classrooms, must take more leadership in the restructuring of public education" (p. 5). Empowering teachers, new teacher professionalism, professional practice schools run by teachers, and new rewards were all part of extending greater choice and discretion to the key education professionals—teachers. Trachtman (1991) found the following in her study of teachers at work: "We found examples of new roles for teachers, greater personal satisfaction, powerful collegial relationships and a pervasive professional glow" (p. 222).

Perspectives on Choice in Education

These four kinds of choice in education present a chance to view reform from several perspectives. Certainly, consumer, voter, organizational, and professional choice in schooling involve very different agents, theories, perspectives, and potential outcomes. Once these forms of discretion, autonomy, and choice-making are related to one another, however, their interdependence becomes more obvious. One should also, however, be alert to the inherent contradictions and conflicts among and within these kinds of choice, adding to the complexity (and confusion) surrounding this controversial subject.

Agency. While consumer choice and electoral choice were mainly the effort of individual decision makers, organizational and professional choice engages groups of teachers and others in determining how schools were to be run. The degree to which these agents of change agree or disagree depends to a great extent on their ideologies, policies, means, and ends. Hence consumers come to education to maximize their own gains and to minimize their losses. Their commitment to education is strong because their children will be affected and for long periods of time (from 1 year to 12 years).

Voters, on the other hand, are making a single decision for which the consequences are distant, long term, and often unknown. It is not uncommon for the electorate to select a public official whom they know little about, hear little from, and hardly follow. It may take years for the consequences of electing one school board, Local School Council, or city council member over others to become obvious. Given that elected leaders hardly make policies alone, the voting behavior of a school board or council is rarely related to school district outcomes. Yet the recent reform era has seen increased demands for greater constituent involvement.

Organizational redesign and choice are the least personal and individual because the school system as an organization can be decentralized without particular individual choice being made. Once shared decision making is created through radical restructuring, however, choice is entrusted to those closest to the students: the elected parents, teachers, administrators, community members, and students.

Professional choice depends on the expertise, needs, and demands of teachers. For teachers (like other professionals) to do their job, they must have the discretion to determine the pedagogy in the classroom, the treatment of students, and the pace of activities. To have control over broader school issues, teachers appear willing and able to assume greater responsibility outside their classrooms. This kind of choice is both individual and group because teachers acting alone can hardly know what fellow professionals want and need. And the very nature of a profession (see Lortie, 1970) assumes peer influence, norm-setting, and control. Choice for teachers, then, is embedded in the professional group to which they belong.

Hence choice becomes complex in education because so many agencies are seeking to exercise their influence to affect the school. Parents with choice can select their children's school and program, thus influencing the course of school events. Voters by definition are influencing personnel and policy through the representational process. Organizational reconstruction may promote choice, as groups and categories of groups work together under the rubrics of "site-based management" and "shared decision making." Short of such formal governance, the structure of organizations may include and preclude certain groups, setting directions. Finally, the essence of professionalism for teachers (and doctors, lawyers, engineers, and architects) is the discretion to handle problems and make decisions based on training, expertise, and experience. Hence choice means something very different to a voter than to a parent, to an organization than to a professional. It is the mixing up of these various agents of choice that appears to confuse observers and policymakers in education.

Varying Theoretical Foundations

The study and practice of choice in education can also be understood in the context of the concepts that underlie them.

- Consumer choice is part of a theory of market behavior based in "public choice theory" drawn from economics.
- Electoral choice and decision making are essentially governmental processes coming from the political science literature.
- Organizational decision making is a phenomenon of theories of organizational design and behavior.
- Professional choice and discretion are based on concepts from the sociology of occupations.

Thus choice in education can be understood simultaneously as economic, political, organizational, and sociological, explaining why reformers sometimes find themselves working at different levels and at cross-purposes. (See Table 6.1.) Each of these theoretical areas contains certain classic contradictions; when these areas of choice analysis are juxtaposed, a set of relations and further contradictions appear.

(1) Theories of education markets and consumer choice. How do parents as rational individuals make decisions under varying market conditions, including the process of "buying" a school: gathering information, visiting potential schools, filing applications, gaining their children's admissions, determining pupils' travel to and from school, and influencing schools once their children are attending (see Weeres & Cooper, 1992)? This application of economic reasoning to the study of school choice-making has stirred considerable interest in school change. In fact, the recent school restructuring movement in the United States has centered on trying to redesign education at the local level to make it more responsive to citizen choice over their agents, the schools. By issuing vouchers, for example, the government could convert the public school monopoly into a competitive marketplace where parents, children, and school come together for the benefit of society. Coleman (1990) writes:

> The way in which schools are organized can strengthen this asset [parental choice and involvement] or weaken it. It is clear that one of the aspects of school organization that does the most to strengthen the asset of parental involvement with their child's upbringing is choice among schools which range widely in values and principles on which they are built. This choice exists when parents are free to choose, not only within the public sector, but also among the diverse array of schools that lie outside the public sector. (p. xviii)

These kinds of consumer choice have long existed for middle-class families who have sufficient interest and income to choose schools outside the public system. Furthermore, Tiebout (1956) found that proliferation of suburban public school jurisdictions within a metropolitan area created conditions conducive to individuals' selecting from a range of local communities of business and residential areas, including the best school for their children. The theory argued that from a range of communities parents selected the ones that best suited their needs; that towns (school districts) fine-tuned their public service offerings (housing, transportation, recreation, and of course schools). Parents would then select the "best" town and school district with the least taxes. Efficient metropolitan markets, according to Tiebout, should produce a distribution of small, homogeneous communities, stratified by median income and qualities of government services (schools are one). Those dissatisfied with their children's schooling could leave (or avoid) a community that failed to meet their needs (Hirschman, 1970).

Consumer choice, while the most dramatic of the "choice reforms" of the recent era, is riddled with inconsistencies mainly based around the limits of markets in allocating values and resources. Many economists are skeptical about such models for the study of school reform because market constructs are too simplistic, presuming that consumers possess rationality, perfect information, and fully competitive markets in which to compete.

In fact, some evidence shows that poor, less educated, and non-English-speaking parents find the transactions costs too high and fail to participate, leaving their children out of the process. Further, in large school districts, the chance that certain parental preferences will be met is slim. Urban districts become so bureaucratic that the "market mechanism" is weakened and the ability of large numbers of parents to "bail out" of the system is small. As Weeres and Cooper (1992) explain:

> The nut of the argument in terms of a political economy of education, was that schools existed in "weak market," for all the reasons explained above: the poor had little access; the system closed out real opportunities to chose since monopolies prefer a captive audience, a standard product, and as little competition as possible to preserve their hegemony. Hence, innovation, reform, and new entrants into the school marketplace (private schools, magnet schools, new schools, home education, proprietary schools) all posed threats to monopolies. (p. 78)

Thus the limits of markets are in part endemic to the economic model, which assumes rationality and accessibility for consumers, and in part related to the realities of powerful public monopolies in education. Given these conditions, consumer choice has limits though higher income people often have recourse to "exit" the system (go private or move residences). Changes in the market, such as a variety of available schools and the distribution of resources (tax deductions, vouchers, open enrollment), might certainly increase mobility—and choice for families in the future.

(2) Theories of electoral choice and school democracy. Another body of theory on choice in education centers on extending governmental representation to citizens closest to schools. Theories of democratic government are as old as ancient Athens and have a revered place in the school reform literature. The Chicago experiment is the shining example of using electoral choice as the engine of reform in one of the nation's most troubled school systems. As Richard Elmore explains in the Foreword to *School Restructuring, Chicago Style* (Hess, 1991), Chicago's reform was, first, a "grass roots political movement," not a top-down policy; second, was a reform "based mainly on the theory that schools can be improved by strengthening democratic control at the school-community level"; and, third, was the most radical, affecting the entire system by creating 542 Local School Councils "with significant decision making authority for schools" (p. vii).

The concept was that local parents, community, teachers, administrators, and students could best influence school personnel and policies by enfranchising them to vote for their own representatives. This kind of Village Democracy has worked in communities since the founding of the nation, so the concept goes. A problem with traditional school democracy, where voters select citywide school board members, is the size of the polity and the competing demands upon the political process. Thus "interest-group liberalism" breaks down, according to critics, "because individuals need to mobilize a larger number of other citizens to make their voice effectively heard" and because well-organized interest groups (i.e., teacher unions, business organizations, homeowners' associations, ethnic groups, and even political parties) make the voice and votes of individual citizens relatively weak and ineffective (see Banfield & Wilson, 1963; Greenstone & Peterson, 1973).

Electoral choice, then, has promise as a form of choice-driven reform. It stands in the mainstream of U.S. school reform, although low voter turnout, the weaknesses of individuals and their ability to mobilize fellow voters, and the disproportionate power of interest groups blunt the use of constituent choice in educational innovation. The Chicago reform may be different because voting and "voicing" are *school site specific* and engage the parents, teachers, administrators, students, and surrounding community of each and every school. But even here, questions arise about the ability of Local School Councils to make real change (given the continued authority of the central office and school board, plus state and federal regulations).

(3) Theories of organizational decentralization and school reform. A third theory of choice in education attempts to explain how radical organizational change can extend choice over policies to those actually charged with implementing them (schoolteachers and administrators). Here we have moved from political science and economics to organizational design (OD) and organizational behavior (OB). These theories trace their roots to Max Weber (1947) and the structural-sociological perspective (Bidwell, 1965) and more recently to the seminal work of Bacharach and Lawler (1980), which examines the politics of organizations. Granting choice to school site actors, through radical decentralization (the "devolution revolution"), is a form of micropolitical behavior in which devices are created in each school to allow choices to be made that improve students' education.

During the 1980s and early 1990s, hundreds of school districts experimented with various forms of school site choice, often called "site-based management," "shared decision making," and "self-managing schools" (Caldwell & Spinks, 1988). All these concepts of choice rest on a two-step process of decentralizing authority to school and sharing that authority among those most affected. As Levine and Eubanks (1992) explain, "Responding to a variety of national and local concerns as well as ideologies stressing possibilities for improving productivity in schools through enhanced employee participation, many school districts initiated empowerment approaches to expand and formalize participation in decision making by teachers and other parties as part of the operation of decentralized site councils" (pp. 61-62).

As Weeres and Cooper (1992) explain, "The institutional design of public education at the local level relies mainly on markets [as discussed above], though school districts are also distinctly 'democratic' settings in which voters express a variety of conflicting preferences and educators attempt to meet those demands through a proliferation of rules, structures, and procedures" (p. 77). The problems with forms of shared choice-making are many, most endemic to asking teachers to take time away from their jobs to help manage schools.

As observers found,

> In addition to issues involving time, energy and technical assis-tance, frequently mentioned constraints include: (a) lack of inter-est of some or many teachers in participating in some types of decisions; (b) absence of school-wide perspectives on many prob-lems and possibilities of change; (c) lack of consensus among faculty but conversely, stifling of initiative when consensus does emerge; (d) reluctance to take responsibility for decisions; and (e) lack of adequate knowledge base and relevant research to inform decision making. (Levine & Eubanks, 1992, p. 65)

(See also, Brown, 1990; Duke et al., 1980; Malen, Ogawa, & Kranz, 1990; Mann, 1990.) Furthermore, many district leaders seem unwilling to relinquish real control to school site choice-makers, a problem only made worse, it seems, by restrictions imposed by local, state, and federal regulations and teachers' contracts.

(4) Theories of professional choice and school reform. The last body of theory is as old as sociology itself: the study of occupations in general and professions in particular. Unlike economic, political, and organ-izational theories of choice, professionalism itself by definition is predicated on the notion that incumbents work under conditions of considerable uncertainty (responding to the urgent, changing needs of groups of children) and will enjoy the necessary trust and auton-omy to make relevant choices. Conley (1991, p. 315) explains that "the professional model assumes that the teacher is a decision maker [exercising choice within an autonomous setting] who creatively adapts knowledge to unique and varied problem situations, expands skills beyond 'textbook knowledge' and continuously refines profes-sional judgment, initiative, and decision making." And as Murphy (1991) argues,

> The redesign of teacher work is based on a number of important premises: One is that teaching is a moral activity and as such should be subject to the control of teachers themselves. A second is that teachers are intellectuals and should, therefore, take the

lead role in discussions about the nature and purposes of schooling. . . . [Third], teaching is a profession and as such should be guided by professional canons rather than by bureaucratic rules and regulations. (p. 28)

Teachers already work in isolated settings where considerable choice and discretion are common. The recent move is to extend this control to the entire school—empowering teachers to make key decisions and to exercise choice as professionals. Sometimes these new opportunities come from new positions as "master teacher," "mentor teacher," "teacher-facilitator," and "lead teachers," and sometimes teachers become part of a decision-making group. Hence choice may be expanded individually or through group and peer participation.

Like consumer, voter, and organizational choice, professional discretion is limited in education by the socialization of teachers (taught to teach and let others govern the school), the structure of the work setting (isolated classrooms), their workday (broken into set, rigid periods), and other demands on them (meeting students, grading papers, holding parent conferences). Furthermore, as Malen and Ogawa (1992, pp. 189-190) explain, school districts are loath to transfer real choice, authority, and resources to teachers in their schools. Thus "plans tend to shift task responsibility but not delegate decision-making authority," and when districts do, they reserve key areas (finance and personnel) at the central office while handing over trivial areas in which teachers already participated (program and curriculum).

Hence we have examined the complexity of school choice in education, based on at least four very different choice perspectives (consumer, voter, organizational, and professional). Further, each of these perspectives, based on economic, democratic, structural, and occupational theories, contains inherent difficulties for real choice-making: Consumers are constrained by the "transaction costs" of making choices, particularly if the parents are poor; voters find their "voice" limited by the size of the district and the power of organized lobbying groups; organizational choice is constrained by the micropolitics of schools that placed greater control in the hands of the bureaucracy; and teachers have limited opportunity to exercise real authority in systems that lock these "professionals" into isolated, routine jobs and keep much of the authority at the central level.

While reforms have been made in all four areas of choice-making (magnet schools for consumers, site-based voting for the school site electorate, organizational decentralization and site-based decision making, and professional empowerment of teachers), until we have a means for bringing these four kinds of choice together, they remain disparate, even competing reforms. In the next section, using Karpik's "logics of action" (1978), we shall attempt to show how these reforms either can cancel one another out or can work in synergy to strengthen the "choice movement" in education.

Logics of Action

Of interest, school choice reforms can be interpreted very differently depending on the perspective of the group involved. As Bacharach and Mundell (1993) point out, it is critical to explain, in Weber's words, the "notion of action—subjective meaning which actors give to their positive and negative decisions" (Aron, 1967, p. 282). That is, in understanding the politics behind school choice perspectives, we need to examine the "logic of action," the decision rules that give shape and meaning to what various groups do. Hence, in trying to fit these four kinds of school choice into some coherent framework, it is essential to understand the logic of each reform and how these belief systems relate to one another. As Bacharach and Mundell (1993) wrote:

> These implicitly assumed logics of action in turn manifest themselves in explicit belief systems which govern behavior in organizations. Specifically, in organizations, logics of action can be manifest as broad ideologies and specific policies. By ideology, we mean broad beliefs which legitimize specific actions and intents. By policies, we mean behaviorally-anchored beliefs which guide and direct specific actions. Whether logics of action are manifested as broad ideologies [such as beliefs in privatization in education] or as specific policies [school decentralization], these belief systems (logics of action) implicitly govern decisions about both goals and means, thus indirectly linking them together. (p. 7)

By analyzing the logics of action of each of the four kinds of educational choice, we can explore the conflicts among these educational choice perspectives and locate areas in which consumer, voter, organizational, and professional choice can be aligned to make real reform possible.

Conflicting Logics of Action

Much has been made of the contradictions within each kind of choice: the limits of choice on the part of consumers of education, the electorate, those operating in organizational structures, and among professionals (teachers). When taken together, these four choice perspectives may be seen as exemplifying conflicting or mutually supporting "logics of action," to use the recently published concept of Bacharach and Mundell (1993), depending on the intent of reformers.

Markets versus democracy. Consumer choice, so the argument goes, presses schools to be responsive and efficient, for fear of losing "customers," while democratic values (logics of action) cause schools to proliferate a bureaucratic structure to meet the varied, competing demands of the "public." In their important book *Politics, Markets, and America's Schools,* Chubb and Moe (1990) have explored the relative advantages of markets versus democracy as the governing force in education. The authors concluded "that the system's familiar arrangements for direct democratic control do indeed impose a distinctive structure on the educational choices of all participants—and that this structure tends to promote organizational characteristics that are ill-suited to the effective performance of American public schools" (1990, p. 20). Democracy, it seems, creates bureaucracy, which in turns stifles the "choices" of educators, while marketization removes school policymaking from the public domain (a private, consumer logic of action) but forces greater choice at the school site.

Hence consumer choice (a market logic of action based on the "invisible hand" of client demands and producer services) and voter choice (based on democratic notions of the logic of representation) may be incompatible because the individual client becomes subject to the generalized "will of the people." And, in reverse, the will of the people leads to laws and policies to be implemented, enforced, and reviewed, which create rules and regulations that can rob schools and their staff of their autonomy.

Hence schools may find themselves caught between two different logics of action: consumers demanding, say, more programs for the gifted while the laws may require "mainstreaming" of all children in heterogeneous groups. To accommodate all these conflicting pressures, public schools generate their own logic of action (centrally controlled and bureaucratic) and thus become rule-bound, procedural, standardized, all of which may prevent schools from responding quickly and easily to demands from their patrons, the parents. Ironically, parents-as-voters may exercise choice that conflicts with their available choices as parents-as-consumers. Thus the logics of action may be running against one another, if Chubb and Moe are to be believed.

Resolving the market (consumer)–democratic (voter) dichotomy. What if the context of school democracy were changed, moving it from the arena of the "system" and placing it at the school? Would this new logic of action resolve some of the tension between consumer and electoral choice? Under such an innovation, parents would select a school, the way investors buy stock in a company, and would then gain access to that school's democratic governance by being able to elect school trustees (as stockholders elect directors). Imagine Chicago with its Local School Councils working around parental choice. This change would disarm the process of bureaucratization that Chubb and Moe fear in democratically run schools.

The process would be simple: Parents would select a school the way they now select a private or magnet school. Once accepted, the family would gain a "vote" in determining who would govern their school— and could even themselves serve on the Local School Council. Democracy, here, would not lead to a bureaucratic structure, with over-regulation and top-down controls. In fact, the logics of action (localist, market oriented) of the electoral and consumer choices would be in sync. This arrangement would solve other problems as well.

Having parents (clients) on the school's governing council eliminates the problem that lone "voters" face. Parents as voters would become an electoral group, voting together to benefit both their own children and others in the school. The logics of action would change, from the parent as consumer to parent as constituent of his or her own school. Self-interest (one logic) would become collective interest (a community logic) around membership in a school. Similarly, the loneliness of the voter (a common problem in the logic of electoral action) is replaced by connectedness with the school and the needs of the group.

Democracy versus professionalism. Electoral choice and professional discretion are not always compatible because again the "will of the people" may not be the best decision in the eyes of professionals. These two logics of action are in conflict over the source of authority (majoritarianism versus training and knowledge), a problem often seen in the relationship between the superintendent of schools (as the professional manager) and the elected school board (representing "the people"). The assumptions behind these two logics are important to understand. Democracy rests on the notion that "ordinary people," elected by their peers, can "represent" the best interests of the group. Professionalism is based on just the opposite reasoning (logic): that laypeople should not be making "expert" decisions but should yield to the expertise of the trained specialists. The differences between these two logics of action (democratic versus professional) are made worse by the tendency for democratic systems such as school districts to create elaborate structures to enforce rules, as Chubb and Moe demonstrated. Hence democracy plus bureaucracy together make professional activity that much more difficult, as the "will of the people" is translated into the tyranny of the bureaucracy.

Further, the building of the "one best system" was an attempt to create a professional system to buffer the teachers and school administrators from the "interference" of the lay community. School governance evolved into a board of laypeople making general policies and the professionals carrying out the day-to-day decisions. The more formalized the system, the more schools became impervious to both democratic influence and professional control. Instead, a "bureaucracy" took over that had its own raison d'être, its own culture, and its own power. Neither the elected school board nor the professionalized teachers could get their way with the "system," leading to demands for radical decentralization, teacher empowerment, and consumer choice.

The school choice movement of recent times confronts all these conditions and has come upon a possible solution. Electoral choice and professional discretion might work best together at the school site, where elected officials can relate directly to school professionals without the intervention of the "system" (bureaucracy, state and federal controls). Thus the logics of action can change from bureaucratic control to localized professional expertise and electoral action. Under local school participation, both electoral choice and professional discretion would be centered at the school, not the whole system. Teachers' choice would then lead the electorate, and the two could work together to handle the problems.

Organizational choice versus professional discretion. Yet a third conflict in logics of action may occur between an organizational perspective and a professional set of choices. The organization—particularly a centralized one—values control, standardization, and accountability while professionals prefer autonomy, mutual support, and discretion. Hence teaching has long been considered something short of a real *profession;* perhaps the term *semiprofession* (Etzioni, 1965; Lortie, 1965) will do. As schools began in the 1980s to decentralize decision making, moving "choice" into the schools, teachers were often vexed if not downright resistant. After years of protecting their prerogatives and professional discretion, shared decision making (an organizational logic of action) threatens to draw them out of their classrooms and to entangle them in the messy business of making decisions and rules to live by.

One effect of the school choice movement of the last 10 or so years was to decentralize choice-making, which often but not always meant the engagement of teachers in helping to set policies. Even shared decision making, however, is not always welcomed by teachers who value their own choices (autonomy logic of action). One can only assume that, as schools become more self-governing and "participation" among teachers in local school decisions becomes more prevalent, then the two logics of action (professionalism and organizational maintenance) will become closer in character and the two groups (teacher-professionals and school managers) will work out an arrangement. Richard Elmore (1991) describes the conditions under which the professional and organizational "logics" are brought together—as under a voucher scheme:

> Schools act as small autonomous firms, operating under the minimum constraints necessary to prevent monopoly or discriminatory practices. Consumers are direct recipients of government funding, which they, in turn, use to purchase education from providers [consumer choice, in our framework]. Staffing, attendance, and content decisions are made by mutual consent among consumers and providers, with no central planning or control, other than the minimum necessary to assure that certain

conditions of consumer access and market structure are met [site-based organizational and professional choice]. (p. 34)

Doyle (1990) argues that "in a public practice option, teachers would be required to set their own standards and establish conditions of work and performance. To make such a system work, an old idea would have to be revised, namely school site budgeting. . . . But in a teacher-run school, expenditure decisions would have to be made by teachers" (p. 112). Whatever the means, professional choice and discretion, like consumer choice and organizational decision making, would work best at the school site, where teachers, administrators, parents, and the school itself could become self-determining.

The Future of Choice in Education

After a decade of government pressure, "choice clearly raises provocative questions and stimulating policy issues," according to Boyd and Walberg (1990, p. x). Yet, as this chapter has shown, choice itself is highly complex, even confusing, because it comes from so many quarters, with so many different meanings, policies, and purposes (logics of action). Consumer choice depends on a marketplace of resources and diversity and the ability to select from among available schools. Voter choice requires an active electoral process, candidates willing to run on the issues, and some assurance that elected officials will attend to education issues. Organizational choice rests on the structure of the system, the level to which choice is devolved to the subunits (schools, programs, staff), and the legitimacy of mechanisms to determine how values, resources, and personnel are used. And professional choice and discretion depend jointly on teachers' willingness to assume control and responsibility and structures to engage professionals in the process.

Each of these types of choice contains certain endemic limitations:

• *Consumer markets suffer from high transaction costs, uninformed consumers, inadequate or limited choices, and the general fear that marketizing education will destroy the dream of universal, free, and equitable "public" education for all (regardless of income, ability, ethnicity, location, interest).*

- *Voter choice has a rather rocky history, with low turnout, inarticulate candidates, and the "politicians' disease" of telling the electorate what they want to hear and doing little after taking office.* Further, the school system has learned well how to isolate and neutralize even the most well-meaning school board member—who is soon socialized into doing what the administration wants.

- *School district organization has made real school-level choice-making difficult.* While top administrators seem willing to discuss sharing their authority, some teachers are finding out the hard way that systems will be systems. Even the legislated decentralization in Chicago ran into the snags in coping with the residual power of the central office that continued to control resources and raise the costs of making policy in the schools.

- *Professional discretion has been slow in coming.* Teachers were so badly treated, so patronized, and so isolated for so long that many cannot trust assurances that their "input" and needs will be considered by a top-heavy system bent on control. Teacher empowerment came mainly through unionization; only recently have teachers begun to act as decision makers on issues closer to their daily work: school mission, programs, curricula, budgets, and personnel, and to forgive and forget, and to trust the authorities.

These forms of choice are not necessarily compatible unless schools are restructured in a major way. As discussed, the logics of action of consumer markets may conflict with democratic choice-making. Market-driven schools may be unfriendly places for teacher professionals. Voters may have trouble influencing teachers who hide in their classrooms and resent the "lay" interference.

The future of education choice, in whatever form, most likely rests with making schools, not districts, the unit of concern and centering most of the choice-making there. Thus, as shown in Figure 6.1, decentralization of control (a change in the logic of organization) would enable voters to have a real voice in how "their school" is run (a localist democratic logic of action), would focus consumer and producer interaction (a market logic), would allow teachers to become part of the decision-making process (a professional logic), and would remove at least some of the conflicts between and within these types of educational choice.

Without anchoring school choice in schools, there seems little hope that choice-making can continue in education. Schools must become the centers for parents as consumers, places where professionals practice their craft, and settings for governance and decision making. To the degree that communities can establish school-centered education, choice has a fighting chance regardless of who is in the White

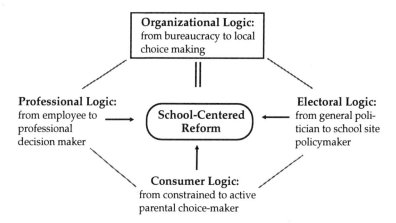

Figure 6.1 New Logics of Action for School Choice

House or the statehouse. Each kind of choice hardly works in isolation or at the district level alone because districtwide elections somehow fail to connect with the needs of many schools. Professionals require a venue for their activity, colleagues with whom they can work, and purview over their immediate work environment. The entire enterprise, then, rests on establishing a school with authority, resources, and, more important, devices for engaging staff, students, parents, and elected officials in joint efforts to harness choice to school improvement.

As Boyd and Walberg (1990) explain,

> Advocates of parental choice believe that it unleashes strong incentives for school improvement. When consumers can "vote with their feet," educators get clear signals about their performance. Without such signals, advocates say, spurs for improvement remain weak, and monopolistic indifference thrives. Choice also benefits educators. When teachers have more voice and choice about what they teach, and the kind of school and program with which they are affiliated, their professionalism, creativity, and commitment to their work are enhanced. Choice for both teachers and students creates communities of shared values, which foster effective schooling. Even those who would impose a state or even a national curriculum can leave the means of organization and teaching to local decision making. (p. x)

But choice in education means different things to different people. To parents, it may mean selecting a school; to teachers, it may signal autonomy and discretion; to the electorate, it may stimulate voting for a favored school board candidate; and for policymakers, it may mean devolving authority for the schools. Whatever the interpretation, these varying views can either pull together or (fall) apart. Centering educational choice-making in schools may help to solve some of these problems: that is, creating a place where the electorate, parents, teachers, and administrators can share their common purposes and exercise their choice for the benefit of all. Schools through choice have a chance of becoming places that young people seek to attend and where real learning can occur.

Chris Wilcox, an 18-year-old high school dropout, for example, testified at a White House workshop that school choice had saved his future. He had been welcomed into an interdistrict (regional) "second chance" magnet choice program in Minnesota, where he succeeded. In his words, "I probably would not have graduated. Choice not only gave me a chance to personalize my education, but it also gave me the confidence that I can make something of myself and control my destiny" (Nathan, 1989, p. 222).

Note

1. Special thanks to Professors Samuel Bacharach and Bryan Mundell for their brilliant paper on "logics of action," which provided the framework for this chapter.

References

Aron, R. (1967). *Main currents in sociological thought* (Vols. 1, 2). New York: Basic Books.
Bacharach, S., & Lawler, E. (1980). *Power and politics in organizations: The social psychology of conflict, coalitions, and bargaining.* San Francisco: Jossey-Bass.
Bacharach, S., & Mundell, B. (1993). Organizational politics in schools: Micro, macro, and logics of action. *Educational Administration Quarterly, 29*(4), 423-452.
Banfield, E., & Wilson, J. (1963). *City politics.* Cambridge, MA: Harvard University Press.
Bidwell, C. (1965). The school as a formal organization. In J. March (Ed.), *The handbook of organizations* (pp. 972-1022). Skokie, IL: Rand McNally.
Boyd, W., & Walberg, H. (1990). *Choice in education: Potential and problems.* Berkeley, CA: McCutchan.

Boyer, E. L. (1992, December). Foreword. In Carnegie Foundation, *School choice*. Princeton, NJ: Carnegie Foundation for the Advancement of Teaching.

Brown, D. (1990). *Decentralization and school-based management*. London: Falmer.

Caldwell, B. J., & Spinks, J. M. (1988). *The self-managing school*. Philadelphia: Falmer.

Carnegie Foundation for the Advancement of Teaching. (1992). *School choice: A special report*. Princeton, NJ: Author.

Chubb, J., & Moe, T. (1990). *Politics, markets, and America's schools*. Washington, DC: Brookings.

Clark, D., & Astuto, T. (1986). *The significance and permanence of changes in federal educational policy, 1981-1988*. Bloomington, IN: UCEA, Policy Studies Center.

Coleman, J. (1990). Preface: Choice, community, and future schools. In W. Clune & J. Witte (Eds.), *Choice and control in America education: Vol. 1. The theory of choice and control in American education* (pp. ix-xxii). New York: Falmer.

Conley, S. (1991). Reforming paper pushers and avoiding free agents: The teacher as a constrained decision maker. In S. B. Bacharach (Ed.), *Educational reform: Making sense of it all* (pp. 313-324). Boston: Allyn & Bacon.

Doyle, D. (1990). Teacher choice: Does it have a future? In W. Boyd & H. Walberg (Eds.), *Choice in education: Potential and problems* (pp. 95-120). Berkeley, CA: McCutchan.

Duke, D., et al. (1980). Teachers and shared decision making: The costs and benefits of involvement. *Educational Administration Quarterly, 16*, 93-106.

Elmore, R. (1991). Foreword. In G. A. Hess, *School restructuring, Chicago style*. Newbury Park, CA: Corwin.

Etzioni, A. (Ed.). (1965). *The semi-professions and their organization*. Glencoe, IL: Free Press.

Fernandez, J. (1990). Dade County public school's blueprints for restructured schools. In W. Clune & J. Witte (Eds.), *Choice and control in American education: Vol. 1. The theory of choice and control in American education* (pp. 223-250). New York: Falmer.

Finn, C., Jr. (1986). Decentralize, deregulate, empower. *Policy Review, 37*, 58-61.

Finn, C., Jr. (1990). Why we need choice. In W. Boyd & H. Walberg (Eds.), *Choice in education: Potential and problems* (pp. 3-20). Berkeley, CA: McCutchan.

Greenstone, J. D., & Peterson, P. (1973). *Race and authority in urban school politics: Community participation and the war on poverty*. New York: Russell Sage.

Hess, G. A. (1991). *School restructuring, Chicago style*. Newbury Park, CA: Corwin.

Hirschman, A. (1970). *Exit, voice, and loyalty*. Cambridge, MA: Harvard University Press.

Jones, T. (1990). The politics of educational choice. In W. Boyd & H. Walberg (Eds.), *Choice in education: Potential and problems* (pp. 241-262). Berkeley, CA: McCutchan.

Karpik, L. (1978). Organizations, institutions, and history. In L. Karpik (Ed.), *Organization and environment: Theory issues and realities* (pp. 15-68). Beverly Hills, CA: Sage.

Levine, D., & Eubanks, E. (1992). Site-based management: Engine for reform or pipe dream? Problems, prospects, pitfalls, and prerequisites for success. In J. Lane & E. Epps (Eds.), *Restructuring the schools: Problems and prospects* (pp. 61-82). San Francisco: McCutchan and the National Society for Studies in Education.

Lortie, D. (1965). The balance of control and autonomy in elementary school teaching. In A. Etzioni (Ed.), *The semi-professions and their organization*. Glencoe, IL: Free Press.

Lortie, D. (1970). *Schoolteacher: A sociological study*. Chicago: University of Chicago Press.

Malen, B., & Ogawa, R. (1992). Site-based management: Disconcerting policy issues, critical policy choices. In J. Lane & E. Epps (Eds.), *Restructuring the schools: Problems and prospects* (pp. 185-206). San Francisco: McCutchan and the National Society for Studies in Education.

Malen, B., Ogawa, R., & Kranz, J. (1990). What do we know about school-based management? In W. Clune & J. Witte (Eds.), *Choice and control in American education* (Vol. 2, pp. 289-342). London: Falmer.

Mann, D. (1990). It's time to trade red tape for accountability in education. *Executive Educator, 12*(1), 26, 28.

Murphy, J. (1991). *Restructuring schools: Capturing and assessing the phenomena.* New York: Teachers College Press.

Nathan, J. (Ed.). (1989). *Public schools by choice: Expanding opportunities for parents, students and teachers.* St. Paul, MN: Institute for Learning and Teaching.

Tiebout, C. (1956). A pure theory of local expenditures. *Journal of Political Economy, 64,* 571-579.

Trachtman, R. (1991). Voices of empowerment: Teachers talk about leadership. In S. Conley & B. Cooper (Eds.), *The school as a work environment: Implications for reform* (pp. 222-235). Boston: Allyn & Bacon.

Wasley, P. (1991). *Teachers who lead: The rhetoric of reform and the realities of practice.* New York: Teachers College Press.

Weber, M. (1947). *The theory of social and economic organizations* (A. Henderson & T. Parsons, Eds. & Trans.). New York: Free Press.

Weeres, J., & Cooper, B. (1992). Public choice perspectives on urban school reform. In J. Cibulka, K. Wong, & R. Reed (Eds.), *The politics of urban education reform* (Yearbook of the Politics of Education Association). New York: Falmer.

SEVEN

Cost Analysis as a Tool for Education Reform

DAVID H. MONK

JENNIFER A. KING

The fiscal implications of reform within education are receiving increasing amounts of attention from policymakers within the United States. Partly, this may stem from a fear that the kinds of education reforms now being explored will generate significant financial obligations that risk thwarting reform initiatives. Concerns have been raised, for example, about the magnitude of costs associated with shifts toward performance-oriented assessments of pupils' higher order cognitive skills ("By All Measures," 1992).

The increased interest in costs may also stem from the growing competition education reformers face for public revenues. The aging of the population, for example, is generating significant new demands for health care services. So long as real economic growth remains

AUTHORS' NOTE: This chapter has been prepared as part of the research of the Finance Center of the Consortium for Policy Research in Education (CPRE), a consortium of the University of Southern California, Rutgers University, Cornell University, Harvard University, Michigan State University, Stanford University, and the University of Wisconsin–Madison. The work was supported by grant R1178G10039 from the U.S. Department of Education, Office of Educational Research and Improvement. The views expressed are those of the authors and are not necessarily shared by USC, CPRE or its partners, or the U.S. Department of Education. We would also like to thank James Cibulka for his assistance in providing access to relevant publications used in this research.

stagnant or sluggish, demands for new social services such as these generate pressures on existing as well as new education programs to realize economies.

It is desirable, in light of this growing concern over cost and related efficiency issues, to take stock of what cost analysis has to offer those concerned with the design, implementation, and study of education policy and school reform. This is the central task of the current chapter. Our goal is to supply an overview of what cost analysis can and cannot contribute. We also seek to provide insight into how cost analysis can be made into a more useful tool for education reformers.

The chapter begins with a comparison of contemporary applications of cost analysis within education and those in related areas of public policy. We use the results of these comparisons to generate a series of trial explanations for the differences across the fields that exist. We next draw on these propositions to help interpret several recent attempts to apply cost analysis to the evaluation of contemporary reforms in education: (a) the reform of education for at-risk students (King, 1993) and (b) the reform of pupil assessment practices (Monk, 1993). These ongoing cost analyses provide good examples of both the strengths and the weaknesses of contemporary cost analysis.

We reach the general conclusion that, while isolated numerical estimates of costs are of interest and can be generated by cost analyses, these are perhaps the least valuable and most problematic of the contributions cost analysis can make to ongoing reform efforts. In particular, we develop the thesis that a good cost analysis can provide the reformer with insight into the origins and implications of costs that need to be dealt with if the reform is to enjoy success in the field. We contend that this more conceptually oriented type of cost analysis is highly promising and ought to be pursued more seriously as part of the growing interest in the fiscal dimensions of reform.

Comparative Analysis

It has been argued that cost analysis is rarely conducted as part of reform evaluations within education (Catterall, 1988; Haller, 1974; Levin, 1991a). We became curious about the degree to which this apparent lack of interest in cost is more characteristic of education compared with other areas of public policy, and we carried out a comparative study to gain some insight into the magnitude of the differences that exist. We sought answers to two questions: (a) What tendency is there for evaluation research in education to be more or less attentive to costs than evaluation research in other areas of public policy? (b) What differences are there in the nature of those cost studies that are conducted in education compared with other areas of public policy?

We first identified two major vehicles researchers use to publish the results of reform evaluations, one focused on education and the other focused on a broader range of public policy domains. We chose two scholarly journals as the sources of our data: *Educational Evaluation and Policy Analysis* (EEPA) for education and the *Journal of Policy Analysis and Management* (JPAM) for the broader areas of public policy. *EEPA* is a major outlet for policy-relevant research in education; the same can be said of *JPAM* in the broader area of public policy. *JPAM*, from time to time, includes analyses of education policy, but as a general rule its focus is much broader.[1] We concentrated our attention on articles published in these two journals during the past 5 years.[2]

A brief explanation of why we relied on the contents of these two journals for our comparison is warranted given that program evaluation is certainly not limited to these two forums. Such studies are frequently conducted at particular sites and not released into the public domain. Our reasons for focusing on these two journals are threefold. First, site-based evaluations are difficult to access comprehensively; it would be a difficult, if not impossible, task to consider all site-based evaluations. It is simply much more realistic to rely on established networks, such as *EEPA* and *JPAM*. Second, scholarly journals such as these exercise a degree of quality control over the studies they include. This offers some measure of validity to the evaluations compared in our analysis. Finally, both *EEPA* and *JPAM* are well-regarded, established journals focusing on policy evaluation. Practically speaking, this offers an accessible and comparable medium through which to examine and compare evaluations in the field of education and those in broader areas of public policy.

A series of coding conventions facilitated the comparisons. Each evaluation study was categorized in one of three ways: 0 = no mention of cost, 1 = a simple or cursory mention of cost but with little or no analysis, and 2 = some extended treatment of one or more aspects of cost. For each evaluation that dealt at some length with cost, we further categorized the nature of the cost treatment. We identified the following types of treatment:

A = This type of study moves beyond counting resources that are easily valued in dollar terms. Typically these studies involve efforts to assign value to resources not traded explicitly in markets. A good example would be the inclusion of the value of young students' time.

B = This type of study considers cost from multiple perspectives and recognizes that different parties bear different aspects of cost.

C = This type examines costs over time. These studies have a longitudinal feature.

D = This type explicitly compares cost to measures of effectiveness. These are studies that include either a cost-effectiveness or cost-benefit feature.

E = This type of study explicitly compares costs with measures of effectiveness across two or more alternative courses of action. Note: Every study coded E is also coded D.

For each evaluation in our sample,[3] we assigned as many letter categories as seemed appropriate given the description of the study. The fact that some studies received multiple letter ratings explains why the sum of the letter columns exceeds the count of evaluations assigned a "2."

The results of our comparison of evaluation studies across the two journals appear in Table 7.1. The results provide a clear answer to our first question. Based on our assessment of published research, cost analysis plays a substantially smaller role in evaluation research within education compared with other areas of public policy. More than 75% of the evaluation studies surveyed within *EEPA* contained no explicit treatment of costs compared with roughly 20% for *JPAM*. As further evidence of the relative lack of attention devoted to cost issues within education, consider the fact that during the past 5 years no fewer than six articles and comments in *JPAM* were devoted to methodological discussions of cost analysis in evaluation; the corresponding number within *EEPA* was one.[4]

The answer to our second question is also reasonably clear. The incidence of different types of treatments is roughly comparable across the two journals: The spread never exceeds 16.2 percentage points and the direction of the inequality is split rather evenly. Moreover, the respective percentages of studies coded "2" (i.e., those that provided some extended treatment of cost) that received two or more letter ratings are quite similar: 62.5% for *EEPA* and 66.7% for *JPAM*.

Table 7.1. Examination of Cost Treatments in Evaluation Studies Within and Outside of Education Policy Analysis

Journal	0	1	2		A	B	C	D	E
Educational Evaluation and Policy Analysis[a]									
Total evaluations (n = 57)	43	6	8		3	5	3	4	2
% of evaluations	75.4	10.5	14.0						
% of evaluations rated 2 (n = 8)					37.5	62.5	37.5	50.0	25.0
Journal of Policy Analysis and Management[b]									
Total evaluation studies (n = 57)	11	28	15		7	7	7	10	2
% of evaluations	20.4	51.9	27.8						
% of evaluations rated 2 (n = 15)					46.7	46.7	46.7	66.7	13.3

NOTE: 0 = little or no mention of cost, 1 = simple or cursory treatment of cost, and 2 = some extended treatment of cost; A = deals with resource not easily measured in dollars, B = considers multiple perspectives on cost, C = has a longitudinal feature, D = compares costs with measures of effectiveness, and E = explicitly compares costs with effectiveness across two or more alternatives.
a. Volumes 10(1) to 14(3).
b. Volumes 7(2) to 11(4).

It therefore appears that the main difference between education and other public policy fields lies in the willingness to conduct or interest in conducting cost analyses in the first place. According to our indicators, differences (across fields) in the nature of those cost studies that are conducted are relatively small.

We discern three possible explanations for the low levels of attention being devoted to cost issues by evaluators of education reforms. First, it may be that the technical properties of education production are less well understood than is the case for the corresponding production processes in other realms of public policy. A number of the *JPAM* studies concern phenomena such as the effects of salt applications on road and automobile surfaces. These are relatively straightforward "production" processes whose technical properties are reasonably well understood. In such cases, the analyst can broaden the inquiry to include consideration of the cost dimension.

In the case of education, in which the technical properties of the production process are not well understood,[5] evaluators may simply assign their highest priority to assessing the effectiveness of the reform in question. Cost is no less relevant, but the thinking may be that not much can be done with the cost dimension until there is evidence suggesting that a reform is having the intended results. Later, we question the wisdom of this view and suggest that insight into the origins of cost can help analysts understand the effectiveness of their reforms in the first place.

Second, it may be that it is easier to obtain measures of costs for areas of public policy that do not involve education phenomena. In other words, education may tend to involve more resources for which it is difficult to assign economic values. Outside education, where the focus is on concerns like the impact of economic activity (e.g., stripmining or oil spills) on the environment or the effects of government policy on welfare dependency, the costs of the activity in question may correspond more directly with the measures of expenditures available within financial records.

If this was the case, however, we would expect to see a relatively heavy emphasis placed on nondollar types of resources by those education evaluators who deal with the cost dimension. And yet, according to Table 7.1, a slightly smaller percentage of the cost studies appearing in *EEPA* dealt with resources not easily measured in terms of dollars than was the case for studies appearing in *JPAM*. Education cost analysts may be responding by concentrating their attention on those resources for which economic values are available. The real effect of the alleged difficulties associated with assigning value to important education resources may be simply to discourage even cursory treatments of cost issues.

Finally, there is the explanation emphasized by Levin (1991a). According to Levin, an important reason for the neglect is the absence of appropriate training for those who carry out evaluations of reform within education. Of course, the alleged neglect of training itself may be explained by the first two reasons for the disinclination of education evaluators to consider costs. Alternatively, it may be that students of educational evaluation are either less capable of understanding or just less interested in conducting cost analyses. Levin holds that valuable cost analysis tools are already available to students of education reform and that new and even more powerful tools are emerging.

Notice how Levin's remedy differs from remedies that are reasonably associated with the first two explanations. If the first two explanations are the real sources of the neglect, providing more conventional training for students of education evaluation will have only marginal effects. The first two explanations suggest that the problem is more deeply rooted and challenge the relevance of conventional cost analysis techniques. The first two explanations also underline the importance of developing the new and more powerful cost analysis tools that Levin anticipates.

We shall return to the question of remedies in the final section of the chapter. For now, we turn to more detailed descriptions of two recent applications of cost analysis to the development of education reform.

Critiques of Ongoing
Cost Analyses Within Education

The Costs of Reforming Education
for At-Risk Students[6]

In response to the growing concern for at-risk[7] students in U.S. schools, several researchers have developed and tested experimental programs designed to better meet the needs of educationally disadvantaged students. Robert Slavin's Success for All schools, Henry Levin's Accelerated Schools, and James Comer's School Development

Program are three comprehensive[8] elementary school-level models that have been receiving attention from those concerned with the educational opportunities for at-risk students.[9]

The three models are fundamentally alike, sharing major goals and advocating similar reforms for schools serving large numbers of at-risk students. And yet they differ in how they approach the problem, in what specific strategies they use, and with whom they charge responsibility for accomplishing reform. These differences have important implications for the relative costs of the three models. Consequently, a comparative cost analysis of the three approaches is of considerable interest to policymakers whose responsibilities include balancing educational improvements for at-risk students with their respective costs.

Unfortunately, serious limits attend the ability of cost analysts to develop cost estimates for these alternative reforms (King, 1993). Most notably, all three reform initiatives involve difficult-to-value resources, costs that extend beyond budgetary concerns. For instance, all three models place additional responsibilities on principals, teachers, parents, and students. These personnel resources might require few, if any, additional out-of-pocket expenditures but are nonetheless very real costs requiring consideration.

While dollar values might be constructed for principal and teacher time by converting salaries into hourly wages, this technique may not be appropriate for valuing parent and student time. Cost analysts typically search for the value of the *best* opportunity forgone when a resource is used in a particular way. In the case of parents and students, the best opportunity need not be the opportunity most easily assigned a dollar value.

For instance, one method of valuing parent time might involve the salary-to-wage conversion discussed above for teachers and principals. Accordingly, the time of highly skilled full-time working parents would be more valued than that of unskilled and unemployed parents. One's wage, however, does not necessarily represent the best opportunity forgone. In particular, this approach has great potential for undervaluing the time of low-wage-earning parents. Consider a parent who earns a very low wage yet is highly skilled and effective at child care. The market value of the latter might be higher than that of the earned wage, so this parent's best forgone opportunity is staying home with his or her young children. An unemployed parent sitting at home is not necessarily a slack or wasted resource. This problem also exists for valuing teacher and principal time, although the difficulties are not as evident at those levels. As the analyst considers volunteer inputs, the problem becomes more of a crippling obstacle.

Even more problematic is the task of valuing the time of young students because there is no market value for unemployable individuals. It stands to reason that the most valuable alternative use of student time involves learning rather than earning opportunities. But the economic value of forgone learning opportunities is hard to quantify and does not necessarily lend itself to dollar metrics.

Such difficult-to-value resources can lead to equivocal and potentially contradictory results. If the analyst simply totals program expenditures and ignores the difficult-to-value resources, Slavin's model is likely to surface as the most costly and Levin's as the least. Yet, depending on how the difficult-to-value costs are handled, any of the three models might arise as the most costly. Such apparently contradictory results are problematic for policymakers.

The Costs of Performance Assessment

The New Standards Project began in 1990 and is a joint effort of numerous states and school districts located throughout the nation[10] to develop radically new approaches to student assessment that are capable of driving fundamental reforms in what students are taught and how schooling organizations function. The project vests considerable faith in the potential for reforms in the assessment of student performance to effect major improvements in education. Much of the project's early work has focused on the development of these new types of student performance assessment. It is an ambitious undertaking by any measure and it draws on private foundation as well as public support provided by its constituents.

Early in the planning for this project, there arose concerns about whether the costs of the performance assessment techniques that were emerging as the centerpiece of the project were sufficiently high to call into serious question the viability of the entire reform. These concerns prompted the commissioning of a cost analysis, the results of which are now available (Monk, 1993).

Policymakers' interests in cost projections are certainly understandable. Compared with conventional student assessment complete with its emphasis on machine scorable multiple choice items, performance assessment is believed to be very resource intensive. Ted Sizer voiced a relevant concern in a public presentation where he asked whether the additional resources required for the new approach to performance assessment would be better spent on school reform in some other way ("By All Measures," 1992, p. S4).

As reasonable as questions about the costs of performance assessment may be from a policymaker's perspective, they are highly problematic for a cost analyst, however. Two problems in particular need to be solved before estimates of the costs of performance assessment can be obtained.

First, there is the matter of timing. Large-scale performance assessment is a new idea and the programmatic details are still being developed. It is difficult to "cost-out" an activity whose characteristics are still being developed. The reformer's reasonable interest in having at least first approximations of the magnitudes of resources that will be required for the reform prompts a reliance on assumptions that can make the analysis highly artificial and potentially misleading.[11]

Second, for the analysis to move beyond an exercise in totaling likely expenditures of resources to a bona fide cost analysis, the analyst must have some inkling about both the benefits associated with the new assessments and the benefits that would be forgone if the old assessment approach were dropped.

The seriousness of the first problem will diminish as the New Standards Project develops. The second problem is much more serious and is not likely to be solved by the further refinement of the New Standards Project. The root cause is ignorance of how educational practices translate into desired outcomes, and this is a reality that is not likely to change in the near term. The analyst finds him- or herself with little to fall back on but assumptions about likely benefits.

In the case of the New Standards Project, the requisite assumptions tend to be quite arbitrary due to the experimental nature of the enterprise. Monk attempted to reduce the arbitrariness of the assumptions he was forced to make by generating cost estimates for alternative sets of assumptions. These alternative sets varied in how optimistic they were about the effectiveness of performance assessment relative to the resources that would be required. While this strategy has some merit and is about all that can be done given the interest in generating numerical estimates of costs, it remains arbitrary in an absolute sense and the analyst is in the unenviable position of having to make assumptions about precisely what it is the analysis is intended to reveal.

Moreover, there is real risk that the numerical estimates generated through such an exercise will take on lives of their own and begin to have unwarranted influence on policymakers' thinking. The problem will only be compounded by the degree to which the "best case" numbers point in a different direction for policy than do the "worst case" numbers. The image of different lobbyists citing the same study as justification for diametrically opposed policy initiatives is not comforting. One likely result will be a further erosion of public confidence in the use of scientific research as a basis for public policy. Policymakers and the public at large are not likely to be very interested in the careful caveats and codicils that are sprinkled throughout the New Standards paper on costs.

Despite the problems and frustrations associated with the cost analysis of both programs for at-risk students and new types of pupil assessment, it does not follow that cost analysis is irrelevant or inherently unhelpful to those seeking to improve educational systems. In the final section of this chapter, we offer our view of where the real strength of cost analysis lies, even in the near term when we lack access to unambiguous measures of key inputs' economic value as well as a deep understanding of education production.

Expanding the Role of Cost Analysis

Conventional cost analysis is facilitated by having access to clear measures of important resources' economic values as well as a good understanding of the technical properties of the relevant production processes. Neither of these conditions holds currently for education, and we have offered examples of the resulting difficulties for the education cost analyst. Does it follow that cost analysis is either irrelevant or inapplicable to education?

Our answer is no, for several reasons. First, we have already seen that some cost analyses have gone forward in education and that while small in number they appear to be similar to the kinds of cost studies that have been conducted in other areas of public policy. Moreover, a number of these education studies are quite well regarded and have been influential in policy debates.[12] Thus, although the requisite conditions may not be met in a strict sense, this does not prevent progress from being made.

Second, we are convinced that there is more to be gained from cost analysis than the "bottom-line" numerical estimates that tend to dominate the conventional applications. We believe it is possible to broaden cost analysis so that it becomes less dependent on fulfilling the requisite conditions but nevertheless remains highly relevant to those pursuing reforms. This broadened approach to cost analysis is capable of generating insight into the origins and programmatic implications of costs. Our underlying presumption is that such insights have considerable value for reformers, particularly at the design stage of reform efforts.

We believe this broadened approach constitutes a valuable complement to the more conventional cost analysis where the focus is on "bottom-line" numerical estimates of costs, and we close with several examples of what this kind of analysis involves. These examples are drawn, once again, from our ongoing analyses of the costs of programming for at-risk students and the costs of large-scale student performance assessment. Our goal is not so much to solve the problems we identified earlier as it is to illustrate the potential for a greater sensitivity to the presence of sometimes quite subtle costs to be helpful to those pursuing reform.

Cost-Based Insights Into the Education of At-Risk Students

Subtle costs. Recall that a major difficulty in conducting a cost analysis of reform programs for at-risk students is the difficulty of identifying and including difficult-to-value costs. All three models rely on additional principal, teacher, parent, and student responsibilities. Given that these program components do not necessarily involve out-of-pocket expenditures, they can be neglected or mishandled within cost analyses. Yet they are essential ingredients for realizing successful reform. Failure to consider them in the planning stages of program implementation can have serious adverse effects on the reform initiative.

In particular, Levin's Accelerated Schools model requires a great deal of parental involvement. If this cost is not recognized and the model is implemented at a site wherein the parental resources are either not available or not productive, the model has little chance of realizing success and might be rejected altogether. Although the broadened cost analysis we advocate here does not promise (or even attempt) to assign magnitudes to these subtle costs, it does draw attention to their existence and attempts to offer insight into their consequences.

Cost variability. To illustrate the potential for variability to exist in the costs of implementation across sites, consider the results of King's (1993) cost analysis of at-risk student programming. She found that Slavin's Success for All model is the most costly in monetary costs and least costly in additional time required of principals, teachers, and parents. In contrast, she found that Levin's Accelerated Schools model is the most demanding of teacher and principal time and least costly in terms of budgetary costs. Finally, she found that Comer's School Development model runs second in both of the above categories and is most demanding in terms of parent time.

It follows that various conditions of the school or community can favor one model over another so that even the model estimated to be most expensive might be the most cost-effective in a particular setting. Thus a context in which both the availability of resources and the probable effectiveness of the various programs can be forecasted is essential for determining which model is the most cost-effective.

To be more specific, implementation of the Slavin model in a community of highly motivated and committed teachers and parents could involve the waste of quite valuable resources. To put the matter in extreme terms, the Slavin model involves hiring costly teacher resources because it fails to recognize the contributions of the available (and perhaps already present by assumption) outside "donated" resources. Under these circumstances, the Levin and Comer models offer distinct efficiency advantages because they draw explicitly on these outside resources, which we are assuming are both available and productive.

The absence of either teacher willingness to use these "outside" resources or parent availability, however, would seriously limit the Levin model's success, because these resources are central to the approach and little or no provision is made to create them or substitute for them when they are not forthcoming. Slavin's model provides those resources explicitly through additional staff positions, and, consequently, in these circumstances, the Slavin model may be preferable on efficiency grounds despite the nominally higher price tag.

Cost-Based Insights Into the Reform
of Pupil Assessment

Subtle costs. One of the hallmarks of performance assessment is a heavy reliance on group tasks as a basis for the appraisal of how much and in what directions a student's capabilities have grown. A typical task is spread over several days and involves dividing students into teams for various types of group activities.

At a superficial level, the costs of administering the task involve the time the students spend pursuing the activities plus the time the teacher might spend preparing for the activities, plus the materials, space, overhead, and so on that might be involved. We call this "superficial" because it overlooks an important reality of classrooms, namely, the "comings and goings" of students and the costs that arise when students are missing from groups.

These "comings and goings" are much less of a cost issue in the context of conventional assessment, although they generate costs here as well. If a student is absent on the day of a conventional standardized test, some sort of makeup arrangement needs to be made, particularly if the assessment is focused on individual-student performance rather than school-level performance. What the student misses while making up the test counts as a relevant and relatively straightforward cost.

In contrast, consider the analogous costs associated with student absences from performance assessment activities. First, the incidence of absences is likely to be larger because the assessment is spread over several days. Second, the cost is arguably higher for the student who is absent because when he or she returns it will be difficult to reconstruct the group that can pick up precisely where that student left off when the absence occurred. Third, there will be costs imposed on those students who were not absent, because the removal of a member of the team can have important implications for how well the team functions.

Moreover, these costs can manifest themselves in many ways. One possibility is that they will translate into inaccurate scores. In other words, the performance of a given student could depend on presumably irrelevant characteristics such as the absence patterns of his or her group-mates during the assessment. Alternatively, they could require additional resources from the school as efforts are made to provide suitable makeup opportunities, perhaps including the use of role-playing students to help reconstruct a group for a returning student.

Finally, consider the magnitude of the complexity that is involved. As the size of the group working collectively on a task increases, the number of possible ways in which the collective structure of the group can be affected by absences increases dramatically.[13] Note also, from the school's perspective, this count of possible ways in which the group structure can be affected must be multiplied by the number of groups and by the number of days during which the task is completed. The product gives some sense of the number of possible "reconstructions" that would be required to cover the "full costs" of this type of assessment.

These are not major or obvious costs that appear within financial records. They are nevertheless highly important features of what will be involved in a large-scale implementation of performance assessment along the lines conceived of by the New Standards Project. A reformer ignores such costs at considerable risk. They are real and need to be addressed. But notice that numerical estimates of their magnitude are really not at issue. Suffice it to say that they are large enough to have impact.

Interdependent costs. At issue here are costs that can be generated as unintended by-products of reform initiatives by actors at decentralized levels of the educational system. An example can clarify the nature of these costs. Suppose that performance assessment reforms proceed and that as a consequence teachers find themselves responsible for making substantive changes in how they conduct instruction. Suppose further that the reformers anticipate a need for further professional development on the part of teachers to accomplish the necessary change and provide the associated programming, thereby incurring certain costs. Finally, suppose that the amount and nature of the professional development made available to the teachers is, in the teachers' view, inadequate to what is being expected. Thus, from the teachers' perspective, whatever costs were incurred to provide their training constitute only a fraction and perhaps only a small fraction of the full costs associated with gaining the expertise necessary to implement the reform.

The reformer may question the validity of the teachers' view on this matter and may genuinely believe that the provided program is more than adequate, but this may not be persuasive, in itself, to these teachers. Of course, this is all speculative, but this kind of disagreement over resource requirements may be quite common. A good example of this sort of disagreement arose in conjunction with the Texas Examination of Current Administrators and Teachers (TECAT). Shepard and Kreitzer (1987) developed cost estimates of the TECAT, which rose dramatically when they included a valuation of the time teachers devoted to preparing for the test. The state's view was that such preparation time was not necessary, but this was not the view of many Texas teachers who sought to protect themselves from an adverse result at the hands of the test.

These costs can be highly relevant for the behavior of key actors in reform efforts. They can manifest themselves in various ways. For example, they can give rise to additional expenditures on professional development activities (beyond what was originally proposed by the reformers). In such a case, they will appear, at least in part, on financial records. Alternatively, and probably more likely, they will manifest themselves either in terms of low responsiveness of the teachers to the reform measure and/or in the form of less than optimal results of students (either because the teachers were correct in their perceived need for additional training or because of a backlash resulting from the failure to take seriously teachers' views on the matter).

In any of these cases, the costs are important and failure to recognize their potential to exist can threaten the integrity of the entire reform effort. Again, the precise magnitude of the costs is not the central concern.

Cost variability. Finally, we note that, just as was the case for the costs of programming for at-risk students, there is important site-level variation that needs to be considered when thinking about costs of performance assessment. To give just a few examples, sites are likely to vary substantially in terms of how much professional development staff will require before they are prepared to implement the reform. This variation will exist across sites as well as within sites. Students will also likely vary (both across sites and within sites) in how much assistance they will require to grasp the changes in how the assessment system functions. A prudent reformer needs to anticipate the presence of this variation and provide for appropriate offsetting measures.

Conclusion

We think there is considerable merit to this alternative, more conceptually oriented type of cost analysis in education. It places less emphasis on generating questionable numerical estimates of costs and more emphasis on understanding the origins of costs. It also recognizes that costs matter and seeks to understand their influence on how people behave in educational settings. As a consequence, it has the potential to generate considerable insight into the functioning of educational production processes and may even give rise to an improved understanding of how resources are transformed into educational outcomes.

In contrast, we have concerns about the mounting pressures on education reformers to generate numerical estimates of costs or costs in relation to some measure of outcome. We view this as a risky endeavor given the uncertainties and ignorance surrounding the technical properties of the education production process as well as the ambiguity surrounding the actual economic value of key educational resources. The numbers that arise out of these exercises can play mischievous roles in policy debates and once released can be difficult to contain.

We must be careful not to overstate our case, however. We do not take the view that attempts to estimate educational costs or cost-benefit or cost-effectiveness ratios are inherently undesirable, even in the short run. They are especially valuable as part of coordinated efforts to discern costs as well as effects of reform initiatives where careful efforts are made to control for extraneous influences (usually by means of an experimental design) and where efforts are made to accumulate and make collective sense of the results being obtained. There are encouraging signs that reform efforts within education and related fields are moving in this direction.[14] We also agree with Henry Levin that more needs to be done to sensitize students of education evaluation to the importance and complexities of cost analysis.

It is clear that cost issues will play a central role in the debates ahead over education policy. We hope this chapter will help make that role constructive and place into proper perspective the meaning of the explicit cost estimates that are likely to be prominently featured in these debates. We also hope the chapter will stimulate interest among those interested in knowing more about the origins and implications of the sometimes quite subtle costs that can influence the behavior of those located within educational systems.

Notes

1. Within our sample of 54 evaluations from *JPAM*, 6 dealt in some fashion with education policy issues. *JPAM* articles cover a wide range of public policy concerns. Consider the following titles: "A Policy Analysis of Hospital Waiting Lists," "The Effect of Routine Income Withholding of Child Support Collection," and "Costs of the 55 MPH Speed Limit: New Estimates and Their Implications."

2. For *EEPA*, the volume numbers are 10(1) to 14(3), inclusive; for *JPAM*, the volume numbers are 7(2) to 11(4), inclusive.

3. We are using the term *evaluation* to include examinations of broad policy initiatives such as attempts to reduce welfare dependency through the use of training programs of various types as well as more specific examinations of the impact of a considerably more narrowly drawn reform. We experimented with maintaining a distinction between these two types of evaluation studies but found that it yielded little additional insight.

4. The six articles or comments published by *JPAM* were Kolb and Scheraga (1990), MacRae and Whittington (1988), Trumbull (1990a, 1990b), Whittington and MacRae (1990), and Zerbe (1991). In contrast, the only corresponding treatment of cost within *EEPA* was Levin (1988).

5. See Hanushek (1986) and Monk (1992).

6. The ideas in this section are drawn heavily from King (1993).

7. The term *at risk* typically refers to students who evidence low academic achievement, retention in grade, poor attendance rates, and high dropout rates. The term is sometimes used to refer to students coming from families with one or more of the following characteristics: low socioeconomic status, minority status, the presence of a single parent or guardian, or a non-English-speaking environment. For more thorough discussions of this student population, see Levin (1989) and Slavin and Madden (1989).

8. The term *comprehensive* refers to the multifaceted nature of the reforms being considered. All three approaches are composed of numerous and diverse educational interventions that are believed by their proponents to contribute collectively to the improvement of education for at-risk students.

9. For overviews of these three models, see Slavin, Madden, and Karweit (1989), Levin (1991b), and Comer (1980, 1988).

10. As of January 1992, there were 16 states and 6 school districts functioning as full partners in the New Standards Project.

11. It is not obvious, however, that this problem is unique to education, unless one wishes to argue that reforms in education are substantially more radical than those found elsewhere.

12. Examples include Barnett (1985, 1991) and Levin, Glass, and Meister (1984).

13. The relevant formula is $_mC_n = m!/n!(m-n)!$, where m = the number of students in the group and n = the number included in each permutation. Because we want all possible combinations, what we seek is the sum: $_mC_m + {_mC_{m-1}} + \ldots + {_mC_1}$.

14. For examples, see Finn and Achilles (1990), Nye, Achilles, Boyd-Zaharia, Fulton, and Wallenhorst (1992), Walker and Vilella-Velez (1992). For discussion of the use of demonstration projects and experimental designs as a means of identifying the education production function, see Monk (1992).

References

Barnett, W. S. (1985). Benefit-cost analysis of the Perry Preschool Program and its policy implications. *Educational Evaluation and Policy Analysis, 7,* 333-342.

Barnett, W. S. (1991). Benefits of compensatory preschool education. *Journal of Human Resources, 27*(2), 279-312.

By all measures: The debate over standards and assessments (Special report). (1992, June 17). *Education Week,* pp. S1-S20.

Catterall, J. S. (1988). *Estimating the costs and benefits of large-scale assessments: Lessons from recent research.* Paper presented at the annual conference of the American Educational Research Association.

Comer, J. P. (1980). *School power.* New York: Free Press.

Comer, J. P. (1988). Educating poor minority children. *Scientific American, 259*(5), 42-48.

Finn, J., & Achilles, C. (1990). Answers and questions about class size: A statewide experiment. *American Educational Research Journal, 27*(3), 557-577.

Haller, E. (1974). Cost analysis for educational program evaluation. In J. Popham (Ed.), *Evaluation in education: Current applications* (pp. 401-450). Berkeley, CA: McCutchan.

Hanushek, E. (1986). The economics of schooling: Production and efficiency in the public schools. *Journal of Economic Literature, 24*(3), 1141-1178.

King, J. (1993). *Meeting the educational needs of at risk students: A cost analysis of three existing models.* Unpublished manuscript, Cornell University, Department of Education.

Kolb, J., & Scheraga, J. (1990). Discounting the benefits and costs of environmental regulations. *Journal of Policy Analysis and Management, 9*(3), 381-390.

Levin, H. (1988). Cost effectiveness and educational policy. *Educational Evaluation and Policy Analysis, 10*(1), 51-69.

Levin, H. (1989). Financing the education of at-risk students. *Educational Evaluation and Policy Analysis, 11*(1), 47-60.

Levin, H. (1991a). Cost-effectiveness at quarter century. In M. McLaughlin & D. C. Phillips (Eds.), *Evaluation and education: At quarter century* (pp. 189-209). Chicago: University of Chicago Press.

Levin, H. (1991b). Accelerated visions. *Accelerated Schools, 1*(3), 2.

Levin, H., Glass, G., & Meister, G. (1984). *Cost-effectiveness of four educational interventions* (Report 84-A11). Stanford, CA: Stanford University, Institute for Research on Educational Finance and Governance.

MacRae, D., & Whittington, D. (1988). Assessing preferences in cost-benefit analysis: Reflections on rural water supply in Haiti. *Journal of Policy Analysis and Management, 7*(2), 246-263.

Monk, D. (1992). Education productivity research: An update and assessment of its role in education finance reform. *Educational Evaluation and Policy Analysis, 14*(4), 307-332.

Monk, D. (1993). *The costs of systematic education reform: Conceptual issues and preliminary estimates.* Final report to the New Standards Project, Cornell University, Department of Education.

Nye, B., Achilles, C., Boyd-Zaharia, J., Fulton, B., & Wallenhorst, M. (1992). *Five years of small class research: Student benefits derived from reduced student/teacher ratios* (American Educational Research Association paper). San Francisco: AERA.

Shepard, L., & Kreitzer, A. (1987). The Texas teacher test. *Educational Researcher, 16*(6), 22-31.

Slavin, R., & Madden, N. (1989). What works for students at risk: A research synthesis. *Educational Leadership, 26*(5), 4-13.

Slavin, R., Madden, N., & Karweit, N. (1989). Effective programs for students at risk: Conclusions for practice and policy. In R. Slavin, N. Karweit, & N. Madden (Eds.), *Effective programs for students at risk.* Needham Heights, MA: Allyn & Bacon.

Trumbull, W. (1990a). Reply to Whittington and MacRae. *Journal of Policy Analysis and Management, 9*(4), 548-550.

Trumbull, W. (1990b). Who has standing in cost-benefit analysis? *Journal of Policy Analysis and Management, 9*(2), 201-218.

Walker, G., & Vilella-Velez, F. (1992). *Anatomy of a demonstration: The Summer Training and Education Program (STEP) from pilot through replication and post-program impacts.* Philadelphia: Public/Private Ventures.

Whittington, D., & MacRae, D., Jr. (1990). Comment: Judgments about who has standing in cost-benefit analysis. *Journal of Policy Analysis and Management, 9*(4), 536-547.

Zerbe, R., Jr. (1991). Comment: Does benefit-cost analysis stand alone? Rights and standing. *Journal of Policy Analysis and Management, 10*(1), 96-105.

PART II

Reform Initiatives Abroad

EIGHT

International School Reform
POLITICAL CONSIDERATIONS

FRANCES C. FOWLER

WILLIAM L. BOYD

DAVID N. PLANK

Not only in France, but in all of Europe, and in the United States, education—especially secondary education—is on trial. The crisis is a general one, and it is a double crisis:

(1) a crisis of educational institutions whose productivity is extremely mediocre, and

(2) a crisis surrounding the act of teaching itself. . . . We are not living through the end of a golden age . . . but a change of historic dimensions which must be understood.

(HAMON AND ROTMAN, 1984, p. 10;
translated from the French by F. Fowler)

Worldwide social, economic, and technological trends have generated pressures (particularly in economic competitiveness and the "legitimation crisis" of the modern welfare state) that few school systems can satisfy (Coombs, 1985; Plank & Adams, 1989). Consequently, the

153

reform and restructuring of school systems is an international phenomenon (Beare & Boyd, in press). Significantly, analysts have noted
that even noncapitalist nations, such as China and the former Soviet
Union, have felt the need to respond to the twin crises of economic
competitiveness and legitimation (Berman, 1989). The crisis also
touches nations of the Third World (Plank, 1990).

To a great extent, this crisis has been shaped and accelerated by the
globalization of national economies. Reich (1991) argues that large
corporations, which once had clear national identities, are increasingly becoming transnational "global webs." In the future, three major
types of jobs will be available: routine production jobs, in-person
service jobs, and symbolic-analytic jobs. Only the jobs in the last
category will be well paid. According to Reich, nations that wish to
maintain or attain a high standard of living will have to capture a high
percentage of the world's symbolic-analytic jobs for their citizens.
Success will depend upon developing a suitable infrastructure, including an appropriate educational system. As a result of all these
factors, fierce economic competition has developed among both developed and less developed nations.

Rapid economic change, competition with other nations, and severe
economic dislocations place additional burdens on the state. Already
overloaded with the conflicting demands of contemporary societies,
the modern state responds by developing policies that have as their
goal not only solving social problems but also bolstering political
legitimacy (Weiler, 1990). The educational system is a popular site for
these legitimating policies for several reasons. Of course, it is close to
the average citizen. Moreover, it prepares young people for the workforce and, less benignly, sorts and selects them for institutions of
higher education and future employers. Thus, as states cope with
economic change and seek to maintain their legitimacy, they tend to
turn to education reform as a way to accomplish both goals simultaneously.

It would be wrong to conclude, however, that education reforms
are identical around the world. Obviously, developed nations are
likely to adopt reform policies that differ considerably from those of
less developed countries. Even within each group of nations, significant differences appear. The English-speaking countries, for example,
have adopted market-oriented reforms to a greater extent than have
the developed nations of Western Europe. These differences can be
explained in terms of distinctive political traditions and varying

degrees of economic crisis. Similarly, differences exist among the less developed countries. Some of them are pursuing aggressive policies of economic development, while others are experiencing mass starvation or civil war and must accord education reform a relatively low priority. The countries of Eastern Europe represent a special case. They have highly educated populations, but with the collapse of their Communist regimes and command economies, they may lack the resources to maintain the educational systems that they have inherited.

It is the purpose of this chapter to sketch the broad outlines of the major varieties of education reform. Due to space limitations, this discussion must be rather superficial. Therefore an extensive reference section has been included for readers who wish to explore the subject further.

Education Reform in English-Speaking Countries

Most English-speaking nations have experienced a remarkable transformation since 1980 in how people think about educational policy and the management of schools (Ball, 1990; Clark & Astuto, 1986; Harman, Beare, & Berkeley, 1991; Wirt & Harman, 1986). Despite differences in political traditions and social contexts, striking parallels exist between the reforms adopted in these nations, especially Australia, New Zealand, the United Kingdom, and the United States (Beare & Boyd, in press). This continuity flows partly from responses to similar problems and partly from cross-national networks of influence.

In many countries, but especially in the English-speaking world, reform is driven by a conviction that market-oriented reforms (i.e., measures that would unleash market forces in education, as opposed to education systems run as centrally controlled government monopolies) are the key to more effective and efficient education systems. This conviction represents the triumph of neoconservative critiques of the welfare state. Ironically, this success has been fueled in part by the "contradictions of capitalism" suggested by worldwide economic problems such as recession and "stagflation," beginning with the OPEC oil embargo in the mid-1970s. The parallels between the United States and Britain in this triumphal critique in the education policy domain are striking (see, respectively, Clark & Astuto, 1986, p. 5, and

Ball, 1990, p. 45). Australia and New Zealand experienced similar developments as Thatcherite ideology spread across the English-speaking world (Gordon, 1992).

As an approach to education reform, the market model is particularly appealing because it seems to address both the crisis in economic competitiveness and the "legitimation crisis" of the modern welfare state. On the one hand, advocates claim that market-driven reforms will improve the effectiveness and efficiency of school systems. On the other hand, such reforms reduce state involvement in favor of individual consumer choice and policies shaped by the "invisible hand" of aggregate choices. The main alternative to market approaches is decentralization or devolution. Such governmental restructuring lacks a compelling theory of effectiveness but can be claimed to enhance democracy and participation. It can also be combined with market approaches. Britain's Education Reform Act (ERA) of 1988 exemplifies such a combination, holding "Local Management of Schools" (LMS) to the discipline of market-driven consumer choice, with funds following students as they "vote with their feet."

The parallels between the school reform efforts of the Thatcher and Major governments in Britain and those of the Reagan and Bush governments in the United States are remarkable. Some of these similarities came from conscious transatlantic borrowing of policies. For example, Kenneth Baker made a whirlwind visit to the United States and saw magnet schools there. This led to the idea for the creation of City Technology Colleges. Similarly, the idea of school-business compacts or partnerships, especially the example of the Boston Compact, captured substantial attention in Britain. More recently, aspects of the British Education Reform Act (ERA) of 1988 are echoed in Bush's "America 2000" education strategy, announced in April 1991.

Some highlights of the parallels follow:

• *In both countries, reform efforts are driven and justified by the claim that a better educated workforce is needed to enhance economic competitiveness.*

• *In both countries, reforms are simultaneously increasing both the centralization and the decentralization of school governance.* In both nations, more decision-making authority is being shifted to the school level ("School-Based Management" [SBM] in the United States; "Local Management of Schools" [LMS] in Britain). At the same time, there are new centralizing forces: the National

Curriculum in Britain and the new National Goals in the United States—a surprising development, given the U.S. tradition of local control.

• *Both countries have magnet schools, programs for school choice, and school-business partnerships.* In a strange turn of events, the City Technology Colleges in Britain, which were patterned after U.S. magnet schools, may have been the inspiration for the Bush administration's proposal asking industries to contribute to the funding for its "New American Schools."

• *Similarly, the British Assisted Places scheme has a counterpart in unsuccessful proposals for federal vouchers for disadvantaged urban youngsters to attend private schools.* This idea has been adopted in one U.S. city—Milwaukee.

Although the idea of market-oriented reforms is spreading across the world and crops up now in such unlikely spots as Sweden (long the bastion of the welfare state) and Eastern Europe, the natural habitat of the market model is the United States and Britain. Indeed, something like a race is under way between these nations to see which can outdo the other in the pace of market-oriented education reforms. For example, *The Economist* (1991, March) magazine challenged the United States to "Be bold, Be British" in an editorial extolling the virtues of the more radical and comprehensive reforms in education under way there. In February 1992, the darlings of American market-oriented reform, John Chubb and Terry Moe, published an article in Britain's *Sunday Times Magazine* (largely reprinted in Chubb & Moe, 1992) acknowledging the British lead in radical reforms but arguing that these reforms don't go nearly far enough and that all schools should "opt out" (i.e., be made independent) so Local Education Authorities (LEAs) cannot interfere with them.

Although Chubb and Moe's rhetoric has not been matched by public policies in the United States, former President Bush's "America 2000" strategy to "reinvent the American school" by creating at least 535 "New American Schools" with a combination of public and private funding produced a typically American and to some, bizarre, offshoot. A private corporation, Whittle Communications, launched a plan to build at least 200 *private, for-profit* schools around the country by 1996, a proposal dubbed by some "McSchools"—schools akin to McDonald's hamburger restaurants.

As part of these developments, President Bush shifted his position on the question of parental choice of schools. Initially, he supported a bipartisan consensus that policies should foster parental choice but limit it to public (state) schools. Then, in the "America 2000" plan, he espoused government-subsidized choice among both public and private schools. His administration not only expressed admiration for British school reforms but lauded Australia's direct government funding of nonpublic schools. This approach, which is controversial in Australia, began in the 1950s when the large Catholic school sector desperately needed funds. Government funding of Australian parochial and independent schools has subsidized an exodus from government schools, especially secondary ones, in favor of nonpublic schools, which generally enjoy higher prestige (Boyd, 1987; Hogan, 1984). Indeed, Anderson (1991) concludes that "if present trends continue, public (schools) will become a safety net, to catch the residue of children not catered for by the private sector" (p. 1).

Along with this form of school choice, Australia has pursued devolution and the restructuring of its highly centralized statewide public education systems (Harman et al., 1991). It has made numerous efforts to fundamentally restructure these governance systems with a shift toward school-based management, especially in Victoria. Similarly, as a result of the Picot Report, New Zealand has pursued one of the most decentralized school-based management systems to be found anywhere. Greater choice for parents has also been a goal in New Zealand. Significantly, in both countries, devolution has been used by governments both to reduce the legitimacy problem and to help manage (and mask) resource retrenchment problems (Gordon, 1992). Insofar as greater choice for parents has been achieved in the English-speaking world, it clearly has increased freedom for consumers—but it may do little for efficiency and innovation. To the extent that greater choice increases the number of schools, it may, as in the Netherlands, increase costs without resulting in innovation (Louis & van Velzen, 1990-1991).

Education Reform in
Western Europe

Like the English-speaking countries, the 15 major nations on the western part of the European continent experienced a change in the mid-1970s. At that time the *Wirtschaftswunder* ("economic miracle" in German) or *Les Trente Glorieuses* ("thirty glorious years" in French) ended. Rapid economic expansion gave way to a period of slower growth marked by unemployment and inflation. As in the English-speaking countries, the public tended to blame the school system—especially teachers—for these problems (Neave, 1992). Soon thereafter, European leaders noticed, too, that Japan was capturing an increasing share of their domestic market (Berman, 1989; Neave, 1988). One European response was to accelerate the evolution of the European Economic Community (EEC) toward economic integration and political union. Another was to develop a number of new education policies both to boost government legitimacy and to meet the challenges of economic competition (Bell & Gaffney, 1990). These reforms differ somewhat from the market strategies espoused by English-speaking countries, however.

To understand this difference, one must understand the European perspective. During the last 20 years, the English-speaking countries have experienced relative decline. The United States is no longer the unchallenged leader of the world in standard of living, and on a number of social and economic indicators the English-speaking nations now fall in the bottom half of the developed world (Reich, 1991; Thurow, 1992). In contrast, many of the countries of Western Europe have experienced a relative increase in status. In spite of the economic slowdown, their productivity growth has continued, leading to higher living standards (Thurow, 1992). As for education indicators, the international comparisons that reveal that the United States performs in the poor to average range also reveal that several European countries perform well. Western Europeans are not complacent, but they do believe that they must be doing some things right. Therefore radical changes seem unnecessary to them (Husen, Tuijnman, & Halls, 1992; Neave, 1988).

Moreover, the market reforms espoused by many in the English-speaking world are incompatible with the beliefs of most Western Europeans. Germany, for example, prides itself on its *Sozialmarktwirtschaft* (social market economy), which recognizes both the importance of the market and the need for the state to guarantee its proper functioning (Thurow, 1992). Thus the German educator Detlef Glowka (1989) reacted to the British education reforms described above in this way: "The [British] tendencies towards privatization and commercialization of the education system would encounter massive resistance in the [Federal Republic of Germany] and would not be supported by a political majority. School and vocational training are regarded as social tasks which can only be regulated by the state" (p. 330). Glowka's view is widely held in Western Europe.

Given this reluctance to "unleash market forces," what does education reform in Western Europe look like? The reforms in this part of
the world can be described as a two-part strategy: (a) restoring lost
legitimacy to the educational system and, beyond it, the state and (b)
significantly raising the general population's educational level to
support industrial policies aimed at capturing high-tech and flexible
production industries.

A major component of European education reform strategies has
been to change education so as to regain, maintain, or increase the
legitimacy of the political system. Many European thinkers do not
understand the "educational crisis" as primarily educational. Rather,
they perceive it as a much deeper problem—as an ongoing crisis in
the economic system. Because the political and economic systems are
so intertwined, the economic crisis undercuts the legitimacy of the
state. Much of this crisis in legitimacy is played out in the educational
system because it is close to the people (Berman, 1989; Broadfoot, 1985;
Neave, 1992).

Western European reforms to bolster legitimacy seek to make
schools—and, beyond them, the state itself—appear more efficient
and benign. Reformers have worked to improve efficiency in two
ways. First, they have adopted a wide range of assessment programs
to measure student performance. For example, in 1986 the Netherlands implemented a national assessment program that measures the
academic achievement of 8- and 11-year-olds. In 1989 Sweden administered its first national tests to second and fifth graders. In the 1980s,
Portugal, Spain, and France passed legislation that mandated the
systematic evaluation of educational performance both by upgraded
inspectorates and by external evaluation agencies (Broadfoot, 1985;
Husen et al., 1992; Laderriere, 1990). As Broadfoot (1985) points out,
this increased educational assessment not only provides data for
evaluation, it also provides "new, positive, impersonal, and . . . un-
contestable norms" that mask the school's selection processes behind
a "benign scientism" (p. 284).

European school systems are also trying to use their funds more
efficiently. Recently they have developed new ways to monitor expenditures to understand how they develop over time and how different
categories of expenditures change. In addition, numerous European
systems have adopted differentiated accounting systems and program budgeting (Broadfoot, 1985; Husen et al., 1992). Such reforms at

least create the impression that the government is managing public funds well.

Another type of reform that seems to be aimed primarily at increasing the legitimacy of the school system is the restructuring of teacher training programs. In the last decade, virtually every country in the EEC has changed teacher training in significant ways. Most commonly, the number of years of education required for teachers has been increased. Preparation programs have also been moved into higher status institutions, often into universities. It is hoped that teachers with better credentials will be subject to less public criticism (Neave, 1992).

As suggested above, such reforms as devolution and decentralization are not always designed to "unleash market forces" but to provide opportunities to participate actively in decision making. Over the last decade, many such reforms have surfaced in Western Europe; even the highly centralized French system has undergone some decentralization. These changes are consistent with various forms of *cogestion* (comanagement) and *Mitbestimmung* (codetermination), which are used in the governance structures of many European businesses. Governments seem to hope that, if they involve more citizens in school governance, both the educational system and the state that operates it will seem more benign and participative—and thus more legitimate (Berman, 1989; Weiler, 1990).

A second major strategy of school reform in Western Europe is to raise the educational level of the masses. This strategy must be understood in the broader context of European industrial policies. European countries often pursue long-range programs in which government and business cooperate in targeting and capturing market share in high-tech and flexible production industries. The example with which English speakers are most familiar is probably Airbus Industries, but many others could be mentioned (Thurow, 1992). In Reich's (1991) terms, Europeans are trying to capture more symbolic-analytic work for their citizens. Obviously, a highly educated workforce is an essential part of the infrastructure needed to support such strategies.

One component of this strategy is the provision of high-quality preschool programs for large portions of the population. European preschool enrollments have soared in recent years. France and Belgium are the leaders; more than 90% of all French and Belgian children attend preschool by the age of 3. Preschools serve all segments of the population but are frequently promoted as a way to raise the academic potential of at-risk children (Husen et al., 1992).

Enrollments have also increased rapidly at the upper-secondary level. France has the most ambitious program, with a policy goal of bringing 80% of all young people to the level of the *baccalauréat* (equivalent to the first year of American college) by 2000. Between 1985 and 1989, French upper-secondary enrollments increased by an average of 7.4% *annually.* Other countries have implemented similar, though less ambitious, programs. Increased enrollments tend to be in high-level technical curricula such as computer science and electronics. In Austria, France, Germany, the Netherlands, and Sweden, more than 40% of all secondary and postsecondary students are enrolled in such programs (Husen et al., 1992; Lersch, 1988).

The countries of Western Europe have also carried out several curriculum reforms. Mathematics has always been emphasized in European schools, but in the 1980s this emphasis increased. An even stronger emphasis has been placed on science education and the teaching of technology. For example, computer science has become a standard offering in European high schools. Switzerland and Germany have developed the most impressive computer literacy programs (Husen et al., 1992; Lersch, 1988; Neave, 1992).

Another curriculum reform involves modern languages. European leaders believe that language proficiency is essential both to facilitate European integration and to compete in global markets. The EEC has therefore published several reports encouraging member states to revise their curricula to permit young Europeans to achieve trilingualism by the age of 16. This goal implies adding languages to the elementary curriculum and extending language offerings in vocational schools. Although English, French, and German are the most commonly offered languages, others are increasingly available. These include non-European tongues such as Arabic, Chinese, and Japanese (Husen et al., 1992).

European educational reform, then, can best be understood as a dual strategy. European governments believe that, if they are to compete successfully in the global economy, they must develop high levels of cognitive skills in their populations. At the same time, two decades of economic slowdown have eroded the legitimacy of the state in Europe as elsewhere. Thus European policymakers have also developed educational reforms that will, they hope, restore some of that lost legitimacy.

Education Reform in
Less Developed Countries

Movements for education reform in the less developed countries of Africa, Asia, and Latin America as well as in the newly poor countries of Eastern Europe are driven by many of the same pressures as in richer countries. Population growth and persistent fiscal crises require governments to search for educational policies that will reduce costs and increase efficiency so as to maintain quality standards while providing access to as many citizens as possible (Coombs, 1985; World Bank, 1988). At the same time, the provision of education is one of the most basic and visible tasks required of governments. Failure to provide access to education to all who desire it on terms that they regard as acceptable may call into question the government's legitimacy and threaten its political survival (Morales-Gomes & Torres, 1990; Nkinyangi, 1991).

These two imperatives often work at cross-purposes: The exigencies of political survival commonly require quite different policies than those that enhance economic efficiency. Indeed, policies aimed at increasing the efficiency of the educational system may undermine the legitimacy of the government. Efforts to increase the fees paid by students, to reduce labor costs, or to alter the school calendar encounter strong opposition from students, teachers, and parents. Opposition from educated, cohesive, articulate interests threatens government survival.

Similarly, the implementation of policies intended to shore up the legitimacy of the government may be beyond the means available to public officials. For example, the right of all citizens to basic education is enshrined in virtually all national constitutions, and the goal of providing primary education for all children is readopted by governments and international agencies every decade, most recently at the World Conference on Education for All in Jomtien, Thailand (WCEFA, 1990). Despite these declarations, however, millions of children remain out of school; enrollment rates are, in fact, falling in many countries.

The dilemma posed for governments that are trying to achieve competing objectives increases the political urgency of educational reform while virtually eliminating the possibility of "success" in educational policymaking (Plank & Adams, 1989). Any significant change in the structure and operation of the educational system or in the distribution of educational resources is almost certain to damage the interests of one or more powerful constituencies. Educational reforms are therefore undertaken only at the peril of the government's survival. At the same time, however, failure to address educational problems evinces a lack of commitment in the eyes of both domestic and international audiences. Inaction in the face of what is widely perceived as a crisis threatens both domestic political support and the government's claim on international aid.

The consequence of this dilemma is a style of politics familiar in countries around the world, in which governments have much to gain from the announcement of policy initiatives and much to lose from their implementation. Under these circumstances, reform rhetoric stands in for reform; the declaration of good intentions takes the place of action that might lead to its realization. In adopting such strategies, politicians and public officials seek to gain the benefits that derive from active engagement with crises while avoiding the costs that inevitably accompany changes in the prevailing distribution of resources (Plank, 1990; Weiler, 1988).

The nature of educational reforms and the rationale for them vary with the economic circumstances and aspirations of different governments (Reich, 1991). In the newly industrializing "little tigers" of East Asia, for example, governments invest heavily in education to provide their citizens with increasing levels of knowledge and skill and so gain comparative advantage in the world economy. In much of Africa and Central America, in contrast, governments must struggle to maintain current rates of primary school enrollment and literacy, so as not to fall even further into poverty (Kelly, 1990). Governments in the newly poor countries of Eastern Europe and Central Asia face a painful choice between maintaining the costly social services provided under socialism and permitting erosion in the quality of their highly educated workforces, which represent their principal asset in global economic competition.

In developing countries, the reform agenda is defined to a large and growing extent by policy prescriptions from the international aid agencies, especially the World Bank (Plank, in press; World Bank, 1992). There are two main reasons. First, in many countries, the revenues that public officials can generate locally are no longer sufficient for the responsibilities assumed by the government in education as in other sectors. Local revenues are fully committed to the payment of salaries and the maintenance of existing programs, meaning that the discretionary resources needed to fund new initiatives must be sought abroad. The power to provide or withhold resources from governments gives the donors tremendous leverage over educational policies. They decide which reforms they will fund and may withdraw support from governments that adopt policies of which they disapprove.

The disproportionate influence of international aid agencies over educational and policy research in developing countries is a second way in which aid donors exercise control over policies. Most educational research in developing countries is conducted by or under the auspices of the principal aid agencies, primarily because the human and financial resources available to them far exceed those available to local governments or universities. Unconstrained by local political considerations, moreover, the policy preferences of the international aid agencies are guided to an unusually large degree by research-based assessments of "what works." As a result, the linkage between educational research and educational policy is much tighter than in developed countries (Boyd & Plank, in press; Samoff, 1991).

Because of the pervasive influence of the international aid agencies, the educational reforms adopted in developing countries around the world tend to look much the same. For example, many countries are currently engaged in macroeconomic policy changes under the auspices of the IMF and the World Bank. These changes, which are commonly subsumed under the heading of "structural adjustment," include substantial reductions in public employment and public expenditure. The education system often accounts for the largest shares of both, so governments pursuing adjustment policies are advised by their donors to adopt educational reforms that will reduce costs and increase efficiency.

One widely adopted strategy for reducing public expenditure on education is to shift the costs of schooling from public agencies to parents and communities. Governments have sought to impose or increase fees at all levels of the educational system, and many have delegated responsibility for the construction and maintenance of schools to local authorities (Bray, 1988; Jimenez, 1987). A second strategy adopted in many countries involves attempts to reduce the real value of teachers' salaries, which constitute the largest share of educational expenditures. The measures undertaken in this regard include the encouragement of multiple-shift schools or multigrade classrooms, in an effort to increase pupil/teacher ratios without commensurate increases in teachers' pay, and the introduction of instruc-

tional radio and other curricular innovations aimed at reducing the
teacher's role in the classroom (World Bank, 1990). The political
dilemma of educational reform thus remains unresolved. As a result,
the political survival of many governments is increasingly dependent
on a complex and perilous balancing act between the policy changes
necessary to ensure the continued flow of foreign assistance and the
maintenance of educational policies and services that advance the
interests of key domestic constituencies. Inherent in the current focus
on efficiency and cost reduction are two dangers: first, that reducing
services and increasing fees will undermine the government's political support, and, second, that the deterioration of social infrastructure
that has been built up over long periods will deny poor countries their
best chance of escaping from poverty. Currently, however, developing
countries' governments have few options except to accept the reforms
prescribed for them by the international aid agencies while delaying
their implementation for as long as possible.

Conclusion

This chapter began with a quotation from two French researchers,
Herve Hamon and Patrick Rotman, who wrote in 1984: "We are not
living through the end of a golden age . . . but a change of historic
dimensions which must be understood" (p. 10). It seems wise to
reiterate that point here. As new education policies are adopted and
new programs are launched in rapid succession, it is easy to lose sight
of the broader picture. For example, it is easy to implicitly interpret
the current education reform movement as primarily a American
phenomenon without seeking to situate it in the broader context of
international education reform. It is also easy to restrict oneself to the
mere description of specific education reforms without trying to
situate them within the broader context of relevant economic, political, and sociological changes and theories about those changes. Such
easy approaches to education reform do not, however, lead to a deep
and nuanced understanding of what is occurring in the United States
and elsewhere. As we move through economic, social, and technological changes of "historic dimensions," it is essential that we bear in
mind both the international context and the theoretical implications
of what is happening.

References

Anderson, D. (1991, November). *The unstable public-private school system in Australia.* Paper presented at the First National Conference of the National Board for Employment, Education, and Training, Canberra, Australia.

Ball, S. (1990). *Politics and policy making in education: Explorations in policy sociology.* London: Routledge.

Beare, H., & Boyd, W. (in press). *Restructuring schools: An international perspective on the movement to transform the control and performance of schools.* London: Falmer.

Be bold, be British: A lesson for America's schools. (1991, March 23). *The Economist,* pp. 19-20.

Bell, D., & Gaffney, J. (1990). [Editorial]. *Contemporary European Affairs, 3*(4), 1-4.

Berman, E. (1989). *A comparative analysis of educational reform.* Paper presented at the annual meeting of the Comparative and International Education Society, Boston.

Boyd, W. (1987). Balancing public and private schools: The Australian experience and American implications. *Educational Evaluation and Policy Analysis, 9*(3), 183-198.

Boyd, W., & Plank, D. (in press). International policy studies. In *International encyclopedia of educational research* (2nd ed.). New York: Pergamon.

Bray, M. (with Lillis, K.). (1988). *Community financing of education: Issues and policy implications in less developed countries.* New York: Pergamon.

Broadfoot, P. (1985). Changing patterns of educational accountability in England and France. *Comparative Education, 21,* 273-286.

Chubb, J., & Moe, T. (1992). *A lesson in school reform from Great Britain.* Washington, DC: Brookings.

Clark, D., & Astuto, T. (1986). The significance and permanence of changes in federal education policy. *Educational Researcher, 15*(8), 4-13.

Coombs, P. (1985). *The world crisis in education: The view from the eighties.* New York: Oxford University Press.

Glowka, D. (1989). Anglo-German perceptions of education. *Comparative Education, 25,* 319-332.

Gordon, L. (1992). *International influences and market educational reforms in New Zealand.* Paper presented at the annual meeting of the American Educational Research Association, San Francisco.

Hamon, H., & Rotman, P. (1984). *Tant qu'il y aura des profs* [As long as there are secondary teachers]. Paris: Editions du Seuil.

Harman, G., Beare, H., & Berkeley, G. (Eds.). (1991). *Restructuring school management: Administrative reorganization of public school governance in Australia.* Canberra: Australian College of Education Press.

Hogan, M. (1984). *Public versus private schools: Funding and directions in Australia.* Ringwood, Australia: Penguin.

Husen, T., Tuijnman, A., & Halls, W. (1992). *Schooling in modern European society.* Oxford: Pergamon.

Jimenez, E. (1987). *Pricing policy in the social sectors: Cost recovery for education and health in developing countries.* Baltimore: Johns Hopkins University Press.

Kelly, M. (1990). *Education in a declining economy: The case of Zambia.* Washington, DC: IBRD.

Laderriere, P. (1990). How should we assess in education? *Contemporary European Affairs, 3*(4), 28-34.

Lersch, R. (1988). Praktisches Lernen und Bildungsreform [Practical learning and education reform]. *Zeitschrift fur Padagogik, 34*, 781-779.

Louis, K., & van Velzen, B. (1990-1991, December-January). A look at the Netherlands. *Educational Leadership*, pp. 66-72.

Morales-Gomes, D., & Torres, C. (1990). *The state, corporatist politics, and educational policy making in Mexico.* New York: Praeger.

Neave, G. (1988). Education and social policy: Demise of an ethic or change of values? *Oxford Review of Education, 14*, 273-283.

Neave, G. (1992). *The teaching nation.* Oxford: Pergamon.

Nkinyangi, J. (1991). Student protests in Sub-Saharan Africa. *Higher Education, 22*, 157-173.

Plank, D. (1990). The politics of basic education reform in Brazil. *Comparative Education Review, 34*, 538-560.

Plank, D. (in press). Review of three recent education reports by the World Bank. *Economics of Education Review.*

Plank, D., & Adams, D. (1989). Death, taxes, and school reform. *Administrator's Notebook, 33*, 1-4.

Reich, R. (1991). *The work of nations.* New York: Knopf.

Samoff, J. (1991, March). *External assistance to African education: The development of the financial-intellectual complex.* Paper presented at the annual meeting of the Comparative and International Education Society, Pittsburgh, PA.

Thurow, L. (1992). *Head to head.* New York: William Morrow.

WCEFA Interagency Commission. (1990). *Final report: World Conference on Education for All.* New York: Author.

Weiler, H. (1988). The politics of reform and nonreform in French education. *Comparative Education Review, 32*, 251-265.

Weiler, H. (1990). Curriculum reform and the legitimation of educational objectives: The case of the Federal Republic of Germany. *Oxford Review of Education, 16*(1), 15-27.

Wirt, F., & Harman, G. (Eds.). (1986). *Education, recession and the world village.* London: Falmer.

World Bank. (1988). *Education in Sub-Saharan Africa: Policies for adjustment, revitalization, and expansion.* Washington, DC: IBRD.

World Bank. (1990). *Improving primary education in developing countries: A review of policy options.* Washington, DC: IBRD.

World Bank. (1992). *Adjusting educational policies: Conserving resources while raising school quality.* Washington, DC: IBRD.

NINE

Pursuit of School Quality in England and Wales

PETER RIBBINS

HYWEL THOMAS

In July 1992, the Department of Education and Science (DES) changed its name to the Department for Education (DFE) and published a White Paper on Education titled *Choice and Diversity: A New Framework for Schools* (DFE, 1992). This is modestly described as "a landmark, 30,000 word document [which] sets out an evolutionary framework for the organization of funding of schools into the next century" (p. 1). The legislation that it requires will be the *eighteenth education act produced by the Conservative government in the last 14 years.*

It is with mixed emotions that the educational establishment will examine its claims of "far reaching proposals to complete the transformation of the education system of England and Wales begun in the 1980s" (p. 1). As such, this may well be an appropriate time to attempt an overview of these years of school reform. Limitations of space and the extent and complexity of the reforms that have taken place over the last 14 years mean that this overview will be selective. This chapter will focus on the government's programs of reforms since the election of the third consecutive Conservative administration in July 1987. Even this will amount to a less than comprehensive discussion because we will be unable to discuss such significant reforms as the introduction, in 1992, of a system of teacher appraisal. It also means that a number of important reforms including the attempt to integrate children with special needs within mainstream schools that has taken place since the 1981 Education Act and the bid to introduce a much more strongly vocational dimension within the upper-secondary curriculum through the Technical and Vocational Initiative and its Extension after 1982 cannot be considered further. Within these limitations, this overview will be based upon a review of aspects of the *context*, *content*, and *character* of recent legislation in terms of its implications for the *substance* of schooling and for the *system* as a whole within which schools in England and Wales are located.

The Context of Schools Reform

Focusing upon the nature of the changes that have taken place in system terms, the writers of the White Paper suggest that "five great themes run through the story of educational change in England and Wales since 1979: quality, diversity, increased parental choice, greater autonomy for schools and greater accountability" (DFE, 1992, p. 2). In a lecture given to the National Conference of the British Educational Management and Administration Society a few weeks after the publication of the White Paper, David Forrester (Head of Schools Branch 4 at the DFE) placed the pursuit of quality at the center of the government's agenda of educational reform. But what this means and why it should be so is less clear.

Nick Stuart, a deputy secretary at the Department of Education and Science (DES), draws upon the language of *economics* to describe this concern for quality. He writes of a growing conviction in government circles that the economic well-being of the nation "was being adversely affected by the performance of an education service that was neither as good as it could be or as good as it needed to be." In a later paper, which sought to explain why the issue of quality had grown in importance since the 1970s, he broadens his argument. Three things had brought quality to the forefront. First, there were *economic arguments* of the kind discussed above. Second, there were *political arguments* that overlapped with economic arguments: "At a time when most people gave priority to controlling and in due course reducing public expenditure as a proportion of GDP, education as a public spending priority lost its edge. Conservative's priorities were pensions, health and law and order together with defense. Demography was also working against the service" because of a declining birthrate from 1971. Finally, there were *educational arguments,* which following Callaghan's "Ruskin speech" (see below) saw "an increasing questioning of performance. HMI inspection evidence confirmed the impression of low expectations, limited curriculum planning and vague objectives. International comparisons began to show up our performance particularly in relation to average or below average performers" (Stuart, in press).

Such arguments have been challenged. Critics suggest that the impulse for contemporary educational change can be better explained as a function of the conflicting ideological prejudices that have characterized the activities of the Conservative party in power. This thesis has been powerfully made but may need to be qualified. To understand why, contemporary debates on educational reform must be located in historical context.

Lawton (in press) suggests that "in 1944 the question of improving education was seen largely as a question of *quantity*—extending the benefits of education to a larger proportion of the population. . . . Significantly, the content of education—the curriculum—was not seen as an issue and was not even mentioned in the 1944 Act." This view is widely shared. When and why did questions start to be raised that turned upon issues of *quality*? Stuart (in press) offers one account. In the 1970s, "parents were beginning to question more and more whether their children were being sufficiently stretched." At the same time, among parents and politicians, "confidence in new approaches to teaching began to ebb." Such a view might be expected of the official known to have drafted much of the 1988 act but it has been advanced by others. Lawton (in press), for example, has claimed that "unquestioning attitudes" to the nature of "what should be on offer" to pupils "began to change in the late 1960s and early 1970s as parents, employers and eventually politicians increasingly asked critical questions about quality and provision." He identifies various reasons for the breaking down of the postwar consensus, including a growing conviction that "schools were not solving the nation's social and economic problems." Like Stuart, he identifies a speech, "critical of education, particularly the lack of coordination between schools and industry," given by James Callaghan at Ruskin College, Oxford, in 1976 as an important turning point.

How and why a Labour prime minister came to make such a speech are the subjects of a detailed study by Chitty (1989). The speech, he argues, needs to be interpreted at a number of important different but interrelated levels. First, it "marked at the very highest political level the end of the phase of educational expansion which had been largely promoted by the Labour party and at the same time it signalled a public redefinition of educational objectives. . . . It was also an attempt to wrest the populist mantle from the Conservative opposition and pander to perceived public disquiet at the alleged decline in educational standards." Second, it "marked a clear shift on the part of the Labour leadership towards policies which would facilitate greater governmental control over the educational system. This was obviously necessary if government ideas on the curriculum were to be implemented." Finally, and above all, the "speech represented a clear attempt to construct a new educational consensus around a more direct subordination of education to what were perceived to be the needs of the economy" (pp. 95, 96).

Such accounts share the idea that a case for greater centralization of power over schools was being made in the Labour party and by its leadership some years before the election of the Conservatives in 1979. Although Lawton (in press) believes "such centralism would probably have continued irrespective of what political party was in government," he nevertheless claims "the election of Margaret Thatcher marked a clear swing to the right in terms of economic, social and educational policies." This swing should not be interpreted in terms of traditional Tory thinking but as a result of the growing influence of the "New Right" on the policies of the Conservative party on a wide range of issues in the 1980s (Belsey, 1986; Gamble, 1988). "New Right" ideas inform much of the 1988 Education Reform Act. It can also be seen in the claim that "central to everything the Government has done since 1979 has been a search for higher quality for the nation's children in our schools. This has comprised a national curriculum, greater choice and accountability, more autonomy and proposals for frequent inspection" (DFE, 1992, p. 2).

The idea that Conservative educational policy has, since 1979, been characterized by radical thinking has been widely contested, however. Chitty (1989) points out

that for at least the first seven years of its existence, the new Conservative government was prepared to operate largely within the terms of the educational consensus constructed by the Labour leadership of 1976. Education was accorded comparatively little space in the 1979 and 1983 Conservative election manifestos and on each occasion the programme outlined was hardly far-reaching and there was no suggestion that the system itself should be overhauled. (p. 194)

The impetus for radical change, when it came, was signaled, inter alia, by the appointment of a new secretary of state (Kenneth Baker) in May 1986 and by the prime minister in a BBC series, *Election Call*, broadcast in June 1987 in which she remarked that "I wish we had begun to tackle education earlier. We have been content to continue the policies of our predecessors" (reported in *The Guardian*, June 11, 1987). With their unexpectedly conclusive election victory in June 1987, the third Thatcher administration finally found "the confidence and determination to adopt truly radical strategies" (Chitty, 1989, p. 197). The nature of its reforming agenda was set out in four pages devoted to "raising standards in education" in the Conservative election manifesto of 1987. This identified four major reforms designed "to establish choice and competition as dominant features of a new education system." First, a "national core curriculum . . . [S]econd . . . governing bodies and headteachers . . . would be given control over their own budgets. . . . Third . . . reforms . . . designed to increase parental choice . . . and fourth, state schools would be allowed to opt out of local authority control and become independent charitable trusts financed centrally" (p. 207).

The Content of Schools Reform

Making sense of the reforms implemented between 1987 and 1992 is not easy. First, they are complex, wide ranging, and far reaching. The Education Reform Act of 1988 alone contains 238 clauses, many with numerous sections and subsections, and 13 schedules, and it has been estimated they give the minister over 200 new powers. Subsequently, the act has spawned many circulars setting out the detailed regulations required to make it a practical reality (these include DES, 1988b, 1988c, 1988d, 1989, 1991a, 1991b). Second, over the last 4 years, the reforms set out in the act have continued to be developed, changed, and added to, and in 1992 the government has made clear that at least one more substantial education act will be required to bring its legislative program to an end. Finally, taken as a whole, the reforms appear to contain a fundamental contradiction. On the one hand, they require the implementation of a national curriculum and national system of pupil assessment, which seems to centralize unprecedented levels of power over the *substance* of schooling in the hands of the national government. On the other, they seek to create an educational market shaped by patterns of demand through the exercise of individual parental choice and supply enabled by the local management of schools, which appears to decentralize decision-making power at the level of the school *system*. In examining the government's agenda for reforming schools, we shall consider how far it is possible to explain and resolve this conflict.

Schools Reform: Centralization and Uniformity

Since the middle of the last century, there have been several attempts by ministers and their officials to determine directly or indirectly what happens within schools and classrooms. With one or two important exceptions, these, until the last few years, have been tentative and short lived. For the most part, there has been a consensus that too much centralization of control over the substance of education is undesirable and may even be dangerous.

In the postwar era, ministers, when asked about how far they could exercise control over the school curriculum, have usually responded with indifference or diffidence. George Tomlinson is reputed (Chitty, 1989, p. 48) to have expressed the view in one version that "Minister's now't to do with the curriculum" (Smith, 1957, p. 162) and in another that "Minister knows now't about the curriculum" (Lawton, 1980, p. 31). Anthony Crosland is reported to have said that "the nearer one comes to the professional content of education, the more indirect the minister's influence is. And I am sure that this is right." Developing this theme, he was prepared to extend this self-denying ordinance to officials as well as ministers: "Generally I didn't regard either myself or my officials as in the slightest degree competent to interfere with the curriculum. We are educational politicians and administrators, not professional administrators" (Kogan, 1971, pp. 172-173). Since the mid-1970s, ministers, even prime ministers, have shown themselves unwilling to accept such limitations on their powers. In examining what has happened and why, we shall focus upon the introduction of a national curriculum and a national system of assessment.

Toward a national curriculum. In its election manifesto in the run up to the election of June 1987, the Conservative party indicated that, if elected, it would give a high priority to reforming education. Within weeks, the first of six consultation documents was issued. It set out the government's proposals for a National Curriculum for all pupils between 5 and 16 (DES, 1987). These proposals were not well received by the educational establishment (Goldby, 1987). Some were opposed in principle to the notion of a national curriculum, others objected to the idea that the national government should play a leading role in determining the nature and content of such a curriculum, but most were critical of aspects of what was being proposed. Why did ideas commonplace in much of the rest of the world generate such hostility?

To understand why this should be so, it is necessary to stress how successful the educational establishment has been for well over 100 years in resisting the idea that either Westminster or Whitehall should have a significant voice in determining the purpose and practice of the school curriculum (Corbett, 1973; Manzer, 1970). Within such a scenario, the role of the DES and the secretary of state is marginalized, and, it seems, control over the curriculum is exercised in effect mainly by schools and teachers.

Such a situation might have led to damaging levels of curriculum diversity and discontinuity within and between the primary and secondary sectors. Some believe that this has happened. O'Hear and White (1991) conclude: "The old system, in which schools and teachers were far more free to set their own aims and work out their own curricula, was too susceptible to grassroots vagaries of enthusiasm and vision and included too few mechanisms for matching what was learnt between primary and secondary schools, or even between one class and the next" (p. 5).

Others argue that what is remarkable about the long period of decentralization of control over the curriculum in England and Wales is the level of continuity that has characterized curriculum thinking and practice, particularly in the secondary sector, for over a century. In this context, the case for a *common curriculum* for all pupils that had *breadth* and *balance* could be said to have been first made by the Clarendon Commissioners in 1864 and was repeated by Morant in 1904 in his attempt to impose a national curriculum by regulation from the Board of Education. Furthermore, the curriculum he advocated bears a striking resemblance to that which is proposed in the 1988 Education Act (Ribbins, 1992b, p. 3).

In any event, the government took scant note of criticisms during either the consultation or the legislative process that led to the Education Reform Act of 1988. The act set out a framework for a national curriculum for pupils from 5 to 16 years, which was to be a "balanced and broadly based" *common curriculum* that

  (a) promotes the spiritual, moral, cultural, mental, and physical development of pupils at the school and of society and
  (b) prepares such pupils for the opportunities, responsibilities, and experiences of adult life (DES, 1988a, p. 1).

Ten subjects plus religious education were specified. The *core subjects* were English, mathematics, and science and the *foundations subjects* were technology, a modern language, history, geography, art, music, and physical education. For each subject, attainment targets ("the knowledge, skills and understanding which pupils of different abilities and maturities are expected to have by the end of each key stage") and profile components were to be identified. Each attainment target was to be defined at 10 levels in terms of statements of attainment. The curriculum content for each subject was to be set out in programs of study ("the matters, skills and processes which are required to be taught to pupils of different abilities and maturities during each key stage"). In addition to this subject-based specification of the main curriculum task, a series of *cross-curricular* skills, themes, and programs were identified.

Since 1988 various criticisms have continued to be made of the national curriculum requirements as these have emerged. Some claim that the 1988 act did not establish appropriate criteria for an adequate national curriculum (O'Hear & White, 1991). Others question the ways in which the curriculum framework outlined in the act has been translated into practice. Certainly, the task of constructing a workable national curriculum has proved to be unexpectedly difficult. There have been problems at each of the four key stages but, as we shall see, these seem to have been most intractable in the cases of key stages 1 and 4. In particular, the idea of a broad and balanced common curriculum for all pupils up to the age of 16 has been significantly qualified since 1988. Sweetman (1991) points out that advocates of the national curriculum as originally envisaged had claimed that "it would do away with the divisive banding which took place at the end of Year 9 . . . as 14-year-olds were assigned to academic or vocational tracks" (p. 9). In practice, this has not happened because the "National Curriculum was barely in place before it became obvious that Key Stage Four at least could not survive in the form envisaged" (Chitty, 1992c, p. 39).

In explaining why this has happened, Sweetman's (1991) analysis of the limitations of the methods of curriculum development employed since the reform act is telling. First, he stresses that little attempt at the time or since has been made to justify the 10-subject model upon which proposals for the national curriculum are based. This illustrates the extent to which traditional curriculum ideas, particularly in the secondary school sector, are resistant to change. Second, it seems that some of those committed to traditional school subjects who might have been expected to oppose a national curriculum did not do so because they "could see how their own subject might be defended once they were defined in subject terms. English teachers, unhappy about what seemed to be the disappearance of English Literature, media studies and drama from the secondary curriculum, saw how they might be extended to all students in a rewritten scheme of syllabus" (Sweetman, 1991, p. 8). Third, the development model relied heavily on "establishing subject working groups, which were then largely left in isolation to define their own parameters of subject content and status." This "had some bizarre consequences. Science, one of the first subjects to be developed, appropriated major sections of the traditional geography curriculum." Curriculum imperialism of this kind was not restricted to science. Several of the working groups used "strategies . . . which were diametrically opposed to any real cross-curricular perspective." Sweetman concludes "the outcome of all this was predictable. An unteachable curriculum was developed where any desirable activity became compulsory" (p. 8).

The consequences have been severe for key stage 4, and the government has been forced to set aside

the advice of the National Curriculum Council [NCC] for all ten subjects of the national curriculum to remain compulsory until 16 [and has] decided only science, maths and English should remain sacrosanct after 14. Pupils would be able to "drop" art, music and history or geography with physical education treated "flexibly." All pupils would have to study modern languages and technology, but would not be obliged to take GCSEs in them. (Chitty, 1992c, p. 40)

These decisions have raised the specter of the reappearance of the kind of multitrack, differentiated curriculum for different categories of pupils from the age of 14 onward, which the national curriculum seemed designed to prevent.

The development process described above has also resulted in acute problems at key stage 1. Not only have those in primary schools faced the prospect of reinventing their curriculums in subject terms, but they have, like their secondary colleagues, also had to struggle to try and force a quart into a pint pot. In consequence, at the time of writing, the NCC is considering the need for "a leaner and more manageable curriculum, with the current range of subjects trimmed down to their essentials" (Hofkins, 1992, p. 1). The chairman of the NCC is reported to have mentioned "the idea of making only English and maths statutory at key stage 1, with a degree of flexibility in other subjects" (p. 1) as an alternative. While he has made it clear that this would not be his preferred option, it does bear an ominous and striking comparison with the developments in key stage 4 described above.

Much of this discussion has assumed that implementation of the government's national curriculum proposals necessarily entails a concentration of control at the center. In determining the extent to which this is intended by the 1988 Education Act, it is necessary to look carefully at the provisions set out in Section 4, which states:

(1) It shall be the duty of the Secretary of State . . . (a) to establish a complete National Curriculum as soon as is reasonably practicable . . . ; and (b) to revise that Curriculum whenever he considers it necessary or expedient to do so.

(2) The Secretary of State may by order specify in relation to each of the foundation subjects—(a) such attainment targets; (b) such programs of study; and (c) such assessment arrangements; as he considers appropriate for that subject.

Read out of context, these subsections seem to give the secretary of state considerable powers but, as Marland (1991) points out, Section 4, subsection 3, also "contains a firm denial of the Secretary of State's right to control anything other than the definition of the National Curriculum components" since "an order made under Section 2 may not require—

(a) that any particular period or periods of time should be allocated during any key stage to the teaching of any matter, skill or process forming part of it; or

(b) that provision of any particular kind should be made in school timetables for the periods to be allocated to such teaching during any such stage."

For these and other reasons, Marland (1992) concludes that in determining their curriculum schools need to be aware that each aspect of the national curriculum has to be incorporated, but it is schools who decide when, how, and in which context. The powers over the curriculum that headteachers and governors are legally entitled, even required, to exercise remain considerable. It is not "the DES or the Secretary of State [who] are controlling the totality, shape, style or delivery pattern of a school's curriculum. The school is the center of curriculum planning" (Marland, 1992, p. 19).

Toward a national system of pupil assessment. The case that schools and teachers are at the center of the delivery of any national system of pupil assessment can also be made. To understand why, we need to examine the proposals for assessment contained within the 1988 act and the way in which they have been developed in practice. The act required that pupil achievement be assessed at four *key stages*: 7 (KS1), 11 (KS2), 14 (KS3), and 16 (KS4). For some, so important are these proposals that they talk of the act and its subsequent elaboration as introducing a national system of assessment rather than implementing a national curriculum.

A detailed account of the evolution of a national system of pupil assessment is beyond the scope of this chapter. Suffice to say that this has turned out to be one of the most controversial aspects of the government's reforming agenda. In this case, conflict was not restricted to the usual debates between the secretary of state and the educational establishment. Chitty (1992b) suggests that "from the beginning, Prime Minister Margaret Thatcher and Education Secretary Kenneth Baker clashed over the nature and status of external testing in the national curriculum. Thatcher wanted externally set tests. Baker, by contrast, accepted the need for an element of school based assessment" (p. 56). The task of producing a workable scheme was given to the Task Group on Assessment and Testing (TGAT) in July 1987. They were given the difficult task of producing proposals within 6 months, and this was compounded by terms of reference that required them to produce a scheme that enabled "assessment . . ., at one and the same time, [to] provide detailed support for individual learning and the kind of information required to create a competitive school market-place" (Butterfield, 1992, p. 193).

In an attempt to meet the very different purposes for assessment contained in its terms of reference, TGAT proposed a much more sophisticated and complex approach than many had expected. The model it advanced was of 10 specified levels of attainment across attainment targets in each national curriculum area. The report generated much interesting discussion and much hostility. For some, the model had "inherent contradictions" (Butterfield, 1992, p. 196) and, for others, it was an "uneasy compromise" (Chitty, 1992b, p. 57). In any case "the story of assessment since 1988 has been one of gradual abandonment of the Task Group's complex proposals. . . . The Right's obsession with standardized, pencil-and-paper, 'objective' tests has now triumphed, largely because it has proved almost impossible for teachers to implement the Task Group's complicated structure" (p. 58).

Schools Reform: Decentralization and Diversity

The government has suggested that "the essential conditions to achieve excellence . . . are those of diversity and choice. By the next century, we will have achieved a system characterized not by uniformity but by choice" (DES, 1992, p. 64). If this is to happen, schools must become more autonomous and more responsive to changing patterns of parental demand: They must be able to come with each other in a much looser framework of control.

Discussions of these reforms, by opponents and supporters alike, have made much use of the concept of the "market." Yet in any conventional definition, "market" does not easily fit either the existing or even the projected system of maintained schools within England and Wales. An examination of this paradox is beyond the scope of this chapter and has in any case been presented elsewhere by one of the authors. In this, Thomas (1992b) analyzes relationships between "markets" and "hierarchies" through a model that examines the interaction of two independent but related dimensions—the *locus of decisions* (from decentralization to centralization) and the *locus of interest* (from self to other). It is against this recognition of the conceptual complexity of these reforms that we turn to an examination of the system levels of changes that the government claims will create greater decentralization and diversity within the schools sector.

The 1988 Education Act's proposals for greater school autonomy have come to be known as the Local Management of Schools (DES, 1988c, 1991b). Since April 1990, school budgets for staffing, premises, and services have been increasingly delegated from local education authorities to schools, where they will be under the final control of the governing bodies. These budgets are funded by a formula that is largely determined by the numbers of pupils attending a school. The continuing employment of staff will depend upon the ability of the school budget to meet anticipated expenditure. Budget deficits may require staff dismissals and there are already a number of cases in which this has happened. These changes and their implications for the employment prospects of staff are expected to lead to increased levels of competition among schools over the enrollment of pupils, an expectation reinforced by changes in regulations that mean that in the future schools will have to admit pupils to their capacity (DES, 1988c, 1991b).

Taken together, these changes have many of the features of an educational voucher system and have been characterized as a pupil-as-voucher scheme (Thomas, 1988). Schools that are successful will attract more pupils and more funds and will, as a result, be able to appoint staff of their choice. Those schools that are unsuccessful (or simply in areas of declining enrollment) will have fewer pupils, less money, and will need to dismiss staff. LMS is an integrated package, introducing more competition as a way of strengthening accountability and, according to its supporters, improving quality and raising standards. As with the impact of the curriculum reforms described earlier, it is only with time that the real effects of LMS will become apparent. What is evident, however, is that LMS and more open enrollment are not the only devices being used to generate greater diversity, competition, and choice.

Other devices include the setting up of Grant Maintained (GM) Schools (DES, 1988d, 1992). The 1988 act allows governors of all secondary schools and most primary schools, following a favorable ballot by a majority of the parents who vote, to apply to the secretary of state for maintenance by grant from the central government and to cease to be maintained by the LEA (Local Educational Authority). As such, "GM schools are self-governing schools. That autonomy is at the heart of the GM school idea, and at the heart of the Government's educational policies" (DES, 1992, p. 19). Progress has been slow from the government's point of view. Despite significant financial entice-ments, particularly during the transitional period, by September 1992, only some 300 schools, the great majority drawn from the secondary sector, had opted for GM status. Even so, the government claims that "on a simple projection of current trends, there could be over 1,500 schools by April 1994. By 1996 most of the 3,900 maintained secondary schools, as well as a significant proportion of the 19,000 maintained primary schools could be grant maintained" (DES, 1992, p. 19). Many of the proposals contained in *Choice and Diversity* are designed to try to ensure that this happens.

A second device is the establishment of a network of City Technol-ogy Colleges (CTC). These colleges were described as an aspect of the government's attempts to add a vocational dimension to the choice of schools available to parents. Like the GM schools, they were to be self-governing but, unlike them, it was always intended that they be funded partly by the private sector. In any event, very few firms were willing to respond with significant financial support. Initially, 24 colleges were intended but, with the treasury having to find the lion's share of the funding required, progress has been slow. It seems un-likely that there will be more than 15 CTCs by the end of 1993. But the government has not been discouraged. The 1992 White Paper an-nounced plans to encourage the creation of Technology Colleges. These are to be much like CTCs but will not be confined to urban areas. No details are offered as to how many such colleges are anticipated (DES, 1992, p. 46).

Finally, the government also intends "to promote much greater diversity and specialization by schools, particularly in technology" (DES, 1992, p. 45). Specialization, it is stressed, "does not mean selec-tion, which implies choice by the school; instead it means increased choice by parents and pupils. The greater the choice, the greater the opportunity for children to go to schools which cater for their partic-ular interests and aptitudes" (p. 45). As a key part of this policy, the government claims to be "establishing, through its Technology

Schools Initiative, a network of maintained secondary schools with enhanced technological facilities, and a commitment to providing courses with a strong vocational emphasis. One hundred secondary schools, both LEA maintained and GM, have been selected this year to become the first of this wider network of Technology Schools" (p. 45).

The developments described above are intended to increase the scope of parental choice and in doing so sharpen competition between schools for the recruitment of pupils. Such competition will be given a further stimulus by two additional factors designed to inform the exercise of parental choice: first, through the implementation of pro-posals made in *The Parents Charter* requiring schools to publish in-formation on aspects of their performance exam results, rates of unauthorized absence, and the routes taken by older pupils at the end of their compulsory period of schooling (DES, 1992), and, second, through the setting up of a new national inspectorate and program of inspection. In arguing the case for this, the government claims that

> previous local authority inspection arrangements in some areas were shameful—irregular and unsystematic visits followed by unpublished reports with little or no evaluation . . . too often there was no clear distinction between inspection and advice . . . although there has been some improvement since 1989, it has been too slow and uneven. The Government could not let this continue . . . from next year, all schools will be subject to regular and rigorous inspection under the watchful eye of the new and powerful Chief Inspector of Schools. (DES, 1992, p. 3)

In addition, plans are being made for setting up a new schools' inspectorate responsible for "regularly investigating how schools are getting on, and making the results of that investigation freely, regu-larly and easily available to parents and the local community." Its immediate task "is to complete for the first time ever a Doomsday Book-like survey of the quality and achievements of all of England's schools, and to do so within a four year period" (p. 8). At the time of writing, a consultation paper suggesting a framework for the inspec-tion of schools has been issued (DES, 1992) and the first training has begun.

Reservations have been expressed about all these initiatives. It has been suggested that parental choice works best in the cases of those

schools that are unpopular and undersubscribed. In the case of popular and oversubscribed schools, it may well be that it is schools that
are choosing parents. Concerns have also been expressed about the
inspection proposals. Some fear it will not be possible to attract and
train sufficient numbers of high-quality inspectors within the time
frame set. Others doubts if such an approach will have much impact
upon the improvement of quality. It could be that the government has
exaggerated the advantages of the rigid division it wishes to make
between inspection and advice. In some of the best of the LEA
schemes, the two have been used as mutually supportive dimensions
of an effective approach to school improvement (Ribbins & Burridge,
1992). Furthermore, ironically, while the DFE is advocating tough
systems of external inspection, the Department of Trade and Industry
(DTI, 1991) warns: "To believe that traditional quality control techniques, and the way that they have always been used, will result in
quality is wrong. Employing more inspectors, tightening up standards . . . does not promote quality" (p. 10).

The Character of Schools Reform

Various attempts have been made to explain the contradictions that
appear to lie at the heart of the government's policies for school
reform. We shall be able to consider two of the most influential
explanations: those that consider the contradictions to be deep and
serious and those that see them as superficial and trivial.

Explaining Ambiguity

Those who believe that ambiguities in the educational reform
agenda of the government are deep and serious most commonly
explain their existence by reference to the existence of the conflicting
ideas of the different factions of the "New Right" and their influence
over the nature and shape of educational policy.

First, what is the New Right? For Chitty (1989), "the New Right
encompasses a wide range of groups and ideas, and there are many
internal divisions and conflicts. What the term could not be said to
signify is either a unified movement or a coherent doctrine" (p. 211).
Even so, its adherents appear to share a common commitment to

the paradoxical doctrine of "free economy/strong state," as Gamble (1988) elegantly puts it. Chitty (1989) suggests that "this combination of potentially opposing doctrines means that New Right philosophy has contradictory policy implications and the ambiguity owes much to a basic division between those on the one hand who emphasize the free economy, often referred to as the neo-liberals, and those on the other who attach more importance to a strong state, the so called neo-conservatives" (p. 212).

In the making of educational policy, three New Right groups have been important: the Institute of Economic Affairs (IEA) (the source of much neoliberal thinking), the Center for Policy Studies, and the Hillgate Group (the source of much neoconservative thinking). For different reasons, both wings shared a belief in the need for decentralization at a system level and for the development of market conditions for education. Where they disagreed was over the need for the kind of centralization entailed by the introduction of a national curriculum. As Ranson (1988) observes, in the decision to legislate a national curriculum, the Hillgate Group's view that the curriculum provides a means of incorporating a statement of the nation's culture and values—and that central prescription was necessary—was to be more influential on Conservative policymakers than the views of the IEA that the content of the curriculum should be resolved by the choices of parents in the educational marketplace.

Resolving Ambiguity

Those who believe that ambiguities in Conservative educational policy are superficial tend to claim that it is possible to identify a common strand informing its centralizing and decentralizing dimensions. Both, they argue, can be seen as a challenge to the dominant role hitherto played by educationists and the educational establishment over key aspects of educational policymaking and practice. Thus, in defending its policies, the government has often taken the view that "parents know best the needs of their children—certainly better than educational theorists or administrators, better even than our mostly excellent teachers. Children themselves, as they grow older and mature, often have a well developed sense of their needs and a good grasp of the quality of the teaching they receive" (DFE, 1992, p. 2). Educational theorists are listed above as first among those to be criticized. This is no accident because, as its members now recognize, it is for the educational research community that ministers have reserved their worst scorn. At its annual conference in September 1992, the president of the British Educational Research Association is reported to have presented a grim picture in which "relationships between researchers and ministers, never positive in recent years, had become increasingly sour and marginalised . . . instead of being valued by those in power, specialist knowledge had become an object of derision" (Abrams, 1992, p. 17).

For Thomas (1989), it is this challenge to the "producer interest" that has led to a set of reforms that simultaneously seek to centralize and decentralize control of educational policy and practice. Viewed as a challenge to the producer interest, this contradiction assumes a greater coherence. By centralizing control over aspects of policy, such as for the school curriculum, the reforms attempt to reduce the control of professional educators in this area. By decentralizing control over human and physical resources to the governing bodies of schools, the reforms both reduce the power of education administrators within local government and require headteachers to work more closely with their governors in managing the school (Ribbins, 1989). Moreover, because the particular form of decentralization selected introduces more competition into a marketplace in which parents will have more opportunity to choose between the quality and type of service apparently on offer in different schools, the power of the client as consumer is enhanced in relation to that of the producer.

The legislation that has driven through the government's schools reforms rarely mentions teachers (Ribbins, 1989). Because its purpose is to challenge the "producer interest," it is concerned with setting the agenda for teachers—and other professional educators—but not with involving them in the process of setting that agenda. Educational reform may have significant economic roots but it must be enacted within a political arena. It can be argued that the interactions between government and teachers that have shaped the nature of contemporary schools reform entered the political domain as a consequence of Callaghan's Ruskin College speech in 1976 and the "Great Debate" that followed. In part, this debate examined, sometimes critically, the ways in which teachers had used their autonomy in the past to shape the substance of schooling. It was taken further in response to the reforming agenda of the Conservative party expressed in 1979 in electoral slogans that suggested: "Educashun isnt wurking." Underlying such slogans was the view that, if standards of pupil achievement were to be increased significantly, producer control over the curriculum and its delivery must be diminished. Rather more slowly, the government came to believe that this would need regulation from the center and might even require the imposition of a national curriculum.

The 1980s were also a period that saw an erosion of the relative incomes of teachers, and this in turn led to 2 years of industrial action by the teachers. A government that had rewritten so much labor legislation showed itself frustrated in its inability to prevent the teachers from taking full advantage of their relatively open employment contracts, which allowed them to disrupt work in schools and to do so with very little financial penalty. For the government, this provided further evidence of the negative effects of "producer control" and of the need for legislation that gives greater power to site-based managers and governors and that makes staff tenure depend on cash-limited pupil budgets. In such an account, the centralizing and decentralizing dimensions of the government's reforms of schools can be explained as complementary aspects of a policy designed to restrict "producer control" and diminish "professional power."

Conclusion

Since it came to power in 1979, and particularly since 1988, the Conservative government has been pushing through a major agenda of schools reform. Whether the outcomes of these reforms will match the intentions of the reformers is, at yet, unclear. Despite the exclusion of educational professionals from the making of policy, they cannot be excluded from its implementation. How teachers interpret their roles and responsibilities will have a crucial bearing on how the reforms work in practice. This is especially true, of course, of those reforms that focus upon issues of substance. It is schools and teachers who have to interpret curriculum reforms, and no amount of inspecting what they do is likely to change this. But it is also true of system-level reforms such as the level of competition between schools, the nature of governor involvement in making policy for schools, the quality of the information provided for parents and others, and the character of their involvement with LEAs or such other bodies as may exercise some kind of a responsibility for aspects of their work in the future.

In conclusion, there are many factors that will influence the way in which the government's schools reforms are implemented and many groups will play a significant part in determining how effective they are. Among these, the contributions of parents, pupils, governors, central and local officials, inspectors and advisers, researchers and teacher trainers, and especially teachers will be important. But the evidence is already suggesting that it will be headteachers who will be crucial in shaping the implementation of these reforms. Much will depend upon how they interpret their new powers both within the school and in terms of its relationships with other schools. They can choose how far they intend to share these powers with other staff within the school and how far they will collaborate with other schools. It is possible that we may be about to enter an era of "cutthroat" management. If this happens, individual schools may make progress but it is hard to believe that schools as a whole will improve. Much will depend upon how headteachers see themselves in terms of the interests of pupils generally: Will this be as protectors or predators?

References

Abrams, F. (1992, September 18). Little comfort for derided researchers. *Times Educational Supplement*, p. 17.

Belsey, A. (1986). The new right, social order and civil liberties. In R. Levitas (Ed.), *The ideology of the New Right*. Cambridge: Polity.

Butterfield, S. (1992). Whole school policies for assessment. In P. Ribbins (Ed.), *Delivering the national curriculum*. London: Longman.

Chitty, C. (1989). *Towards a new education act: The victory of the New Right?* Lewes, England: Falmer.

Chitty, C. (1992a). What future for subjects. In P. Ribbins (Ed.), *Delivering the national curriculum*. London: Longman.

Chitty, C. (1992b). *The education system transformed*. Manchester, England: Baseline.

Chitty, C. (1992c). Key stage four: The national curriculum abandoned? *Forum, 34*(2).

Corbett, A. (1973). Education in England. In R. Bell et al. (Eds.), *Education in Great Britain and Ireland*. London: Routledge & Kegan Paul.

Department of Education and Science (DES). (1987). *The national curriculum 5-16: A consultation document*. London: Author.

DES. (1988a). *Education Reform Act*. London: Her Majesty's Stationery Office.

DES. (1988b). *Education Reform Act: Local management of schools* (Circular 7/88). London: Author.

DES. (1988c). *Education Reform Act: Admission of pupils to county and voluntary schools* (Circular 11/88). London: Author.
DES. (1988d). *Education Reform Act: Grant maintained schools* (Circular 10/88). London: Author.
DES. (1989). *Education Reform Act: The school curriculum and assessment* (Circular 5/89). London: Author.
DES. (1991a). *Implementation of more open enrollment in primary schools* (Circular 6/91). London: Author.
DES. (1991b). *Local management of schools: Further guidance* (Circular 7/91). London: Author.
DES. (1992). *The Parents Charter: Publication of information about school performance in 1992* (Circular 7/92). London: Author.
DFE. (1992). *Choice and diversity: A new framework for schools* (White Paper). London: Her Majesty's Stationery Office.
DTI. (1991). *Total quality management: A practical approach.* London: Author.
Gamble, A. (1988). *The free economy and the strong state: The politics of Thatcherism.* London: Macmillan.
Goldby, M. (Ed.). (1987). *Perspectives on the national curriculum.* Exeter, England: University of Exeter, School of Education.
Hofkins, D. (1992, September 25). Stripped down to absolute essentials. *Times Educational Supplement*, p. 1.
Kogan, M. (1971). *The politics of education.* London: Penguin.
Lawton, D. (1980). *The politics of the school curriculum.* London: Routledge & Kegan Paul.
Lawton, D. (in press). Defining quality. In E. Burridge & P. Ribbins (Eds.), *Improving education: The issue is quality.* London: Cassel.
Manzer, R. (1970). *Teachers and politics.* Manchester, England: Manchester University Press.
Marland, M. (1991). *Governing the school: The legal responsibilities for the curriculum.* Unpublished manuscript.
Marland, M. (1992, September 4). How to make use of the acts. *Times Educational Supplement*, p. 19.
O'Hear, P., & White, J. (1991). *A national curriculum for all.* London: IPPR.
Ranson, S. (1988). From 1944 to 1988: Education, citizenship and democracy. *Local Government Studies, 14*(1), 1-21.
Ribbins, P. (1989). Managing secondary schools after the act: Participation and partnership. In R. Lowe (Ed.), *The changing secondary school.* Lewes, England: Falmer.
Ribbins, P. (Ed.). (1992a). *Delivering the national curriculum.* London: Longman.
Ribbins, P. (1992b). Reproducing the subject based secondary school. In P. Ribbins (Ed.), *Delivering the national curriculum.* London: Longman.
Ribbins, P., & Burridge, E. (1992). Improving schools: An approach to quality in Birmingham. In H. Tomlinson (Ed.), *The search for standards.* London: Longman.
Smith, W. (1957). *Education: An introductory survey.* Harmondsworth, England: Penguin.
Stuart, N. (in press). Quality in education. In E. Burridge & P. Ribbins (Eds.), *Improving education: The issue is quality.* London: Cassel.
Sweetman, J. (1991). *The complete guide to the national curriculum.* Newton Regis, England: Bracken.
Thomas, H. (1988, December 2). Pupils as vouchers. *Times Educational Supplement*, p. 23.

Thomas, H. (1989). Who will control the secondary school in the 1990s? In R. Lowe (Ed.), *The changing secondary school*. Lewes, England: Falmer.

Thomas, H. (1992a). *Markets, hierarchies and management in education*. Unpublished manuscript.

Thomas, H. (1992b). Policy-making in educational reform. In *Update of Module 2 of E333 Policy making in education*. Milton Keynes, England: Open University Press.

TEN

Benevolence in
Canadian Public Schools

DANIEL J. BROWN

Problems and Opportunities

Public schools everywhere are widely acknowledged to possess some
very daunting problems. Two kinds of difficulties emerge as rather
critical for schools in Canada. One is a general shortage of resources
as a consequence of competing societal priorities, the reduction in the
proportion of persons with direct ties to schools, and the perception
that public schools have not achieved their educational goals, as
described internationally by Boyd (1987). The other major vexation
is called "bureaucracy," a summary label used to describe the rigidi-
ties associated with the large district organizations in which schools
are embedded. Public schools are seen as having little autonomy to
meet local needs. Rather, they are tightly held by networks of procedures that stem from the democratic control of school districts and
their accompanying administrative apparatus as asserted strongly by
Chubb and Moe (1990). The outlook for public schools is ominous.
They may be considered institutions in peril.

Various efforts at educational reform are under way in Canada. This
chapter discusses an initiative that addresses the two problems of
shortage and rigidity. Called "voluntarism" or "benevolence," it is an
avenue whereby most schools are able to acquire acutely needed
resources for local needs and to build important connections among
their parents and surrounding neighborhoods. While not a cure-all,

voluntarism may have considerable potential to do much good for public schools, although this potential is rarely acknowledged among persons interested in educational finance. This chapter introduces the topic, presents a very brief summary of an investigation into benevolence in some Canadian public schools, and then offers some policy directions.

Exactly what is *voluntarism* for schools? Let's start with what it is not. While the term is associated with parental choice of schools, it is not used in that sense in this chapter. Resources, rather than choice, are the focus. It does not mean general parental participation, which includes parental control of schools and parental help with children's homework. Concern is with giving. It does not mean methods of gaining private resources through exchange mechanisms, such as student fees, grant seeking, and contracts. That particular topic is the subject of a further study. Rather, voluntarism means individual giving to public schools. Giving is a one-way transaction in which reciprocation is indefinite or long term. While schools receive gifts in the forms of time, money, and goods from parents, nonparents, and business organizations, the gifts of time from individual people are the ones most evident in this study. The terms *benevolence* and *voluntarism* will be used synonymously throughout this chapter.

Not much is known about voluntarism in schools. The largest study to date is Michael (1990), which is chiefly concerned with the need for more volunteers in U.S. schools and the description of notable district-level programs linked to the National Association of Partners in Education. Other work has covered volunteers to some extent but is more concerned with the broader effects of parental participation. Most prior studies do not link volunteers to the general problem of school resources.

The research reported in this chapter was generated within a larger study on voluntarism begun in 1987 and supported by the Canada Council. My students and I interviewed 120 principals, teachers, and volunteers in British Columbia. Schools and persons were selected on the basis of their activity and knowledge associated with benevolence at the school level. They encompassed differing socioeconomic status levels; rural, suburban, urban locations; and a range of leadership behaviors. The data were augmented with documents and reports and the general literature on volunteers and analyzed according to the guidelines provided by Miles and Huberman (1984). For the larger study, see Brown (1993).

Initial Results of the Study

Volunteers and Their Works

Gifts come to schools in myriad ways. Many center on food, such as bake sales and lunch programs. Others involve team coaching or transportation of students. Some are clerical, such as assistance in school libraries. Others imply extended contact with students, such as tutorials or mentor programs. Many involve donations of time to help the school gain other resources—fund-raising. Some persons aid schools by being speakers or secretaries. Benefactors often report that they do what teachers do not have the resources to accomplish. The time donated is toward both curricular and extracurricular activities. Some schools receive up to 15 volunteer hours per student per year. For instance, an urban elementary school principal described his parent advisory group as consisting of 32 persons with 2 representatives for each classroom. He counted 67 parent volunteers for his school of 300 students. While some gave only 1 hour per week, he observed that 5 to 6 were on hand full time every day, greatly increasing the ratio of adults to students in his school. The fact that some schools receive substantial donated time is not surprising. Weisbrod (1988, p. 132) indicates that the value of volunteer time is 50% more than dollars donated to nonprofit organizations. Jencks (1987, p. 336) says that, while willingness to give money may have declined recently, the propensity to give time to social causes has increased during the last decade.

Who are these people who give their time to schools? Although volunteers are a diverse lot, it is possible to put together a rough profile of parental participants for the schools in our study. They are chiefly women and Caucasian. Many do not work outside the home or have part-time employment. Most speak English well and are judged to be comfortable in their schools. Many have a personal history of volunteer work. A profile of nonparents (persons without school-aged children) was not possible to build. When observed, nonparents included the following overlapping groups: alumni, university students, business people, grandparents, teachers, and retired persons. Who does not volunteer? Many people who might be expected to volunteer do not. For instance, a survey revealed that over 70% of the parents in a sample of elementary schools never helped

(Social Planning and Research Council of British Columbia, 1989, p. 125). Further, because most volunteers are parents, many schools have a relative paucity of nonparents among their benefactors. Two other groups received frequent mention among our respondents: recent immigrants and those who do not drive a car.

Why do volunteers give their time to schools? Administrators, teachers, and the participants themselves were asked this question. Their predispositions may be clustered in the following ways. Reasons concerning the welfare of their own children, the enjoyment of being in the classroom, and concern for children generally all featured prominently. The early stage of volunteering was associated with the welfare of the donors' own children and the need to escape the confines of domestic life. A later stage was seen to be motivated by self-fulfillment, development of new skills and knowledge (some being useful for employment), and the assumption of responsibility for the children of others. The strength of connections with students, teachers, and others in the school grew as volunteers moved from the earlier to the later stage. Such social bonding may be seen as a trust relationship in which the interests of schools and its benefactors are shared.

The Administration of Giving

How are these complex sets of activities, their participants, and the attendant motivations managed? School administrators appear to have a key role in the overall recruitment, selection, assignment, and recognition of volunteers. For some schools, the administration of benefactors is a formal process; for others, informal. Recruitment and selection may be carried out by general invitations or by direct contact by teachers or donors themselves. The amount of training appears to be small and usually provided by teachers. Recognition may be personal or given to all benefactors at once by the school.

Two critical roles in the attraction of volunteer resources emerged from our data—those of principals and teachers. School administrators played a key function in "opening the doors" to volunteers and making them welcome. One elementary principal said, "Many adults have had negative experiences in school. These people are intimidated by the school and must be made to feel welcome." When benefactors were made welcome, they were given responsibilities and developed a sense of "ownership," a pattern cultivated by a number of principals, who fostered this bonding through the recognition of their donors. Principals were alert to the pattern of greatest volunteer interest on the part of parents of children in the primary grades (Epstein, 1990, p. 129) and targeted that group for invitations. Administrators of small schools, particularly in rural areas, made a point of fostering community contacts to bring additional resources into their schools. Some even maintained databases of volunteers and their contributions so they could be invited to support their schools on future occasions.

Teachers also figured prominently as people who took special initiatives to invite the participation, usually by personal contact. Their welcome and later recognition was viewed by the volunteers as very important. Teachers took care to match the benefactors' abilities with tasks. For instance, donors who spoke little English were given jobs that did not require that proficiency. Yet, in some schools, volunteers did not receive this treatment. As mentioned by one, "Walking into the staff room for the first time to get a cup of coffee, it was overwhelming. I felt that I shouldn't have been there, that I was intruding on the teachers." Principals reported on the discomfort that some teachers have with working alongside adult participants. It appears that there is a mutual fear of teachers and potential volunteers in some schools.

Some Effects of Voluntarism

There are a number of effects of giving on schools. And some of the effects are quite profound. The most obvious effect is the provision of resources in the form of time, funds, and sometimes goods. Such resources support the curricular and extracurricular programs that benefit children directly. Dollars raised via fund-raising buy goods and services that are otherwise not available. These resources are discretionary in the sense that they are spent at the school site for needs that the school determines. They are not channeled from district offices via staffing or space formulas and tied to specific expenditures. Rather, these private resources are allocated within the school by school personnel. And they are *marginal* in the economist's positive sense of the term, sometimes making the difference between the ability and inability to render critical educational services. As one headteacher said, "We couldn't run the school the way we want to without volunteers. If we had to do everything ourselves, lots would be left undone."

Students appear to benefit from voluntary resources in two ways. One is academic learning. While data addressing academic achievement were not included in our study, the extensive review by Henderson (1988, p. 149) showed that parental efforts made a significant difference. Another effect is student social learning. The principals, teachers, and volunteers in our study affirmed that the presence of additional adults had an impact on student attitude and discipline. Schools were perceived to become more familial as the ratio of adults to students increased. An elementary principal mentioned, "Extra adults are potential role models—particularly from a cultural and gender perspective. . . . From a more abstract standpoint, [students] see the adult community concerned about education." A teacher said, "[Students are exposed to] different personalities to deal with. Many of our students have limited outside contacts. They can find out that others are trustworthy and caring."

What about the adults and others who participate in giving? Do they realize some of their own goals? Benefactors report that they make a contribution and receive recognition for it. As their participation continues, they identify more and more with the school, thus their interests and those of the school blend. They also gain skills and learn a good deal about schools. As a by-product of their efforts, they form bonds with others—administrators, teachers, staff, and "the kids."

What about effects on the school and community? As the school becomes more familial, its network of relations is extended into the neighborhood. Volunteers become advocates for the school. One urban principal captured the phenomenon this way: "Backyard ambassadors, goodwill agents who can spread meaningful firsthand observation. They get an understanding of the difficult and the positive. They have more credibility in expressing themselves in the community than we have ourselves." This social effect was seen as being very valuable by the principals we interviewed. For instance, when some were asked if their schools would stop fund-raising if additional moneys were supplied by their school boards, most replied that they would not. Principals considered the growth of social capital shared with their parents and neighborhoods to be a major asset of their schools.

Does success at the attraction of private resources reduce school boards' willingness to support schools? Although that suspicion was harbored by some interviewees, there was no evidence offered to support that hypothesis. The ebb and flow of funding levels from boards or the province may have been affected by the financial health of the province much more than by school activities.

There are two effects that present difficulties as a result of the attraction of gifts to schools. Our study found that workloads for administrators were increased as a consequence of the need to manage volunteers, the funds they raise, and the programs that result. While most administrators we interviewed acknowledged that the benefits were worth the costs, the burden was apparent when high levels of voluntarism were evident in their schools. There may be an optimal number of volunteers or volunteer hours for each school, although the data from this study did not permit that number to be ascertained. If so, schools with excesses of volunteers would find that the benefits they receive from the additional volunteer would be less than the costs incurred from the addition of that volunteer. Too much of a good thing, perhaps? The workload of teachers is also likely increased. While many more tasks were accomplished and some teachers' minor tasks were taken over by volunteers, management of the volunteers often requires additional teacher time.

The other problem associated with the use of volunteer time is found in the resistance of some support staff unions. They showed a concern for the possible subtraction of paid positions and sometimes for the security of their members' jobs. Such fears were expressed more strongly when the tasks performed by volunteers were ones that union members had performed previously. Some support staff locals succeeded in discouraging volunteers by specifying in contracts that certain clerical tasks and tutoring functions may be undertaken only by paid labor.

Factors Influencing Voluntarism

The neighborhood context of the schools we studied appears to have a strong impact on the ability of those schools to attract voluntary resources. Elementary schools in which the parents worked in professional/managerial occupations, earned relatively high family income, and had greater numbers of years of education were associated with extensive voluntary participation. One vice-principal said, "When you call for 50 volunteers and 80 respond, what do you do?" His remark also indicates the willingness of parents in upper-middle-class schools to donate their time. The outlook in schools in working-class or poor neighborhoods is rather different. Volunteers are much fewer. Principals say that it is most difficult to "get them out." Parental participation in all forms appears to be much less evident. There is also some indication that the quality of that participation is lower. For instance, the ability to mount successful fund-raising campaigns may be less because such skills are not as evident in neighborhoods where occupational status, income, and educational levels are lower. These findings from our study are well established in the literature on socioeconomic status and schools. An excellent source is Lareau (1989, p. 115), who observes that working-class neighborhoods have fewer resources of time or money and are also characterized with greater transiency. Further, she notes that working-class parents view education as a form of work. To them, work and family are separate.

The evidence gleaned from our study also indicates that this strong socioeconomic pattern may be overcome. Under certain conditions, schools in working-class neighborhoods were found to have a considerable number of volunteers. One school of 280 students had five full-time volunteers and many other part-time donors. Another school was able to build an adventure playground with volunteer labor. Still another, in the poorest section of a large city, was the recipient of many gifts of time, money, and goods, far more than its counterparts in wealthier surroundings. Why would some "poor" schools be rich in volunteers?

The answer to this question appears to lie in the actions of the principals. In this study, they had moved deliberately to make their parents welcome in their schools, having "open door policies," wherein parents were given open invitations. The principals also attracted nonparents, such as other family members, university students, or other persons from the community. These principals insisted that almost all parents, whether rich or poor, care about their children. The literature backs up our findings. McLaughlin and Schields (1987, p. 157) say that low-income parents become involved if the school takes the initiative. They assert:

There is strong evidence that low-income and poorly educated parents *want* to play a role in their children's education. . . . Conventional wisdom to the contrary, parents who lack knowledge themselves do not necessarily lack interest in the schools their children attend. What's lacking, in most schools and school districts, are appropriate strategies or structures for involving low-income parents. (emphasis in original)

Such willingness to participate may not be restricted to volunteer time. Jencks (1987, p. 322) observes that lower and higher income families give a greater fraction of their incomes to charitable causes than do others. The relationship between effort and income may be U-shaped.

Another major factor impinging on giving to schools is the ethnicity of neighborhoods. A number of the principals whom we interviewed had encountered difficulties in attracting volunteers to their schools, particularly from Asian groups who had moved to Canada. The most frequently occurring explanation was that these groups had no tradition of parental involvement in schools in their native lands. A recent Swiss immigrant benefactor give this account:

Where I came from, voluntarism, basically, was nonexistent. The school was not interested and actually discouraged parents from participating. Teachers looked at students as their domain and didn't want parents to interfere. The only time that was tolerated was once a year [students] went on a field trip and they needed a couple of parents to come along to supervise.

Contrarily, there were some schools in our sample that had a substantial number of European or Asian volunteers. Again, their participation was associated with the efforts of principals and teachers to make them feel welcome and to match their tasks to their abilities. For instance, participants who spoke little English but excellent Chinese were asked to make telephone calls in Cantonese or to help in the Mandarin kindergarten class. A university student volunteer offered this insight from her experience:

I am attracted to the kids and I can see something happening, some response, and that's what keeps me coming back. I can identify with them. I had that problem [English]; some can't speak very well. I remember, I used to sit in the back of the library. Also, [there is] the feeling of being caught between two cultures— trying to retain your own culture while desperately trying to fit into a new culture at the same time.

It appears that, when efforts are made to reach minority groups that might not otherwise participate, they too become willing and are able to donate time to schools.

Aside from socioeconomic status and neighborhood ethnicity, there is one other factor that emerged from the data in our study. It is the belief, particularly as expressed by principals, that a reduction in funding by the provincial government spurred efforts by some schools to attract private resources via giving. During the recent recession with its accompanying cutbacks to schools, many schools were successful at fund-raising for computers, seen as very important learning aids. In "normal times," computers would have been allocated by board offices. When faced with the possibility that students would "do without" important services, many schools mounted fund-raising campaigns through parental efforts. While some of these principals believed that they should not be required to attract private resources in these ways, they also felt that the benefits were worth the costs. There may be a financial imperative at work here.

General Perspectives

The results of this investigation lead to the following observations: Voluntarism is an avenue whereby substantial private resources are given to some schools; benefactors are typically parents but include nonparents as well; and donors desire to contribute to the welfare of children. Further, the actions of principals and teachers have a considerable impact on the extent and ways in which volunteers are employed in schools.

Benevolence has a number of clear effects on schools. One is the provision of instructional and support services that would not be available otherwise. Another is a set of student benefits, both academic and social. A third is that the adults who donate their time build strong ties to their schools, thus the school-community links are strengthened. Social capital is increased. Fourth, difficulties of school personnel overload and some opposition to voluntarism are encountered.

Three important contextual factors are seen to impinge on school voluntarism. Certain socioeconomic and cultural contexts reduce the probability that gifts will be given to schools. Evidence from some schools, however, indicates that leadership on the part of principals tends to overcome much of the disadvantage of those contexts. Further, the advent of retrenchment for schools may spur their willingness to attract or seek private resources.

How are these results to be interpreted? When the starting point of the individual donor is taken, Coleman (1990) declares persons to be not just purposive but rational, having "interest" in resources, which include virtually any nonhuman component of the world. Not only do individuals have interests, they also have some control over resources of interest to others, particularly their labor. Resource transfers take place. In the case of voluntarism in schools, these one-way transfers occur when the interests of the benefactor are seen to be coincident with the interests of the school. As a by-product of these transfers, "social capital" is built. Coleman (1990) defines the integrative concept of social capital as the sum of authority relations, relations of trust, and consensual allocations of rights that establish norms (p. 304). Boulding (1989) also strongly supports the thesis that social integration is an outcome of one-way transfers. He calls it "the power of love" and associates it with institutions such as the family, churches, and charitable organizations. For Boulding, "The stick, the carrot and the hug may all be necessary, but the greatest of these is the hug" (p. 250).

When the point of view of the school is taken, it becomes useful to consider the school in relation to the institutions in its environment. Coleman (1990) focuses on the modern corporate actors (business, governmental, nonprofit organizations, or schools), which may be contrasted in many ways with primordial actors, such as family and community. Modern corporate actors are seen in conflict with primordial actors whose traditional functions they have usurped. The consequences are in the depletion of social capital, particularly for members of the new generation, who, like "poor little rich kids," may be rich in physical or human capital but poor in sustaining social relationships. Yet, the schools we have studied have recognized their need for additional resources and have built social capital with their neighborhoods. A process of adaptation appears to have taken place, wherein a modern corporate actor (the school) has joined forces with two primordial institutions (the home and community) for mutual support. Such an adaptation may be interpreted within what Morgan (1986, p. 39) calls the organismic metaphor, which perceives the organization to be an open system. This approach focuses on the strength of environmental forces in shaping organizational behaviors. It also stresses system goals and functionality, differentiating between factors that affect the organization, processes that go on within it, and the resultant outcomes. For this study, the factors are the contextual ones that affect resource inputs, the processes are seen as administrative, and the effects are the results of voluntarism in schools.

The concept of goals requires that we ask: What is the goal of schools within the larger social context? Coleman and Hoffer (1987, p. 3) provide two general orientations for the role of education. Education may be offered in one of two conceptually distinct ways. When conceived as public, its intended outcomes, such as assimilation into the larger society and the acquisition of knowledge and skills, are to the benefit of the state. As a consequence of these benefits, the entire populace is required to pay for all the resources to provide the service. Financial and social resource exchanges between the society and the school take place over the long term. When children are educated, they contribute to the society that supported them earlier. The chief means of support is financial rather than social; ownership of education is spread across the society; educational organizations offer their services as an arm of governments.

When conceived as private, education's intended outcomes, such as adoption of neighborhood and family values and the acquisition of knowledge and skills, are to the benefit of the individual and community. Logically, families and neighborhoods are asked to contribute all of the resources required because they are the beneficiaries of the education that their children receive. Resource exchanges between neighborhood and school take place over the short and long term, with social and financial exchanges on a daily as well as a lifetime basis. Ownership of education is viewed as local. Both financial support and social support in the form of neighborhood networks are considered important for all facets of student learning.

When taken as archetypes, these goals offer little room for compromise. It is possible, however, to conceive of schools that incorporate features of both public and private traditions. Such schools would

Table 10.1. Relation of School Goals to Inputs, Processes, and Consequential Effects

| Functions | School Goals | | |
	Societal	Common	Familial
Resource inputs	Solely provincial and local taxation	Mix of taxation, gifts, and exchanges	Tuition, gifts, and other exchanges
Administrative processes	Actions focused within the school	Actions encompassing school and community actions highly dependent upon parents	
Learning contexts	Isolation from home and community	Connection with home and community	Integration with home and community

derive support from the larger society and also be sustained by those in the primordial institutions that are most closely connected with them. A combination of state support, exchange, and voluntarism would be their lifeblood. They concurrently would pursue goals of educational equity and social integration. While most of their resources would come from the wider society, they would be rich in social capital with its attendant benefits. (See Table 10.1.)

Tentative Policies

As described, voluntarism may be considered a proposal for school restructuring, because elements of benevolence coincide with the definition of restructuring as proposed by Lieberman and Miller (1990, p. 761). Voluntarism alters the institutional structures of schools somewhat; it alters the learning environment for students; it builds networks, particularly with parents. Yet, benevolence differs from two important proposals for other kinds of restructuring. School-based management is one movement to reduce bureaucracy and improve accountability (Brown, 1990, 1991). That reform thrust appears to hold considerable promise. Yet, decentralization of public dollars to schools does not act as a safeguard against retrenchment and it does not necessarily promote sustaining social networks for schools. Another movement for restructuring is the movement for school choice (Chubb & Moe, 1990). It promises school autonomy and ample parental control. While the parental choice idea is far more revolutionary than decentralization or voluntarism, claims of its effects are contestable. We simply do not know if the provision of school choice would increase school effectiveness or how it would affect student equity.

Although the aforementioned results of this study are only tentative, the issues that they raise go to the heart of policies on education. While incorporating the long-standing concern about student equity, the vision that this research reflects is one in which schools are bonded with their neighborhoods. They acquire resources from their province or state, from their district, and from their own immediate contexts. Such schools are the beneficiaries of private resources given voluntarily. It appears that voluntarism is a way to solve the problems of discretionary resources and retrenchment initially posed in this chapter. More important, voluntarism is also a way of uniting schools with their communities. If benevolence is seen as a desirable reform, what policies could be adopted for its enhancement?

Proposed School District Policies

High levels of voluntarism in schools were associated strongly with behaviors of principals and teachers that encourage parental participation and build community linkages. Principals and teachers could be selected for their positions on the basis of their demonstrated ability to attract and work with school volunteers. In-service and preservice training for principals and teachers could include knowledge, skills, and attitudes required to build benefactor networks. Potential donors need to be reached and invited to participate, not just by individual schools but through district efforts as well. The overall aim of such a program would be to institutionalize voluntarism, to change it from a sporadic and highly variable phenomenon peculiar to individual schools to one that is widespread.

District resource allocation policies could shift. While most positions would continue to be funded publicly, it is possible to specify some roles and also certain material needs that schools could be required to provide for themselves. While it is expected that administrators, teachers, most support staff salaries, and major capital out-lays would continue to be funded publicly, perhaps 10% of schools' required resources, such as those for some support roles, equipment, supplies, and transportation, could be earmarked for voluntary sup-port. But would such a 90/10 rule be a violation of the principle of equal educational opportunity?

The evidence gathered from this study and elsewhere in the litera-ture suggests that some schools would suffer if simply asked to raise 10% of their resources from voluntary means. Consequently, it is proposed that districts determine the placement of each school on an index of socioeconomic status and ethnicity. Index validity would probably be enhanced by principal involvement in its construction. Schools in the upper-middle-class range need no additional assis-tance. Many of them have well-established networks of volunteers and can serve as sources of information for others. Lower-middle-class schools could use some help. The most assistance would be needed for those schools designated working class and in neighbor-hoods with high levels of immigrants. How could the working-class schools be aided? Placement of additional district resources in those schools would be one way of providing a "level playing field." Principals and teachers known for their ability to establish networks of volunteers under adverse conditions could be moved (voluntarily, of course) to those schools. Coordinators, whose task would be to make bridges to the community, could be placed in those schools. With such resources, working-class schools would share in the payoffs of voluntarism. Would all schools benefit? Perhaps not. Some schools serve children from neighborhoods in which social dislocation is so great that it may not be possible to attract voluntary resources to them. In the few cases where "it can't be done," fully public provision of the resources for schooling or other special actions may be necessary.

Proposed State and Provincial Policies

Voluntarism has been conceived in this study as a grassroots phe-nomenon. This viewpoint implies that it cannot be legislated, it can only be encouraged. The current position of many policymakers is that the public schools are fully publicly supported and that benevo-lence is contrary to their vision of an equitable education for all children. That normative stance, when conveyed to the populace, provides a strong reason for not giving to schools. If, however, policy leaders were to assert that public schools were mostly, but not fully, supported by tax moneys, then the citizenry would have much more reason to support schools voluntarily. If educational leaders were to suggest that community members had the moral obligation to support the school of their choice, then appeals for help from the schools might meet with greater response, particularly from those without children in school.

Would provincial or state resource allocation be altered under a general policy of voluntarism? Paradoxically, it may be necessary to hurt schools to help them. Reduction in funding is perceived to be a reason for an increase in voluntarism. While severe retrenchment would produce considerable disruption and layoffs, minimal increases in resources for schools would produce a climate in which schools could be encouraged to look beyond tax dollars for support.

Are there other policies for voluntarism that provincial ministries of education could pursue? The ultimate responsibility for education rests with provinces and states. While offering moral leadership and controlling most tax resources, they could also provide direction and resources for the administration of benevolence. Grants, personnel, and information would constitute valuable contributions to districts.

General Policy Issues

It is possible that, if the conclusions about voluntarism are correct, benevolence may be a promising avenue for school improvement. Just what is to be the future orientation of schools? Are they to be viewed solely as servers of society or simply as extensions of families? How should a school relate to its community? Is a path of compromise between public funding and grassroots action possible? Glazer (1988) states,

> Certainly the role of the state is crucial. But it must more and more consider partnerships with the variety of voluntary, market, non-statutory organizations and mechanisms that we find in each society according to its distinctive history. And states must ponder the possibility that their own actions undermine the ability of societies to respond to needs as well as or better than the state can. (p. 139)

Could voluntarism be a powerful force in the reform of education? Martin (1985) offers considerable hope for the contribution of benevolence to all forms of humanistic service in Canada in his book imaginatively titled *An Essential Grace*. Belief in the goodwill of individuals persists in Canada and it may be even stronger in the United States (Lipset, 1990). Americans, take note! As Woodrow Wilson observed,

Nothing but what you volunteer has the essence of life, the springs of pleasure in it. These are the things you do because you want to do them, the things your spirit has chosen for its satisfaction. . . . The more you are stimulated to such action the more clearly does it appear to you that you are a sovereign spirit, put into the world not to wear a harness, but to work eagerly without it. (Baccalaureate address at Princeton, June 13, 1909)

The state can pay the bills but it cannot love a school. What kind of schools do we want our children to attend in the twenty-first century? Will they be schools with heart?

References

Boulding, K. (1989). *Three faces of power.* Newbury Park, CA: Sage.

Boyd, W. L. (1987). Public education's last hurrah? Schizophrenia, amnesia, and ignorance in school politics. *Educational Evaluation and Policy Analysis, 9*(2), 85-100.

Brown, D. J. (1990). *Decentralization and school-based management.* London: Falmer.

Brown, D. J. (1991). *Decentralization: The administrator's guide to school district change.* Newbury Park, CA: Corwin.

Brown, D. J. (1993). *Schools with heart: Voluntarism and public education.* Unpublished monograph, University of British Columbia, Department of Administrative, Adult, and Higher Education.

Chubb, J., & Moe, T. (1990). *Politics, markets, and America's schools.* Washington, DC: Brookings.

Coleman, J. S. (1990). *Foundations of social theory.* Cambridge, MA: Harvard University Press.

Coleman, J. S., & Hoffer, T. (1987). *Public and private high schools: The impact of communities.* New York: Basic Books.

Epstein, J. (1990). School and family connections: Theory, research, and implications for integrating sociologies of education and family. In D. G. Unger & M. B. Sussman (Eds.), *Families in community settings: Interdisciplinary perspectives* (pp. 99-126). New York: Haworth.

Glazer, N. (1988). *The limits of social policy.* Cambridge, MA: Harvard University Press.

Henderson, A. (1988). Parents are a school's best friends. *Phi Delta Kappan, 70*(2), 148-153.

Jencks, C. (1987). Who gives to what? In W. Powell (Ed.), *The nonprofit sector: A research handbook*. New Haven, CT: Yale University Press.

Lareau, A. (1989). *Home advantage: Social class and parental intervention in elementary education*. London: Falmer.

Lieberman, A., & Miller, L. (1990). Restructuring schools: What matters and what works. *Phi Delta Kappan, 71*(10), 759-764.

Lipset, S. (1990). *Continental divide: The values and institutions of the United States and Canada*. New York: Routledge & Kegan Paul.

Martin, S. (1985). *An essential grace*. Toronto: McClelland and Stewart.

McLaughlin, M. W., & Schields, P. (1987). Involving low-income parents in the schools: A role for policy? *Phi Delta Kappan, 69*(2), 156-160.

Michael, B. (Committee on the Use of Volunteers in Schools, Commission on Behavioral and Social Sciences and Education, National Research Council). (1990). *Volunteers in public schools*. Washington, DC: National Academy Press.

Miles, M., & Huberman, A. M. (1984). *Qualitative data analysis*. Beverly Hills, CA: Sage.

Morgan, G. (1986). *Images of organization*. Newbury Park, CA: Sage.

Social Planning and Research Council of British Columbia (SPARC). (1989). *Volunteers in the Burnaby school system*. Vancouver, BC: Author.

Weisbrod, B. (1988). *The nonprofit economy*. Cambridge, MA: Harvard University Press.

ELEVEN

Educational Transformations in a "United" Germany

WOLFGANG MITTER

MANFRED WEISS

On October 3, 1990, Germany was legally reunified. The "transitional" phase started by Erich Honecker's overthrow 1 year before had come to a formal end, insofar as the German Democratic Republic (GDR) ceased to exist. Two months later, on December 2, 1990, the first all-German *Bundestag* was elected by the whole voting population of Germany. In the meantime, there were passionate debates about the chances of building an "alternative" East German state, to be based upon a merger of "democracy" and "free socialism." Though now reduced to low-level and limited manifestations, these debates have not disappeared among intellectuals and theologians. Yet this theme had already ceased to be a mass concern on the threshold of 1990, as the slogan "we are the people" was transformed into "we are one people" by the Leipzig "Monday demonstrators." This change in public sentiment was taken up (or accompanied) by West German policy and led to the well-known result. That is why the 12 months between October 1989 and October 1990 must now be considered as an "interim year," including its impact on education (Hörner, 1990).

In legal terms, German reunification has been based upon the "accession" of the German Democratic Republic to the Federal Republic of Germany, according to article 23 of its Basic Law; the alternative provision as contained in article 146—namely, to elaborate a new

Constitution and to have it confirmed by general referendum (of all Germans) was also discussed—but finally rejected.

Schools in East Germany are facing numerous challenges regarding their orientation in the education system and, moreover, in the whole of the social system. The changes they have to undergo affect structural as well as curricular issues. Above all, however, they must cope with the attitudes that have survived the collapse of the Marxist-Leninist ideology. In particular, students must learn how to overcome their internalized shyness of making choices and decisions (Mitter, 1992, p. 51). These challenges are exacerbated by the fact that the problems must be solved with thousands of teachers who had been loyal executors of the hitherto official doctrines. Of course, teacher education is highly involved in the reeducation process. At the end of 1990, all departments and faculties of education at East German universities were dissolved and, over the course of 1991, replaced by newly organized units with former professors and lecturers given the chance to apply for reappointment. In short, East Germany represents a laboratory for educational reform in which there is an overall trend toward adjustment to its West German counterpart dominating the near future. Given that current policy debates in East Germany mirror other discussions about possible all-European or even global interrelationships, however, education in West Germany could hardly be expected to remain unaffected. Although structural and curricular issues had been handled quite smoothly in the late 1970s and 1980s, there are already signs that this "stability" is eroding in West Germany, with calls for an all-German system operating as a stimulus for change.

Aspects of
Adjustment and Conflict

With the unification and the (re)constitution of the East German *Länder* following the elections of October 14, 1990, the "interim year" of more or less "wild growth" came to a sudden end. The following year was characterized by decisions and measures taken by Länder parliaments (Landtage) and authorities to restructure "their" education systems according to their constitutionally warranted "cultural responsibility" (Kulturhoheit). The legal reconstruction of the educational systems in the reconstituted Länder of Eastern Germany has been strongly marked by adjustment to West German models. These processes have been created and reinforced by the following trends.

(1) Equal or similar composition of Länder governments, rooted in coalitions or one-party dominance, has favored the "importation" of structural and curricular peculiarities from West to East. Striking examples can be observed of how cooperation has been built up between Brandenburg and Northrhine-Westphalia, which are dominated or governed by Social Democrats (SPD), and between Saxony and Baden-Württemberg, which are governed by Christian Democrats (CDU).

(2) "Working alliances" have also resulted simply from geographic proximity and have been supported by shared reminiscences of former relations. These alliances have proven to be practical despite contrasting political majorities. This is the case with Schleswig-Holstein (SPD dominated) and Mecklenburg-West Pomerania (CDU dominated), Lower Saxony (SPD dominated) and Saxony-Anhalt (CDU dominated), as well as Hessen (SPD dominated) and Thuringia (CDU dominated).

(3) The East German Länder governments have hired civil servants from the West at various levels of educational administration, up to the position of secretary of state (deputy minister). In contrast to other departments (justice, economy, and so on), the ministers themselves (so far) have been recruited from "native" East Germans only, Mecklenburg-West Pomerania excepted.

There is legitimate criticism, however, that such seemingly supportive engagements often include a tendency to impose "Western" experience and attitudes on "newcomers," without taking their assets and concerns into due consideration. Whether deliberate or unintentional, it is this patronizing behavior that has led critics to apply the term *colonialism* to these relationships. Although such comments should be recognized as exaggerations with regard to the "normality" of educational policies and everyday school practice, they do indicate dark facets of the current situation and call attention to the sociopolitical situation of a "united" Germany in toto. Moreover, it suggests a need to better understand the German people's frame of mind concerning their interrelations with one another.

Considering the close connections that have developed between and among educational administrations in West and East Germany, an external observer is likely to be surprised to notice the emergence of specific structural and curricular features in the East German Länder, which signal their particular needs and interests. Perhaps even more important is the fact that these needs and interests mirror issues and trends relevant to West Germany as well. Without claiming anything like completeness, the following reflections present four such issues. The first two deal with primary and general secondary education, while the third and fourth are devoted to vocational and higher education.

Primary and General Secondary Education

Structural Issues

The education acts recently passed in East Germany (Führ, 1992, pp. 15-23) have focused on the abolition of the Ten-Year General Education Polytechnic Secondary School, the unified comprehensive school that had been established to merge primary and secondary education "under one roof." The lower stage of these comprehensive schools have all been reorganized as separate primary schools, while changes in lower-secondary education are more reflective of the majority political constellations in an individual *Land*. For example, all CDU-dominated Länder have (re)established selective *Gymnasien* (grammar schools), while only SPD-dominated Brandenburg has given priority to *Gesamtschulen* (comprehensive schools). Except for Mecklenburg-West Pomerania, all the East German Länder have refrained from (re)establishing *Hauptschulen* (short-course secondary schools), which represent the nonselective secondary school found in West German Länder. In Brandenburg, the Gesamtschulen recruit primary school-leavers without any selective procedure, with selective Gymnasien and *Realschulen* (middle schools) existing beside them. Saxony, Saxony-Anhalt, and Thuringia, on the other hand, have introduced school types that merge Realschulen and Hauptschulen. In the education acts, these appear under the names "middle school," "regular school," or just "secondary school." This specific trend has been directly caused by the financial need to avoid having to run separate school units in thinly populated rural areas. But it also responds to a trend in West Germany that shows the rapidly decreasing attractiveness of Hauptschulen for "German" parents, particularly in big cities, irrespective of their current political majority.

Whereas in 1960 almost two thirds of students in grades 7-9 attended Hauptschulen, in 1991 the figure was 33.4%. During the same period, attendance rates for this age group increased from 15.6% to 28.7% at the Realschulen and from 20.5% to more than 31% at the Gymnasium. Consequently, in many places, Hauptschulen have already degenerated into "schools for the leftovers," including socially disadvantaged German students, students with learning disabilities, and foreign children of different origin and command of the German language. The last group sometimes represents more than three quarters of the student population in these schools.

It is generally expected that the situation of the Hauptschule will worsen in the future despite measures aimed at raising educational standards, improving equipment, and expanding curricular and extracurricular offerings. Surveys show that the proportion of parents who content themselves with the Hauptschule certificate for their children decreased from 31% in 1979 to about 10% in 1991. At the same time, the proportion of parents who want their children to attain the highest school-completion certificate, the *Abitur* (which is the qualification necessary for general university entrance), increased from 38% to more than 50%. Comparable educational aspirations exist among East German parents, who were included in the 1991 survey for the first time (Rolff et al., 1992, pp. 11 ff.). After reunification, 30% of the relevant age groups transferred from primary schools to an educational track leading to the Abitur—twice the number of transfers that had been customary in GDR times.

A special case is presented by Berlin, which enjoys the status of a Land (like Hamburg and Bremen). In the now-united city, the schools of the East have adjusted almost entirely to the Western pattern, although the establishment of 6-year primary schools stands out as an exception to the West German 4-year "rule." Brandenburg, which is considering integration with Berlin into a joint Land, has adopted the Berlin system at this level. The organization of upper-secondary general education in East Germany follows the West German example in that the Reformed Gymnasium Upper Stage has replaced the former GDR Extended Secondary School (Erweiterte Oberschule). Yet, here again, the East German Länder, except Brandenburg, have followed a separate path by installing a 2-year course instead of the 3-year course that represents the normal pattern in West Germany.

Curricular Issues

It is evident that the syllabi recently introduced in the East German Länder bear the stamp of their Western counterparts. This adjustment was reinforced by the adoption of textbooks issued, in most cases, by West German publishers. Yet, these "quick-fix" measures hardly serve to fill significant gaps. First, West German syllabi and textbooks are predominantly oriented toward methods of instruction based upon communicative interaction between teachers and students; therefore contents and methodological guidelines in the textbooks are aimed at motivating students to independent thinking and learning. This over-all orientation necessarily confronts East German students, and especially their teachers, with unexpected requirements, because the GDR school had been focused on an authoritarian style of instruction, at least generally speaking.

Second, the East German school has to cope with the "socialist" inheritance of ideological indoctrination and must now open educa-tion up to the basic values of human rights, freedom, and democracy. This challenge is radical per se. Teachers and students can meet and internalize it only when they are given the chance to reflect upon the East German past with regard to their own life stories and the history of the GDR in general. West German textbooks that mirror different, if not contrasting, experiences can offer little help. Therefore provid-ing East German schools with textbooks for history, social studies, and so on (or, at least, with Western editions adapted to new requirements) has become an urgent demand that has not yet been satisfied, al-though some West German publishers have discovered the opportu-nity for expansion. On the other hand, the unification of Germany, which was tackled as a theme of "utopian" character before 1989, has confronted the schools in the West with the task of reexamining many a chapter of what was previously taught. All these reconsiderations of subject matter and instructional methods are overshadowed by the challenge to define a "national identity" in the united country with special regard to a multidimensional "Europe" (to be dealt with later in the chapter).

Finally, religious instruction has appeared on the all-German agenda. Since its reintroduction into the syllabi, religious instruction has provoked controversial debate in East Germany, which in turn has produced ripple effects in the West—an occurrence that would have been inconceivable until now. It seems that resistance to giving reli-

gion the status of a "regular" subject can be discerned as the most
visible aftereffect of "socialist education." Of course, such an interpretation comes close to being an oversimplification, because it evades a
crucial problem concerning the position of religion and churches in
modern society anywhere (both of which, in turn, must be addressed
separately!). In West and, recently, East Germany, debates are being
held about offering religious instruction in the form of "comparative
religious studies." In the Land of Brandenburg, these debates have
brought about a provisional curricular arrangement, which is focused
upon a project to examine the viability of an interdenominational unit
called "ethics." While the Protestant church, though rather hesitantly,
has given its consent, the Catholic church has definitely refrained from
joining this project.

Vocational Education

Vocational education in East Germany has also been a theme of
critical discussions. Here, however, controversies do not affect essential structural or curricular issues, nor do they question the achievement level, which enjoys a relatively high reputation in West Germany
and in international comparisons. This esteem refers both to full-time
technical schools and to the "dual" training system that West and East
Germany have retained and continuously extended as a common
"German inheritance"—not withstanding some important structural
differences between the training systems (see Uthmann, 1991).

Critical comments, however, have surfaced as to the technological
backwardness with regard to modern standards characterizing part
of the former GDR variety, particularly in comparison with innovations implemented in West Germany during the past 20 years. Observers have pointed out that many training courses simply cannot
meet the requirements of economic progress in a satisfactory way. The
process of total reconstruction, in which the whole economic system
in East Germany has been involved, has aggravated this crisis of
"dual" training insofar as many former state-owned firms have been
closed, and with them thousands of training positions. New enterprises are growing slowly and there is a shortage of some 70,000
training positions. Special emergency projects (e.g., the establishment
of suprafirm training centers) have not been sufficient to fill the gap.
In this respect, the situation in West Germany is entirely different,

where decreasing birthrates and increasing attendance at Gymnasien by youngsters aged 15-19 have brought about a significant deficit in the number of apprentices. In 1992, for example, 120,000 training positions remained unoccupied.

It is just this crisis of the "dual" system, though differently caused in West and East, that is likely to necessitate fundamental reforms in the whole system of vocational education. Western experiments in arranging special training courses for Gymnasium leavers who do not (immediately) want to enter higher education studies (some 17% of all apprentices belong to this group) can be regarded as one alternative model to overcome the crisis. An open question is, however, whether companies will still be willing to invest up to 100,000 DM in the training of a person who will continue university study at the end of his or her apprenticeship (currently about half of the apprentices holding the Abitur take advantage of this option).

In this context, critical observers also regret that the upper-secondary training arrangement *Berufsausbildung mit Abitur* (vocational training with secondary graduation), which was considered an asset of the GDR system, has not been retained. Such criticism is reinforced by the ongoing development and expansion of similar school units in a good number of Western countries such as France, Sweden, and the United Kingdom.

Higher Education

Universities and polytechnics in East Germany have been exposed to thorough and far-reaching reforms whose outcomes are not yet predictable. On the one hand, departments and faculties in the humanities and social sciences (including education) have been dissolved and replaced by newly organized units. On the other hand, the universities that were mostly deprived of fundamental research (which was monopolized by the now closed Academy of Sciences and a variety of specialized research institutes) are expected to restore traditional ties between research and teaching.

Emphasizing this task does not mean concealing the crisis into which higher education had fallen in West Germany as well during the 1980s. There, the universities and polytechnics have to cope with an ever-growing number of students, which is likely to reach the 2 million mark. The resources allocated to higher education did not at all correspond with the increase in demand in this sector. For example, between 1975 and 1991, student numbers have almost doubled, whereas staff increased only by 20% (scientific staff just 13%). Currently, some 900,000 study places are available for 1.8 million students. Thus the whole system in West Germany has had to cope with a tremendous overload, a situation that significantly affects research capabilities, let alone the various needs for basic and specific organizational and curricular reforms. The universities in the GDR were not affected by such expansion because their admission quota had always been kept at a more or less stabilized level (about 10% of the age group versus 25% in West Germany by the end of the 1980s).

For the time being, recruitment data do not yet signal any significant expansion at East German universities. This, however, should not be considered a static observation (see Führ, 1992, pp. 11, 26-29), because, in view of the high educational aspirations in the East German Länder, it can be expected that the demand for higher education studies will increase and reach West German levels in due course. It is hoped that by then the process of restructuring and extending the higher education sector in the new Länder will be largely completed, thus avoiding the detrimental developments experienced by West German institutions.

Impacts on Education in West Germany

It seems that the overall trend toward adjustment to its West German counterpart will dominate the near future of schools in East Germany. Yet, at this moment, the contours to be recognized of an East German educational system do not yet allow any justified predictions. While the current debates in the new East German Länder indicate uncertainties on the one hand, the aforementioned "deviations" from the "West-bound" trend are not to be overlooked. In fact, one should not be surprised if this trend increases on a medium-term basis. Whether the "assets" of the former GDR system will experience a certain revival (of course, related to the changed socioeconomic and political framework) must remain an open question. In particular, such an "asset" is given, above all, in the field of polytechnic and prevocational education, although its theoretical concept as well as its implementation need to be reconsidered. In this context, the former unit Berufsausbildung mit Abitur comes into the picture again.

On the other hand, education in West Germany can hardly be
expected to be left unaffected by its cooperation with its Eastern
counterpart. This prediction can be permitted for the sole reason that
great numbers of school administrators and university lecturers have
been delegated or invited to East Germany to help reconstruct education, teaching, and research—which is an ambivalent enterprise given
the aforementioned "closing-down" and "reopening" activities. The
experiences of "Western people" under East German "laboratory"
conditions will no doubt influence them and affect their further
professional work "at home" after their return. Moreover, the overall
debates in the public, pushed by, among others, the various teachers'
associations and the media, can be regarded as catalyzing stimuli in
this process of mutual impacts. The following examples are put
forward to justify this hypothesis. First, it seems that the newly
established dual (bipartite) structure at the lower-secondary level,
as enacted in the aforementioned East German Länder, can be considered a reaction to a West German deficiency, all the more so as
some prominent West German educationists have recommended this
model as an alternative to their traditional tripartite system (e.g.,
Hurrelmann, 1988).

Second, current debates in the West German Länder about reducing
the length of primary and secondary education from 13 to 12 years,
which were motivated initially by "European" concerns of equiva-
lence (according to the policy of "harmonization" in the European
Community), have been reinforced by examination of the East German "12-year model." Consequently, this has led to an agreement
reached by the Standing Conference of Ministers of Education (Stän-
dige Konferenz der Kultusminister) that consists of the provisional
recognition of both variations.

Third, a striking interest in private schools in East Germany appears
to be a further significant phenomenon. Currently, this interest can be
interpreted as a symptom of aversion to state control and as a corollary
of people remembering the collapsed "democratic centralism." The
increased interest such schools have also gained in West Germany
(Weiss & Mattern, 1991) allows the assumption that common trends
in West and East Germany coincide. Finally, reacting to the breakdown
of the former "command education" (Kommandopädagogik), teachers, parents, and also students in East Germany have initiated pilot
projects at their schools focused on "quality in education," that is,
developing a "school ethos" for the sake of humanizing communica-

tion, interaction, and learning. Although the first initiatives after the collapse of the "socialist regime" seem to have faded out as a result of the formal "consolidating" effects of the new education acts, some have survived and continue their innovating efforts in the legal form of "pilot projects." So far, they have been small in number, but they have revealed a remarkable commitment that might have a positive impact on comparable efforts that have characterized the West German scene since the beginning of the 1980s.

The Financial Context of Educational Reforms

Any future room to maneuver for educational reforms will be significantly restricted by Germany's precarious fiscal situation. This is primarily a consequence of the financial burdens connected with reunification. Tax revenue in East Germany, whose capital stock experienced almost complete devaluation,[1] is far too low to finance the restructuring of the economy and the adjustment process of the public sector. For an indefinite period, substantial government transfers from West Germany will be needed. In 1991 East Germany received net transfers of 125 billion DM from West German public budgets; in 1992 the transfers amounted to 150 billion DM. Between 1990 and 1994, almost 145 billion DM will be provided by the "German Unity Fund." Up to now, the main burden of transfer payments has been borne by the federal government; the share of the Länder has been relatively small. This, however, will change by the end of 1994 with the expiration of the "German Unity Fund." Then the new East German Länder will be included in the system of revenue equalization between the Länder (Länderfinanzausgleich). The equalization contributions to be made by the financially strong West German Länder will considerably affect their budgets and thus their educational systems, which are funded mainly by Länder revenues (approximately three fourths of the total educational expenditure). The situation will be aggravated by an increase in the number of students in the general education sector in West Germany by more than 17% between the years 1990 and 2005.

The coincidence of budget constraints and increasing educational demand implies that the number of teaching posts cannot be extended in accordance with the increase in enrollments; that is, it will not be possible (for the first time in the last two and a half decades) to maintain the status quo in education. Adjustments have been made, or are planned, by the Länder governments by prolonging the work time of teachers, increasing class size, reducing the prescribed schedule of lessons, and canceling certain reductions of the teaching load (e.g., old age reductions, reductions for administrative activities). Whereas these measures are strongly criticized by teacher and parent organizations, the Länder audit offices, anxious to check the "cost disease" (Baumol) in education,[2] insist on their realization. In recently published reports on the economy of resource use in education (Weiss, 1992a), some audit offices complain that too much of teachers' working time has been withdrawn from classroom instruction and, due to an inefficient school organization, personnel resources are being wasted.

The aforementioned situation demonstrates a basic problem of the differentiated German school system in which different competing schools coexist at the lower-secondary level (grades 5-10). The negative consequences of this structural peculiarity are especially being felt by the Hauptschulen (short-course secondary schools), which, as noted earlier, have experienced a considerable loss of attractiveness in recent years. Particularly in urban settings, many of these schools are significantly undersubscribed, causing substantial "diseconomies of scale." In view of experiences with a formally differentiated school system in West Germany, the adoption of this system (with some modifications) by the new Länder is difficult to comprehend. This is especially the case if one takes into consideration the "demographic implosion" currently occurring in East Germany—a demographic change unparalleled in German history. Specifically, between 1989 and 1992, the number of births in East Germany declined from 200,000 to about 80,000, that is, to 40% of the 1989 figure. This decline will have far-reaching implications for the newly established school structure in the East German Länder (Budde & Klem, 1992). School closures and the establishment of multigrade primary schools in sparsely populated rural areas will be unavoidable. At the lower-secondary level, where several school types compete for a steadily decreasing number of students, the existence of the schools ranked below the Gymnasium (or the corresponding tracks in comprehensive schools) will be jeopardized. This demographic decline will, on the one hand, relieve the budgets of the new Länder while, on the other hand, substantially increase unit costs due to "diseconomies of scale," which are to a great extent a consequence of the school structure imported from the old Länder.

The pressure to overcome these inefficiencies inherent in the German school system will move the question of school structure—which was hotly debated in the 1970s in connection with the proposed replacement of the tripartite secondary school system with a comprehensive one—back onto the political agenda. Of decisive importance for the topicality of the efficiency issue in education was a widely publicized expert report compiled by a private management consultancy firm on the state of the school system in Northrhine-Westphalia ("Kienbaum Expert Report"). The reaction of the public to this report was more disquieting to educational policymakers than the uncovered severe shortcomings of the school system of this federal state and the measures recommended to remedy them. Its reception suggests a massive general loss of confidence in the efficiency of the German school system and a dwindling willingness to provide additional resources for education. This is reinforced by objections (raised especially by finance ministers and economists) to a further increment in the number of civil servants, in view of a substantial increase in future pension payments that is a consequence of the expansion policy of the 1960s and 1970s. According to projections for the former Federal Republic, the proportion of the total tax revenue necessary to finance all personnel expenditures of the federal government, the Länder, and the communities, given the current employment size and structure in the public sector and a constant tax rate, will increase from 45% at the current time to about 67% in 2030 (Färber, 1992). Suffice it to say that this is a politically unacceptable and thus unrealistic magnitude.

To summarize this section, it can be stated that the future fiscal situation in Germany will not provide favorable conditions for educational reforms. Educational policymakers can no longer count on expanding educational budgets as in the past. Instead, they will be forced, for the first time, to make special efforts to ensure a sufficient financial base for the educational system. This implies the fulfillment of a number of "fiscal management" tasks including (a) the full use of possibly redeployed resources, (b) the gradual elimination of inefficiencies (especially by changing the school structure), (c) the establishment of priorities guiding the internal allocation of resources, and (d) the search for new sources of funding in the private sector (Weiss & Weishaupt, 1992). Even in the case of successful "fiscal management" (which seems highly improbable), the room to maneuver for educational reforms will be quite constricted. Consequently, cost-intensive reform measures like expanding all-day schooling and integrating disabled children into regular classes will largely have to be put off for the time being, forcing educational policymakers to place greater emphasis on "cost-neutral" reforms.

Conclusions

This chapter has been built on the assumption that current transformations in the East German Länder coincide with radical challenges affecting the united Germany as a whole. The need for educational reforms is, on the one hand, caused by the wide range of demands presented by science, technology, and the economy. On the other hand, Germany is increasingly incorporated into supra- and international ties, as there are (a) short-term contributions to the consolidation of the European Community, whose initiatives in educational matters have already become relevant; (b) concurrent and growing commitment to the "wider Europe," which entails the revival of former educational cooperation with Germany's neighbors in Central and Eastern Europe, as well as the opening of new commitments; and (c) continuing commitment to projects aimed at supporting education in developing countries and regions.

This "Europeanizing" and "globalizing" orientation must be achieved in a situation in which Germany herself has started her march into a *multicultural society*—although this term and its underlying concepts are controversial among both politicians and the general public. The number of migrants among the "foreigners" has come close to 5 million. In addition, the continual arrival of "ethnic Germans" from Poland, Romania, and the former Soviet Union must be coped with. This task is far more difficult than external observers may assume, because their "return" into the "home country," which their ancestors left centuries ago, involves identity issues, all the more so as many "returners" (especially among the younger generation) do not speak any German. Finally, the situation is further complicated by the vast, and seemingly never-ending, number of people seeking asylum. Controversial debates on whether or to what extent "political" and "economic" motives can be separated only hide the universal and topical foundations of the migration issue.

Within the framework of this overarching transformation process, the observer can identify problems concerning the internal cohesion of the education system per se. This hypothesis can be illustrated by the following three statements:

First, the "revision" of the large-scale reforms that were initiated and implemented in West Germany in the late 1960s and early 1970s must not be simplistically labeled political "conservatism." The search for an explanation must be more open and differentiated. The observer should take into special account that conservatives, but also liberals and even social democrats, prefer to maintain or reestablish separate (parallel) schools at the secondary level of education (preferably in the form of bipartite structures). The recent restabilization of the Gymnasium against the overall trend toward making secondary education more comprehensive that prevails in the majority of the European countries has been affected by the widespread awareness of the importance of new technologies for content, method, process, and achievement in learning. Consequently, a striking public appreciation of excellence and selection has replaced concerns for equity and support (this is particularly evident with regard to the promotion of highly gifted youngsters).

Taking this situation into general account, it is not surprising that the Gymnasium can be considered the unchallenged "market leader" in the esteem of parents. This is even accepted in the meantime—admittedly with some reluctance—by the most radical advocates of the comprehensive school, the GEW teacher union. The "peace" that has been reached after the long-lasting "cultural struggle" over the school structure at lower-secondary level in the 1970s should not, however, hide the fact that the obvious structural deficiencies of the German school system press for political action. There is sufficient evidence that the tripartite school system cannot adjust effectively to shifts in educational demand and that the coexistence of different competing secondary schools tends to increase total system costs. Educational policymakers cannot shirk their responsibilities in this matter, as is suggested by their recently applied strategy of shifting important decisions to school-level negotiations, which has been introduced in the guise of strengthening school autonomy and parent empowerment (e.g., the new Education Act in Hesse—for details, see Weiss, 1992b). It might be that the growing concern for cost and efficiency in education will make it easier in the future to discuss the school structure issue in a less ideologically biased way than in the 1970s, when equity considerations were the main issue.

Whereas the majority of the West German Länder governments hesitate to get (re)involved in this discussion, in a few Länder, promising structural changes have been initiated, for example, the introduction of "Regional Schools" in Rhineland-Palatinate, which combine Hauptschulen and Realschulen. This marks a first step toward the development of attractive alternatives to the Gymnasium within a "bipartite school structure." It could finally lead to a system of two formally equivalent types of schools as proposed by some educationists. According to Hurrelmann (1988), alongside the Gymnasium, with its preparatory-study orientation toward academic subjects, a new kind of comprehensive school should be established as an alternative, one that combines vocational and general educational curricular contents (practical and theoretical learning) and also provides the opportunity to attain (in addition to all other school-completion certificates) the Abitur.

Second, the de facto revival of the Gymnasium and the declining interest in the "comprehensive" concept must not obscure the emergence of a remarkable number of multifarious pilot projects and innovative activities within the traditional school type. We can even point out that the principals and teaching staffs of Gymnasien have fewer scruples in such engagements, because the existence of their schools as such, contrary to that of comprehensive schools (Gesamtschulen), is not in danger or contested. These pilot projects help strengthen the move toward internal school reforms at all levels of the education system. The goals are defined mainly as quality in educational school ethos (also known as "climate" or "chemistry").

Third, a manifest drive among parents and the public in general has crystallized in changing conceptions of schools from governmental institutions to service agencies. The outcomes of this drive result in the increase of competing alternatives instead of the hitherto privileged monopolizing solutions. It is true that, for the time being, public expectations indicate a significant preference for the tripartite system. In a growing number of places, however, principals and teachers of comprehensive schools have succeeded in making their social reputation and in consolidating their positions in and beyond their communities. This trend, taken as a whole, signals changes in public attitudes, tending to more flexibility on the one hand and to more democratization on the other. Among the social groups that have made known their expectations and demands, we must not forget the youngsters themselves who, compared with their "predecessors," seem to have learned better how to express their attitudes and aspirations, including their critical judgments. In this respect, students attending Gymnasien today have little in common with those of previous generations.

The apparent "consolidation" that resulted from the "revision" of the reform in the West German Länder before the breakdown of the Berlin Wall at the end of 1989 was, in fact, far from maintaining the kind of "stabilization" that some people and, particularly, politicians might have dreamed in the early and middle 1980s. The above-mentioned examples seem to intimate that hopes for new innovations may not end in academic debate but may be translated into political and pedagogic action, all the more so as the current social and economic crisis underlines the need for reconsideration and reform.

Finally, it is the situation of the young generation that challenges educators and policymakers to new initiatives. Emotional reactions to the current crisis, prompted by confusion and ignorance, have laid the groundwork for aggression and even violence against "strangers." Young people in East Germany seem to be particularly susceptible to such aberrations, in counteraction to having been indoctrinated with abstract and unreal slogans of "proletarian solidarity" and "socialist brotherhood." Recent acts of violence committed by right-wing youngsters in several East German cities and villages, however, immediately exerted an "awakening" effect on nationalistic and even racist activities among like-minded peers in West Germany. Such outbreaks of a tiny minority might be treated calmly, if they did not signal latent sentiments among ordinary people. Youngsters and young adults, lacking qualifications and therefore permanently confronted with unemployment, can be identified as the group most exposed to such extremism. This radical challenge must be met in a period wherein all industrialized nations (the specific problems of the developing countries are neglected in this context) are confronted with basic value conflicts concerning the moral standards to be conveyed to the young generation. The recent "invasion" of drugs and juvenile criminality into East Germany, together with right-wing violence, only demonstrates the extreme and most detestable concomitants of "Western civilization." Here Germany is included in a crisis of European and, moreover, global scope.

In this connection, one must be aware that many objectionable

phenomena that required, among other strategies, educational coun-
teractions, existed under the former "socialist" roof as well, though
concealed by a regime that denied what should not exist. In this
respect, one can find East Germany in the same boat with other
"postsocialist" countries with comparable outbreaks of extremism,
particularly among youngsters and young adults—which, of course,
should not be used as any kind of excuse for what has become
manifest in Germany to an alarming extent.

Summarizing, however, it is precisely the bulk of the young generation that has accepted the challenges set by the reunification in Germany and by the current social and economic crisis. It is true that this
acceptance is hardly based on any "patriotic pride," let alone enthusiasm. One could rather speak of realistic response to what "must be
done." It seems that the combination of realism, openness, and uncertainty should not be underestimated as a promising perspective,
including its relevance to the education system as a whole.

Notes

1. This is reflected by several indicators: (a) Industrial production in East Germany
declined to one third of the 1989 level; (b) the GDP (Gross Domestic Product) decreased
by almost 50%; (c) former GDR enterprises are not competitive internationally; and (d)
average productivity is only about one third of the West German level. The sharp drop
in industrial production is also the result of the conversion of currency (the introduction
of the DM on July 1, 1990), which led to an enormous decline in exports to the East
European countries. In total, between 1990 and 1991, exports declined to one third of
their former level. The impact of the economic collapse on the labor market is reflected
by the decline in employed persons (1 million became unemployed; Siebert, 1992).

2. Between 1970 and 1990, expenditures per student almost quadrupled, from 1,550
DM in 1970 to 5,700 DM in 1990. In 1970 the student-teacher ratio in the general
educational sector was 26.5; in 1990 it was 15.2.

References

Budde, H., & Klem, K. (1992). Äußere Schulentwicklung in den neuen Ländern:
    Perspektiven und Gefährdungen. In H. G. Rolff et al. (Eds.), *Jahrbuch der Schulent-
    wicklung, Band 7* (pp. 133-157). München: Juventa.
Färber, G. (1992). *Revision der Personalausgabenprojektion der Gebietskörperschaften bis
    2030*. Speyer: Forschungsinstitut für Öffentliche Verwaltung.

Führ, C. (1992). *On the education system in the five new Laender of the Federal Republic of Germany.* Bonn: Inter Nationes.

Hörner, W. (1990). *Bildung und Wissenschaft in der DDR: Ausgangslage und Reform bis Mitte 1990.* Bonn: Bundesminister für Bildung und Wissenschaft.

Hurrelmann, K. (1988). Thesen zur strukturellen Entwicklung des Bildungssystems in den nächsten fünf bis zehn Jahren. *Die Deutsche Schule, 4,* 451-461.

Mitter, W. (1992). Educational adjustments and perspectives in a united Germany. *Comparative Education, 1,* 45-52.

Rolff, H. G., et al. (Eds.). (1992). *Jahrbuch der Schulentwicklung, Band 7.* München: Juventa.

Siebert, H. (1992). *Das Wagnis der Einheit.* Stuttgart: Deutsche Verlags-Anstalt.

Uthmann, K. J. (1991). Vocational education and training in Germany after unification. *European Journal of Education, 1,* 5-12.

Weiss, M. (1992a). Zur "inneren Ökonomie" des Schulwesens. *Recht der Jugend und des Bildungswesens, 2,* 206-217.

Weiss, M. (1992b). *New guiding principles in educational policy: The case of Germany.* Paper presented at the annual meeting of the American Educational Research Association, San Francisco.

Weiss, M., & Mattern, C. (1991). The situation and development of the private school system in Germany. In H. von Recum & M. Weiss (Eds.), *Social change and educational planning in West Germany* (pp. 41-62). Frankfurt/Main: German Institute for International Education and Research.

Weiss, M., & Weishaupt, H. (1992). Überlegungen zur Sicherung der Ressourcenausstattung im Bildungswesen. In P. Zedler (Ed.), *Strukturprobleme, Disparitäten, Grundbildung in der Sekundarstufe I* (pp. 177-201). Weinheim: Deutscher Studien Verlag.

PART III

School Reform in the Twenty-First Century

TWELVE

School Reform and the "New World Order"

JAMES W. GUTHRIE

Policy priorities and pedagogical practicalities currently differ among nations and groups of nations and they assuredly will continue to do so. Nevertheless, throughout the industrialized world, governments are seeking effective policies for enhancing economic productivity through education, employing economic incentives to promote the productivity and efficient administration of schooling, and searching for additional resources to meet increasing demands for education. As the purposes of education are becoming globally more determined, the policies and administrative principles that guide pedagogy will likely become increasingly more predictable. The result, at least in Western-bloc nations, may well be a remarkable international convergence among many of the systemic components of schooling, both higher and lower education.

The purpose of this chapter is to (a) describe the economic and social dynamics propelling education policy and management reform internationally, (b) suggest the probable nature of future education system

AUTHOR'S NOTE: A version of this chapter was presented at the Comparative and International Education Society Annual Meeting (March 1990, Anaheim, California). A subsequent version was adapted for the *Hong Kong Education Research Association Journal* in March 1991. I wish to express my appreciation for the constructive comments on this draft of Harry Judge, Charles T. Kerchner, and Lawrence C. Pierce.

administrative commonalties, and (c) speculate regarding the consequences of these changes for educational administration.

Background

Western nations increasingly view schooling as a strategic instrument for promoting national economic development.[1] The primary
policy objective in these instances is to enhance a nation's supply of
human capital. Generally, the nations involved are ones that have
much materially and are hoping to use their education systems to
acquire more. Conversely, education in many Third World nations is
being shaped forcefully by economic adversity. Explosive escalation
of enrollments, low rates of economic growth, awesome climatic
disasters, disproportionate spending on defense, and staggering levels of foreign debt have resulted in dramatic reductions in per pupil
resources. The result is that education systems in many developing
nations have little by way of resources with which increasingly they
must accomplish more.

Of course, the pedagogical world is not all this black and white. The
labor-intensive nature of instruction has resulted in dramatic post-
World War II increases in schooling costs in Western nations. Thus
there frequently is a policy tension as public officials attempt to use
schooling to enhance national economic productivity while simultaneously keeping an eye open for ways to render schooling more
efficient, shift school spending to the private sector, or reduce growth
of education costs. The policies that result frequently reflect this
ambivalent, and sometimes antithetical, amalgam of purposes.

Similarly, leaders in developing nations, regardless of how hard-
pressed their national treasuries, are intensely aware of the economic
benefits, both for individuals and for the entire polity, of an effective
education system. Thus, even when in the midst of widespread education cost control efforts, many Third World nations simultaneously
aspire to use education to enhance national economic development.

It also should be added quickly that international economic conditions are by no means the only forces shaping modern educational
systems. The picture is made more complicated by the existence of
national education reform efforts that stem from purely political
purposes, are perhaps motivated by a nation's internal ideological

dynamics, and are probably shaped by deep-rooted historical conditions, religious beliefs, and idiosyncratic practices (Barber, 1992).

Thus, given the multiplicity of national motives, and the complexity of national conditions, one cannot help but be struck by the remarkable resemblance of internationally emerging educational policies. This convergence is particularly apparent in Western-bloc nations, and such is the focus of this chapter. The probability appears great, however, that, in time, global economic conditions will propel former Eastern-bloc and nonaligned nations in similar directions.

The explosion in modern electronic means for conveying information, the creation of worldwide consumer markets, the existence of a growing international network of education reform ideas and informed educational policy experts, and vast reductions in the time and costs of international travel are stimulating a globalization of schooling. These forces, however, only transmit ideas. The more likely explanation for their widespread adoption is a common set of growing international economic and social imperatives.

Education's Evolving Economic and Social Environment

Nations throughout the modern world are being shaped powerfully by global economic and social forces. Many of these forces act in common upon all nations. Yet, there are sufficient distinctions to justify consideration of groups of nations. This discussion relies upon what have become conventional groupings, between so-called Western, Eastern, and Third World, or nonaligned, nation categories.

Western-Bloc Nations[2]

Powerful military forces, possession of strategically significant geographic locations, access to valuable raw materials, and widespread capacity in basic industries were once the mainstays of national power and international hegemony. Such is less the case today. Conventional military power is declining in economic significance, as is geography. Strategic resources once came from the ground. Increasingly, they come from the mind. The "new" strategic raw material, upon which economic productivity is ever more dependent, is "human capital" (see, for example, Shultz, 1971). Therefore policymakers increasingly escalate their expectations for the performance of education systems.

Throughout history, technological innovations have redistributed power, enabled a tribe, a people, or a nation to vie for and gain dominance. Fire, ferrous metal, and farming are historic discoveries that transformed nations and transferred power. Modern examples include internal combustion engines, interchangeable parts, electrical energy, and electronic components. The list is longer, but the point is the same. Significant technological revolutions formerly were founded upon sporadic scientific discoveries. Increasingly, such shifts are crucially dependent upon systematic inventions.

Rapid communication, expanding information, and modern organizational arrangements are transforming national economies. They are now global in their competitive outlook, internationally interdependent, insatiable in their quest for technological innovation, and crucially dependent upon the availability of human talent. Reliance upon a narrow intellectual elite appears increasingly outmoded. Modern manufacturing and service industry techniques demand a labor force capable of adjusting to new technologies and making informed production decisions. Educated and highly skilled human intelligence is increasingly viewed as a nation's primary economic resource, and it is needed in large amounts.

Modern economics, however, are not simply boosting or gently nudging an already initiated notion that education systems should enhance a nation's human capital resources. Rather, international economic forces are already beginning to reshape the forms of schooling across national boundaries. This "human capital imperative" is only likely to intensify over time. This globalization of education will occur primarily because nations no longer can easily protect their domestic producers from international economic forces. Failure to respond quickly to technological and organizational inventions can rapidly jeopardize a people's standard of living and a government's political future. Increasingly, even former Eastern-bloc nations find that they are no longer immune to or can wall themselves off from the rapid ebb and flow of international trade, monetary, technological, and financial developments.

The following quotation from an October 1989 *Atlantic* article on economic development crystallizes the complex, intertwined, and rapidly evolving nature of international manufacturing and services industries.

Ford, with one third of its sales from outside the United States, owns 25 percent of Mazda. Mazda makes cars in America for Ford; Ford will reciprocate by making trucks for Mazda; and the two companies trade parts. Each owns a piece of Korea's Kia Motors, which produces the Ford Festiva for export to the United States. Ford and Nissan, Japan's No. 2, swap vehicles in Australia and are planning a joint minivan program in America. Ford and Volkswagen have merged into a single company in Latin America, which exports trucks to the United States.

General Motors holds a 41.6 percent stake in Isuzu, which is starting a joint venture in America with Suburu, which is partly owned by Nissan. GM also owns half of Daewoo Motors, Hyundai's major competitor in Korea. Daewoo makes Nissan cars for Japan and Pontiacs for America; soon it will be selling cars that were primarily designed by GM-Europe to Isuzu in Japan. GM has also teamed with Japan's No. 1, Toyota, to produce cars under both companies' labels in America and Australia. (Morris, 1989, pp. 53-54)

As complicated as the above-described explication is, it probably represents the economic and much of the social future for the industrialized world. Consequently, traditional educational values and institutions are being crowded by government officials who, in response to developing economic and social imperatives, believe that new educational policies and practices are necessary for their nation to become or remain vital.

Expansion of the populations served by schools and colleges, centralized curricula expectations, national educational objectives, expanded uses of standardized tests, growing dependence upon government agencies to collect and analyze school performance data, intensified efforts to link colleges and industry, and altered expectations for educational evaluation are among the predictable practical outcomes of this globalization movement.

Specific educational reform tactics and administrative procedures may differ from nation to nation, depending upon historic development patterns, contemporary politics, current resource levels, and operating structures. For example, in national systems stemming from an elitist schooling model—such as England and the historic members of the British Commonwealth—the clear long-run education reform goal will be to expand the numbers of individuals eligible for and interested in seeking higher levels of schooling. In egalitarian-oriented systems, such as the United States, the long-run goal of education reform will be to elevate achievement standards such that there are larger numbers of well-educated workers.

Regardless of the variety of national tactics, the Western world objective will be substantially the same. The long-run goal will be to use educated intellect as a strategic means for a nation to gain or retain an economically competitive position in the global marketplace. As a consequence, education systems increasingly will adopt similar characteristics. Before turning to a description or prediction of these similarities, however, a comment regarding the remainder of the world's nations appears in order.

Former Eastern-Bloc Nations[3]

Attempting to satisfy intensified citizen demand for consumer goods and responding to Western-bloc industrial competition is and will continue to shape public policy reforms in former Eastern-bloc nations. When it comes to education systems specifically, however, the pace of reform appears slower and the direction is less clear. Internal political events, and ethnic and religious conflict, even if accelerated by external economic forces, may well provoke proposals for more intensely socializing students to new political and regime norms.

Also, domestic economies are deeply stressed in many former Eastern-bloc nations, and public sector resources are carefully husbanded. Hence few public leaders are likely to advocate that entire national education systems immediately be transformed exclusively into engines for the formation of added human capital. There currently are other pressing system objectives to be considered and operating efficiencies to be maintained. Nevertheless, within what was the Soviet sphere, there are increasing suggestions regarding education reforms that are similar to those being debated or adopted by Western nations.

Developing, Nonaligned, Nation Dynamics

If anything, economic imperatives are stronger here than in the two previously discussed national groupings. The economic forces are themselves quite different, however. Many developing nations are massively in debt and suffering badly from poverty. Efforts to gain foreign capital to repay these burdens occupy much of the economy. In addition, their populations, including school-age cohorts, are growing rapidly; they allocate disproportionate amounts of gross national product to defense purposes; and their economic growth is insufficient to bear these burdens and simultaneously elevate standards of living.

A few facts underscore the intensity of the problems (Heyneman, 1989). Less developed nations, those with the lowest resource levels, contained 67% of the world's learners in 1950. By the year 2000, this percentage is predicted by the United Nations to increase to 79%. Conversely, the percentage of the world's learners in more developed nations is declining proportionately.

Many developing nations simply do not have the resources to carry this schooling burden. Foreign debt is a part of the problem. In Brazil, 62% of export revenues are obligated to repay foreign loans. Comparable figures for Morocco, Argentina, Ivory Coast, and Algeria are 43%, 34%, 32%, and 27%, respectively. In 1987 the average figure for debt service to export income for low-income developing nations was almost 22%.

Despite these towering debt service burdens, many developing nations allocate large portions of their public wealth to defense. A United Nations estimate places defense spending at 14% of gross national product (GNP) among the lowest income developing nations.[4]

Given these and other pressures, it is not surprising that per student education spending in low-income developing nations has decreased. In sub-Saharan Africa, for example, higher education per pupil resources have been halved, secondary reduced by 40%, and primary reduced by 23% since 1970. Expenditures on nonpersonnel items, such as textbooks, have been reduced even more dramatically.

Under these enormous resource pressures, Third World nations are frequently occupied with finding more cost-efficient means for delivering school services. Using education systems to promote national economic development is a policy objective, but the shortage of resources renders attainment virtually impossible in the foreseeable future.

What Will Be the Converging Components of Global Reform?

Increasingly the education systems of industrialized nations are beginning to exhibit schooling features in common. As the economic purposes of education intensify, this convergence will increase. National variations will certainly continue to abound, as policymakers tailor individual reform dimensions to the particular circumstances of their polity. Also, higher education reforms are likely to be less uniform than reforms for elementary and secondary schools. Nevertheless, similarities are growing and will likely accelerate. The emerging common components are described in the following sections.

Before proceeding, however, it is important to emphasize that these existing and prospective schooling reforms, while perhaps primarily driven by a desire to enhance a nation's economic productivity, are not exclusively propelled by this purpose. The policy picture is considerably more murky. Many of the emerging systemic reform components will also be justified on the grounds that they may enhance schooling productivity, reduce schooling costs, shift a greater portion of school spending to the private sector, or encourage social mobility and political stability.

The following descriptions and predictions are generic in nature. Particular attention, however, is paid to U.S. and U.K. practical reforms and policy proposals because, for purposes of prediction, they are among the most pronounced and prophetic.

Converging Lower Education Reforms

Lower education reform, preschool through secondary levels, increasingly is characterized by the following common components: (a) extension of publicly funded schooling to lower age groups, so-called preschool; (b) central government curriculum influence; (c) intensified instructional emphasis upon scientific and technological subject areas; (d) expanded use of standardized examinations and centralized evaluation procedures to measure student achievement and school performance; (e) wider dependence upon central government agencies to collect, synthesize, and report upon educational systems' performance; and (f) the devolution of greater operating authority to schools, bypassing conventional units of local educational governance.

Downward Expansion of Institutionalization

This emerging common education component is at least as much a result of current economic changes as it is a policy intended deliberately to change future economies. Involvement of ever larger proportions of mothers in the workplace has created enormous political pressures in industrialized nations to provide publicly financed, or at least publicly subsidized or coordinated, child care. Because schooling is an existing institution, and generally a publicly supported institution, which eventually touches the life of almost every child, a policy connection is frequently made between child care provision and schooling. Increasingly, child care and preschool services are provided, or at least are part of the policy debate, for children as young as 3 years of age.

There is less agreement on the degree to which subject matter content and specific schooling skills should be imposed upon children in preschool programs. The age at which children are capable of learning formally presented material is debatable. There is little controversy, however, regarding the usefulness of school "readiness" training. Increasingly, early childhood programs are expected not only to prepare young children for school in a social sense, train them to follow adult directions, cooperate in a group setting, adhere to schedules, stand in lines, and so forth, but also to assist them in acquiring skills and habits useful in learning to read and count. Thus, even when specifically defined formal instruction is not extended to lower ages, institutionalization of children is occurring.

Downward extension of schooling occasionally is boosted further by national desires to enhance the educational achievement of lower socioeconomic status, "at-risk" youth. The argument is made that some portion of these children's relative inability to benefit from schooling can be compensated for by earlier socialization for schooling and exposure to instruction.

A Centrally Defined Curriculum

Central governments increasingly specify the majority of subjects to be covered in primary and, particularly, secondary schools. This policy objective can be accomplished explicitly by including lists of subject matter areas in statute or regulation or, more subtly, specifying subject matter areas as either secondary school graduation or college admission requirements. In either event, the intent is to ensure that a minimal common core of subject material is conveyed to students.

Curriculum reform expectations are frequently conveyed through central government directives to regional and local operating units. These may include subject matter guidelines, content frameworks, lesson plans, teaching modules, reading lists, bibliographies, lecture outlines, illustrative class activities, suggested experiments and field trips, sample examinations, and so forth. Also, implementation frequently carries with it central efforts to specify the content of or otherwise influence the selection of a common core of textbooks.

Centrally imposed curriculum specifications seldom are intended to occupy the entire spectrum of what a school covers at a particular grade level. Almost always there is room left to supplement the curriculum at the discretion of local officials, governing boards, or educational professionals. Nevertheless, a predictable outcome is to limit discretion for students, or their families, to select from among a wide range of elective courses. In nations that historically have not had a centrally determined curriculum, requirements will become more intense, and individual freedom to choose—by local officials, educators, and households—has been or will be reduced.[5]

The United States continues to have one of the most decentralized systems of schooling of any large nation in the world. Even so, "decentralization" is vastly different today in the United States than a quarter century ago and before. Curriculum reform demonstrates this assertion nicely. State governments have been the major actors in generating contemporary U.S. curriculum mandates. This is no surprise. The U.S. constitutional system places plenary educational decision-making discretion in the hands of state, not federal, officials.

Thus it is particularly interesting to note the strong contemporary national influence on this reform dimension.

Federal government presence takes several forms. One is dramatically visible pronouncements and highly publicized advocacy for added attention to selected subject areas. Further yet, former Secretary of Education William Bennett took the unprecedented step of issuing a model elementary and secondary school curriculum. Had this been done even a quarter century earlier, it would have drawn intense criticism, been labeled an inappropriate effort at federal government influence, and been widely perceived as a blatant usurpation of "local control." In its contemporary setting, it drew hardly a critical comment, except from self-serving subject matter proponents who believed their favorite academic area to be unfairly slighted.

In the United States, national influence over education is exercised through a variety of policy channels. The National Assessment of Educational Progress (NAEP) was reauthorized by Congress in 1988 and expanded to permit an experimental comparison of student performance, state by state.[6] The authorizing statute also called upon the National Assessment Governing Board to develop curriculum objectives for the nation. Presumably, in time, these curriculum objectives will be measured by nationally, as well as state-by-state, administered tests developed by NAEP.

The "summit" meeting of state governors, convened on September 27, 1989, by former President Bush, resulted in a pronouncement regarding the desirability of "National Educational Objectives." In his January 1990 State of the Union Address, President Bush actually proposed seven national education goals. The National Governors Association reinforced these same goals 1 month later. These targets remain to be specified in detail. The revolution, however, is in the concept, a concept that a quarter century previously would have been electoral suicide for any political party. Ironically, under current economic circumstances, *not* to be an advocate for national standards, objectives, and goals may prove to be politically unacceptable in the United States.[7]

More science, more mathematics, and more attention to technology have been particularly prominent among reform requirements intended to intensify instruction and render U.S. schooling more rigorous. In addition, however, English grammar, writing, literature, foreign language, geography, and history have been prominent features of curricular specifications for many states. Less frequently featured are courses in the visual and performing arts, business, crafts, physical and health education, and conventional vocational subjects.

An Emphasis on Mathematics, Science, and Technology

A subset of the movement toward centrally determined curricula is an intensified concern for the subject areas of mathematics, science, and related technology. This emphasis applies to elementary, secondary, and tertiary schooling levels. The justification is easy to understand. Modern economies are constructed on scientific discoveries and technological innovations—hence the desire to use schooling to enhance national capacity for scientific research and technological development. Added expectations for mathematics and science instruction and expanded textbook treatments of science in the elementary grades, additional mathematics and science graduation requirements and college entrance criteria for secondary students, expanded undergraduate emphasis upon science in colleges, and vastly increased facilities and research funding at the graduate level are hallmarks of this national movement.

Many European and Asian nations have a sustained history of intense mathematics and science instruction, particularly at the secondary level. The challenge in such circumstances will be to insert more science and technology into the elementary curriculum and expand the proportion of the age cohort who benefit from secondary schooling. The United States has a less consistent pattern of curricular concern for mathematics and science. Thus, to comply with the human capital imperative, U.S. federal officials and national organizations, as well as state governments, have become active on this technical and scientific curriculum reform dimension. The National Science Foundation has substantially expanded its funding of projects intended to enhance public school science and mathematics instruction. Numerous national organizations such as the prestigious National Academy of Sciences and the National Council of Teachers of Mathematics have issued reports stressing the need to intensify instruction in technically related fields. The initial National Assessment of Educational Progress state-by-state examinations stressed mathematics and science. The Third International Mathematics and Science Study (TIMSS) will be launched in 1994 to offer yet another international comparison of math and science achievement.

Increased Reliance Upon Pupil Performance Measures and Centralized Evaluation Procedures

The evolving mode for determining compliance with centrally issued curriculum mandates, and the increase in mathematics and science instruction, is governmentally developed or authorized standardized tests of student achievement. Through elaborate psychometric procedures, test questions can be tied to curriculum objectives. These tests can be designed to provide data regarding each student's individual performance. More typically, they are expected to assess the overall performance of a school or other management unit, a school district, a province, a state, or a nation. Thus costs savings can be achieved, for what otherwise is an unusually expensive undertaking, by relying upon a variety of sophisticated sampling techniques. The results can be generalized to the intended operating unit, without having to examine every student on every test item.

Expanded Central Reporting and Monitoring

A fourth point of international convergence is the development among nations of expanded government agencies and procedures for reporting and monitoring educational system performance. There are new, or substantially enlarged, government and quasi-government bureaus responsible for collecting, compiling, synthesizing, analyzing, and reporting education-related data. Also, the requirements placed upon operating subunits—states, local education authorities, and so forth—to supply information to the center are being increased. In general, reporting on and evaluation of educational activities have been intensified.

A major component of this added emphasis upon data collection and analyses is the attention given to international comparison. Schooling contains few internally driven standards. This condition, when coupled with increasing global economic competition, renders

international comparative information regarding student performance and school achievement ever more compelling to policymakers
and the public.

Increased Operating Authority for Individual Schools

Education systems are tending to devolve greater operating discretion to individual school sites. This trend involves bypassing interme-
diate agencies—counties, shires, prefects, parishes, boroughs, local
education authorities, and local school districts. The announced intent
of the reform is to empower local school officials, administrators, and
in some instances teachers with the ability to tailor instruction to the
preferences and needs of their clients—pupils and their parents.

This reform appears to be propelled more by desires to enhance
educational productivity than by efforts to increase economic productivity.[8] Making decisions on the rim of the wheel, rather than at
the hub, is how the movement is characterized in England. This
strategy is consistent with modern private sector and organizational
development dogma regarding the usefulness of maximized discretion at operating sites (Peters & Waterman, 1982). By devolving management decisions to schools, it is easier to account for the use of
resources and pinpoint pupil performance. Thus, in addition to the
prospect that it might enhance schooling productivity, school site
management may well have a strong accountability and cost-cutting
flavor to it.

The operational details of school site devolution are inconsistent. In
some models, the only ceding of central office discretion that takes
place is over trivial matters such as the spending of budgeted funds
for instructional supplies. (This typically amounts to only a small
proportion of overall school money, even when per pupil discretionary allocations are aggregated for all students in a large secondary
school.)

At the opposite extreme are models where teachers, as a collective,
make decisions regarding employment and retention of new hires,
allocate budgets, determine discipline policy, and control the daily
school schedule. In between are variations where authority is allocated to principals or heads but not to teachers or hiring discretion is
allocated to a school but selection can take place only from a pool of
recruits compiled by central districtwide authorities (Guthrie, 1986).

School site management is a frequently included rhetorical component of U.S. school reform but has been adopted only haphazardly. In Florida, Miami's schools, a huge urban system, are the most visible showpiece. The Miami superintendent assumed the chancellorship of the New York City schools in 1989 and began to apply the same kind of decentralized management in that system. In 1989, Chicago, the nation's third largest school system, undertook the initial steps of a drastic decentralization move. Teachers in Los Angeles demanded a version of school site management before agreeing to return to work in a May 1989 strike. Many other smaller systems have adopted it. Much is written about it. To date, however, no state has adopted it in toto.

Thatcher government promotion of the school site management principle is among the most extensive in the world. Education Reform Act (ERA) provisions specify that fiscal appropriations pass through local educational authorities, the conventional budget unit, and, with the exception of a small percentage of central authority administrative holdback, proceed straight to school sites. School governing board members are officially specified as responsible for budgetary decisions. Assuming the conventional practices of policy-setting bodies in allocating power, however, this should result in vastly enhanced operational discretion for heads of schools and, to the extent to which they choose to involve them, their staff members as well (Davies & Ellison, 1989).

This sixth point of global convergence—school site decision discretion—appears at first glance to be paradoxical. In the face of growing centralization of school decision making, why would greater operating authority be ceded to school sites? The frequent justification is that, whereas it is necessary for central authorities to specify the *what* of schooling, it is not appropriate, or even sensible, for them to specify the *how*. There are two somewhat antithetical justifications provided for this posture.

One frequently offered rationale for decentralized operational decision making is that teachers are, or at least should become, "professionals." Thus it is demeaning to specify their instructional behavior. Presumably, they know what their student clients need and they are trained to meet those needs. Too great a degree of central direction would be demeaning and thus counterproductive. Better for central authorities to leave instructional decisions to those on the operational periphery—school administrators and instructors.

Another rationale is that too little is known scientifically regarding instruction to take the risk of specifying teaching behavior centrally. Under conditions of technical uncertainty, better to permit "a thousand flowers to bloom." Out of myriad natural experiments taking place in schools and classrooms, perhaps verifiable principles of instruction will eventually emerge that can someday be codified and conveyed from teacher to teacher in a systematic manner.

A third justification, consistent with modern management dicta, is that those closest to the operational point of service delivery are best positioned to make judgments regarding client preferences and the means for tailoring services to them.

A fourth justification is that school-based management facilitates greater parental participation in their children's schooling. The elimination, or at least reduction, of intervening bureaucracies means that parents can have more direct access to schools, administrators, and teachers.

A final justification is that school site management will, over time, enable central governments to reduce the reliance of schools upon school district or local education authority bureaucracies. Such would have, from the standpoint of the center, at least two advantages. It would permit more direct, straightforward communication between the center and the periphery, eliminating a third party in the middle. This, arguably, would render schools more responsible to the center. Additionally, reducing the role played by local education or school district authorities might reduce education costs.

Converging Higher Education Reforms

Higher education reforms also exhibit six evolving trends. These developing policies and practices are also propelled by newly intensifying global economic forces. These higher education trends are related to, but do not simply mirror, lower education changes.

Space does not permit an elaboration upon each dimension. Their significance, however, warrants their being listed here. The six higher education common reform dimensions are (a) overall expansion of tertiary sector student capacity; (b) system building-institutional consolidation and streamlining; (c) efforts to shift a greater proportion of higher education costs to the consumer, that is, students and their families; (d) construction of more direct higher education links to industrial research and development and the overall economy; (e) added emphasis allocated to quantifiable performance measures; and (f) intensified reporting and accountability to central governments.

These six dimensions are different structurally than the new reforms and future expectations for lower education. Nevertheless, the purposes are the same. These changes are intended by policymakers primarily to enhance the ability of higher education to contribute to national economic growth and, secondarily, to enhance the productivity of higher education.

Evolving Prospective Components

In addition to the above-described common dimensions for lower and higher education, modern reform movements among Western-bloc nations frequently will include efforts to (a) infuse schooling with features of the marketplace, that is, competition and consumer choice; (b) enhance teacher professionalization; and (c) identify policies that will enhance the education of underparticipating or unmotivated youth. These three evolving components are further out on the policy horizon and their future likelihood is not yet as evident. Nevertheless, they are being discussed with sufficient frequency to justify mention.

Privatization and Choice

Proponents of this position search for means by which schooling can be rendered more competitive and clients—households and pupils—can be provided with an expanded range of choices about their education. The rationale for these proposals is mixed. The frequent fundamental assertion is that any organization with a guaranteed clientele, or a guaranteed source of financial support, will tend to become self-serving and less sensitive to the preferences and needs of clients. Hence, both to serve clients better and to render the institutions more efficient, steps must be taken to inject elements of the marketplace into schooling. Monopolies must be disbanded and competition encouraged.

Higher education students, at least in 4-year colleges and proprietary schools, generally already have their choice of institutions. Reformers enamored of choice desire to reinforce this condition by

allocating virtually all central government higher education financial
support directly to students rather than to institutions. By making it
increasingly necessary for higher education institutions to compete
for students, the expectation is that they will become more responsive
to the specific manpower needs of the labor market, more sensitive to
client preferences, including preferences for vocational preparation,
and, because colleges and universities then would not be assured of
funding, operate more efficiently in the process. Another prospective
reform strategy is for central governments to provide only a limited
proportion of institutional support, 80% or 90%, for example, to
motivate colleges and universities to generate necessary added funding through their own entrepreneurial and fund-raising efforts.

At the lower education level, there exist a wider spectrum of choice
proposals; some radical, some less so. Among the moderates are
advocates of choice who would restrict household education selection
only to schools in the *public* sector. Other moderated choice plans
restrict selection to schools within the public sector and only for a
particular set of grades, or only if the movement of students enhances
racial desegregation, or only if the household meets specified criteria—for example, the normally assigned school has persistently declining test scores or the household itself is below a minimum income
level.

The more radical plans envision conversion of education, higher
and lower, into a free market where all school services are provided
privately. Government might subsidize, or even to some degree regulate, such services but would not itself be a direct provider.

Choice proponents are highly visible in the United States. As late in
his final term of office as April 1988, former President Reagan said:[9]

> Successful reform won't come about from the top down. Central
> planning doesn't make economies healthy, and it won't make our
> schools work, either. How can we release the creative energies of
> our people? By giving parents choice. By allowing them to select
> the schools which best meet the unique needs of their children.
> By fostering a healthy rivalry among schools to serve our young
> people. Already, the "Power of Choice" is revitalizing schools
> that use it across the nation.[10]

Business representatives frequently advocate radical choice plans.
Representatives of professional education organizations themselves

often advocate less radical, public-sector-limited choice plans. Opinion polls repeatedly reveal that an American citizen majority supports the idea, at least in the abstract ("Poll Finds Grants," 1992).[11]

Despite highly visible advocates and extensive public discussions, and at least superficial public opinion support, policy implementation of the choice idea has been slow to evolve in the United States. As of mid-1989, only 4 of 50 U.S. states had adopted even limited choice plans for lower education, so-called open enrollment plans. By 1992, however, 13 additional states had enacted a variant of a choice plan (Policy Analysis for California Education [PACE], 1992). By 1992 Colorado, California, and Florida were actively flirting with private sector choice plans as ballot initiatives.

Thus it currently is too early to predict the extent to which "choice" will ever emerge as a widespread feature of U.S. lower education.[12] At least with radical versions that would provide public funds to religious institutions, "choice plans" may provoke sufficiently intense constitutional controversies to eventually dampen the enthusiasm of reformers. For the moment, however, the rhetoric surrounding "choice" is sufficiently pervasive and persistent to justify its inclusion as a possible reform component.

"Choice" is closer to being a widespread reform reality in England than in the United States. "Privatization" and "consumerism" were major themes of Thatcher government reforms, and educational "choice" was no exception. The 1988 Education Reform Act (ERA) did not explicitly address "choice" in lower education. Through two mechanisms, however, it enhances the prospect of a more complete "choice" system in the future. For example, if a governing majority obtains central ministry approval, an individual school can opt out of its local educational authority and use public funding to operate virtually as a private institution. Such a school has to adhere to central government dictates regarding the curriculum and testing, but it has no higher authority except its own parent governing board and the Department for Education in London.

The ERA contains a less radical but potentially more pervasive choice feature. Local education authorities are prevented from placing tight ceilings upon enrollments for a particular school and parents are permitted to select from among all public schools within a local education authority. Hence parent choice—open enrollment, within the locally defined public sector—is a new English reality.

It is currently too early to assess how widespread parental transfer decisions will be. Underselected schools, however, run the risk of staff redundancies, and teacher job security—tenure—no longer resides with the local education authority. Thus, in that financial resources follow the pupil tightly under ERA financial arrangements, household decisions to transfer a child from one school to another may have potentially dramatic budgetary consequences for individual schools.

This evolving component has another related facet, "privatization." The proposals are to place various components of system operation out to bid by private providers. This can involve matters sufficiently peripheral as trash removal and food catering all the way to integral features such as remedial reading or foreign language or vocational instruction (Wilkerson, 1992). The policy objective almost always is to render an education system operation less costly. The closer to the core of instruction the proposals come, the more controversial they become, and the greater the resistance by education professionals.

Professionalization

This too is an incomplete or latent component of prospective Western-bloc education reform movements. Where it is to be found currently, it has at least two dimensions, not all components of which are consistent. One is an effort to upgrade the quality of teachers by elevating entry standards. There is substantial policy debate about the most effective manner in which to achieve this objective. One avenue requires teaching-job candidates to have higher levels of academic preparation and/or pass minimum competency tests. Elevating competency can also include requirements for an additional year (possibly at the graduate level) of college preparation. The other policy avenue is to expand the pool of able candidates by liberating applicants from teacher training or pedagogical training requirements.

The second professionalization trend is an expansion of the decision discretion accorded teachers and higher education faculty members. Where this is present, the argument is that central governments may well specify the *what* of schooling, but they should not dictate the *how* of instruction. The latter is well within the domain of professional teachers to determine and it would be demeaning and prove counterproductive for policymakers to attempt to override them.

The first dimension is illustrated in the United States by formation of the National Professional Teacher Standards Board. This agency, formed in 1987 as a result of a national commission report, plans to offer U.S. teachers the option of applying, and taking the necessary examination, for a national teachers certificate (Carnegie Forum, 1986). Presumably, the standards will be higher than what is currently required by most states for a teaching license. If so, then the long-range hope is that local school districts, and perhaps states, will eventually compete for these highly qualified teachers and, in the process, elevate standards for the entire field.

The United States has a growing number of local district examples of expanded teacher discretion. There are still too few to accord this component complete reform status. Nevertheless, examples can be found in at least 20 states. The decision arena for teachers has been expanded in various instances to include participation in the recruitment and hiring of new teachers, the evaluation, including tenure decisions, of probationary teachers, and the evaluation of tenure teachers. Also, teachers in these expanded-discretion settings may take added responsibility for selecting curriculum materials, inservice training opportunities, and administrators.

There appear to be few highly visible English equivalents of this U.S. professionalization phenomena. Indeed, something of the opposite appears to be occurring. Many of the Thatcher government-proposed reforms were perceived by teachers and teacher union officials as having a heavy-handed "teacher-bashing" spirit to them. Thatcher government reforms appeared to be designed to bypass professional educators. In England, these groups were viewed by highly placed government officials as being part of the problem, whereas in the United States the overwhelming posture of reform leaders—governors, business officials, and so forth—has been to cooperate with teachers in the design and implementation of reforms.

Underserved, and Possibly Unmotivated, Youth

Increasing discussion is being allocated to identifying policies for enhancing the achievement and motivation of large numbers of lower socioeconomic status youth who currently may not be participating fully in or benefiting from schooling. Whereas the relationship between education and national economic development is increasingly obvious for policymakers, the same relationship for individuals within a nation is not always as evident. International migrations of political and economic refugees, "guest" workers, alterations in family patterns, centuries of racial and class discrimination, widespread trading in addictive drugs, and an assortment of other symptoms of social distress have created a sizable "underclass" in many industrialized nations.

In addition to their own unhappy personal conditions, individuals caught in debilitating circumstances threaten to increase public welfare costs substantially. Also, undereducated individuals represent lost labor. In many Western nations, youth population cohorts are shrinking. Faced with the prospect of a worker shortage, governments are beginning to assess means for enhancing the education of larger proportions of youth to increase the sophistication of their labor pool. At the moment, no consensus has emerged even regarding the nature of the problem, let alone solutions. The expanding constellation of distressing conditions is, however, provoking policy-level discussion about the problem and its relationship to schooling.

Conspicuously Absent Reform Components: Research and Development

One cannot help but speculate regarding the absence of any significant central government reliance upon intensified educational research or development of technology to enhance schooling productivity and promote human capital formation. What would appear to be a natural response to ever-rising costs of instruction, demands for spreading schooling to ever-wider populations, and desires to link schooling to the growing realities of high-tech automation is virtually neglected by policymakers. This is despite the fact that electronic and optical technology appear capable of revolutionizing instruction, rendering it far more individualized and, eventually, less expensive.

Professional Consequences

New economic imperatives are creating a different environment for educational professionals, even if only by way of the intensity in which these differences present themselves. The overarching change is in the degree to which education policy and practice are being politicized. This fundamental shift toward politics has numerous practical expressions of which the following conditions are illustrative:

(a) an increasing expectation that educational practitioners will be accountable to and schooling results made understandable for generalists and laypersons, not simply educational professionals and government specialists;

(b) educator involvement with greater ranges of, and politically more influential special interest groups and stakeholders directly interested in, educational outcomes;

(c) an expansion of high-level general government agencies interested in, and perhaps responsible for, the management of education and schooling and greater linkages between education agencies, government planning efforts, and the policymaking process;

(d) skepticism regarding evaluations undertaken by educators and a consequent greater reliance upon evaluation generalists, higher likelihood of competing and adversarial evaluations, intensified risk of advocacy imitating analysis, policymakers requiring systemic evaluation strategies, and a greater reliance upon eclectic analytic tactics and expanded measurements; and

(e) added dependence upon internationally oriented performance comparisons.

A Concluding Caveat for the Education Profession

Despite a deep historical connection to industrial development and whatever their immediate connection with the economy, schools have traditionally been expected to fulfill a substantial range of additional functions, both for society and for the individuals and households involved. Acculturating new citizens, promoting religious, linguistic, and political indoctrination, inculcating government principles, ensuring social cohesion and civic order, preparing a citizenry for military participation, facilitating social mobility, developing artistic and aesthetic tastes, assisting in personal adjustment to society, and contributing to individual fulfillment are among the other-than-economic functions variously expected of schools.

Many of these other purposes are now being forcefully subordinated to national economic development in the last quarter of the twentieth century. Nevertheless, regardless of how exciting existing and prospective economically motivated reforms may appear, it is important to be mindful that other functions existed; even if currently diluted, still exist; and no doubt will persist. Professional educators thus should be mindful of the many masters worthy of being served other than or in addition to national economic development.

Notes

1. Once achieving new levels of political stability, Eastern-bloc nations are highly likely to pursue a similar course.

2. This term is probably best defined as the 25 nation members of the Organization for Economic Cooperation and Development (OECD), the post-World War II Marshall Plan successor.

3. This term generally describes members of what was the Warsaw Pact.

4. By comparison, in 1992 the United States allocated approximately 6% of GNP to defense and the rate is declining.

5. An expected reaction from among the advocates of elective courses has already begun to develop.

6. The National Assessment of Educational Progress was initiated in 1966. At that time, however, it was tightly restricted in format to prevent student achievement and school performance comparisons among states.

7. As long ago as September 1989, a Gallup Poll revealed that a larger percentage of 'Americans feared Japanese economic and trade competition than were concerned with a Soviet military threat.

8. In Spain, school-based management was initiated as a means of further democratizing the nation.

9. The Bush administration was initially ambivalent about choice. In his first year in office, President Bush made it clear that he would not be advocating "choice" as a high-level policy priority. By 1992, however, the president had forwarded a household choice plan to Congress and was campaigning for reelection with choice as a major platform plan.

10. This quotation was cited in an unpublished paper by Bruce Cooper (n.d.) of Fordham University.

11. Public opinion polls typically display a majority favoring some version of school choice, perhaps even a version in which private schools participate. For example, an Associated Press poll conducted between August 28 and September 2, 1992, found a 2 to 1 majority among the electorate favoring President's Bush proposed federal scholarship plan for school vouchers. In eight opinion polls conducted from 1970 to 1992, however, the Gallup organization never found more than 51% of the public favoring the inclusion of private schools in a parental choice plan. Polling results appear to be unusually sensitive to the manner in which the choice question is worded. The use of the term *scholarship* by Bush campaign representatives may have disguised the issue of aid to nonpublic schools.

12. Choice has historically been a different policy issue in U.S. higher education. Here there is a substantial history of private and religiously sponsored institutions that have drawn government support—federal, state, and local—for hundreds of years.

References

Barber, B. (1992). Jihad vs. MacWorld. *Atlantic, 269*(3), 53-63.

Carnegie Forum on Education and the Economy. (1986). *A nation prepared: Teachers for the 21st century. The Report of the Task Force on Teaching as a Profession.* Washington, DC: Author.

Cooper, B. (n.d.). *American and British education reforms.* Unpublished manuscript, Fordham University, New York.

Davies, B., & Ellison, L. (1989, September 15-17). *Changing financial provision leads to a radical reform of the English educational system.* Paper presented at the annual meeting of the British Education Management and Administration Society, University of Leicester.

Guthrie, J. (1986). School site management: The next needed school reform. *Phi Delta Kappan, 68*(4), 305-309.

Heyneman, S. (1989, September 26). *Revolution in the East: The educational lessons.* Paper presented at the Conference on Development Through Education, University College, Oxford.

Morris, C. (1989). The coming global boom. *Atlantic, 264*(4), 53-54.

Peters, T., & Waterman, R. (1982). *In search of excellence: Lessons from America's best run companies.* New York: Harper & Row.

Policy Analysis for California Education (PACE). (1992, May). *Choice in the states.* Berkeley, CA: Author.

Poll finds grants for parental school choice favored. (1992, September 7). *San Francisco Chronicle, 201,* 6.

Schultz, T. W. (1971). *Investment in human capital.* New York: Free Press.

Wilkerson, I. (1992, April 22). A city is letting a company run a school district. *The New York Times,* p. 15.

Author Index

Subject Index